LOVE OF KNOWLEDGE

LOVE OF KNOWLEDGE

Tarthang Tulku

Dharma Publishing

Time, Space, and Knowledge: A New Vision of Reality

Love of Knowledge

Copyright © 1987 Dharma Publishing

No part of this book may be copied, reproduced, published, distributed, or stored electronically, photographically, or optically in any form without the express written consent of Dharma Publishing. Dharma Publishing will take vigorous action to enforce its rights under all applicable copyright laws and international conventions. Registered with the Register of Copyrights and the Library of Congress. For information contact Dharma Publishing, Berkeley, California.

Typeset in Mergenthaler Trump Mediaeval and Helvetica Light. Printed and bound in the United States of America by Dharma Press, Oakland, California.

ISBN: 0-89800-169-2; 0-89800-138-2 (pbk.)

9 8 7 6 5 4 3 2 1

CONTENTS

Publisher's Preface   ix

Preface   xiii

How to Read This Book   xix

Working with the Exercises   xxxi

Guide to the Exercises   xxxv

Introduction   xxxix

PART ONE: PATTERNS AND POSSIBILITIES

1 The Promise of Knowledge   3

2 Knowledge Alive in History   11

3 Faces of Knowledge   17

4 No Direction   25

5 Binding Through Identity   33

6 The Known   43

7 Replacing Knowledge with Belief   51

8 Questioning Limits   57

9 The Range of the Knowable   67
10 Adventure of Knowledge   75
11 Disclosing New Potential   83
12 Transforming Time and Space   89

PART TWO: MODELS OF KNOWLEDGE

13 Knowing Through Polarity   99
14 Problematics of Polarity   109
15 Compelling Flow of Time   121
16 Modeling Self-Constructs   129
17 Interpretation at the Core   137
18 The World of the Self   147
19 The Reign of Intentional Knowledge   155
20 Guidance and Direction   163
21 Presenting the Self   169
22 Two Times   179
23 The Onward Flow of Time   185
24 The Self in Question   193
25 Founding Identity   201

PART THREE: SOURCES OF KNOWLEDGE

26 Merging with Time   213
27 World Without Positioning   223
28 No Alternative in Alternatives   231
29 Visionary Realm   239

30 Touching the Limits 249

31 Constricting Circle 257

32 Taking a Stand 263

33 Availability of Knowledge 269

34 Rain of Questions 279

35 Knowledge in Human Being 287

36 Magical Interplay 297

37 Knowledge Through Wonder 305

38 Commitment Without Commitment 313

PART FOUR: KNOWING KNOWLEDGE

39 Encompassing Opposition 321

40 Nothing to Know 329

41 Knowledge Within Negation 337

42 'Emptiness' of Emptiness 343

43 Protecting Against Loss 351

44 Assertion of the Subject 357

45 Knowledge Pervading Being 363

46 Inexpressible Wonderment 371

47 Knowing Implicit Illumination 379

48 Opening Time and Space 387

49 Dance in Time 395

50 Dynamic Intimate Awareness 403

Glossary 413

Index 417

PUBLISHER'S PREFACE

Among the most familiar and basic of the concepts that we use to guide our understanding are Time, Space, and Knowledge. The world we live in appears in space, unfolds in time, and makes itself available through knowledge. Yet we have little understanding of the nature of these most fundamental aspects of existence or of how they operate.

Ten years ago, a pathbreaking inquiry into these questions was initiated with the publication of *Time, Space, and Knowledge: A New Vision of Reality*, by Tarthang Tulku. Carefully crafted to present a vision that went well beyond the bounds of the conventional, this new work (known to its students as TSK) received an enthusiastic reception. The English edition is now in its fourth printing, and translations have been published in Dutch, German, and Italian, with work on French and Japanese translations underway.

Before publication of *Time, Space, and Knowledge*, Tarthang Tulku led seminars in which he explored the new vision. Beginning in 1978, teachers trained by the author offered TSK seminars, workshops, and long-term programs. The first of several nine-month programs was held in 1979, and since that time other programs have been offered around the world. Scientists and philosophers of international renown have taken part in TSK workshops in which they shared the results of their own investigations into time and space.

More than one hundred colleges and universities in America and Europe have made *Time, Space, and Knowledge* required reading in disciplines as diverse as philosophy, psychology, comparative religion, and management. Dissertations and other forms of academic research are in progress, and thousands of individuals have made the TSK vision a focus for study and practice. In 1980, Dharma Publishing published essays by philosophers, theologians, psychologists, and educators exploring the TSK vision in a two volume set under the title *Dimensions of Thought*. These were the first volumes in the "Perspectives on TSK" series, which we hope to supplement in the future.

The TSK vision offers insight into fundamental patterns of human activity and thought, and has encouraged new forms of inquiry in a variety of fields. It has helped individuals clarify their own thinking and has encouraged investigation into the meaning of the truths and conceptual structures we rely on at the deepest level.

At the same time, it has always been clear that numerous readers found the vision difficult to understand and to explore. For some, the complex and tightly structured presentation proved frustrating, while for others initial insights gave way over time to confusion and discouragement.

We are thus deeply pleased to be able to present a work that makes the fundamental TSK vision accessible in new ways. Though challenging in its own right, *Love of Knowledge* is more readily understandable to a mind attuned to conventional ways of knowing. All of us who have had the opportunity to work with it have found that our understanding deepens with each reading. Readers willing to work with the book on its own terms will find their efforts richly rewarded.

Love of Knowledge serves as an introduction to the TSK vision, while also laying the groundwork for further explorations. It stands as an independent analysis of conventional knowledge and a thoughtful assessment of the potential for new ways of knowing. It gives Dharma Publishing great satisfaction to participate in presenting *Love of Knowledge* to the public.

PREFACE

Since the publication of *Time, Space, and Knowledge* almost a full decade ago, I have observed the appearance of a growing number of books on themes explored in that work. This trend seems beneficial, for time, space, and knowledge are topics of the greatest significance for humanity. Every attempt to illuminate their meaning and significance is bound to serve the cause of knowledge and to contribute to human welfare.

I have long wanted to continue my own systematic exploration of the topics introduced in *Time, Space, and Knowledge*. Fundamental issues remained to be examined, and I saw a need to clarify and extend the TSK vision in new directions, so that those familiar with the vision could deepen their understanding, and those who had found the initial presentation difficult could be encouraged to continue their efforts. Students of the vision, including physicists, psychologists, educators, and others, repeatedly asked me to undertake such a task, and their thoughtful questions reinforced my interest.

Initially, I hesitated to publish a sequel to *Time, Space, and Knowledge* out of a concern that the TSK vision might be turned into a set of beliefs. As I saw how well the vision was able to protect itself, however, I realized that there would be little harm in sharing my ongoing inquiries. Due to the press of other projects, it was not until 1984 that I was able to begin dictating the first notes for a new book. In the spring of 1985 I added to these notes in a more systematic way, and a partial rough draft began to take shape. In the fall of 1986 I finally had the opportunity to give this new project my full attention, and the work began to gather momentum.

The material being explored was difficult, and several successive drafts of a working manuscript were prepared. Eventually the more introductory and general sections were collected together for this book; the remaining portions, which deal systematically with elements of the vision presented only in evocative form in TSK, were left for later publication. In light of the great effort that has gone into production of the present volume, I cannot promise that another volume will be ready for publication in the near future, but I fully intend to share the results of my continuing investigations.

Since I am not a native speaker of English, preparation of this work involved special challenges. In orally presenting the ideas and images that came to me, I was not always able to express clearly the meanings I wished to convey. Because of the lengthy gestation period, my sense of how best to organize the material and the specific terminology I was using shifted over time.

The task of dealing with these difficulties fell to the primary editor, Jack Petranker, who worked with great devotion over a period of more than two years, editing and re-editing the notes I had given. I worked closely with him throughout this process, verifying that the presentation was complete and accurate within the limits imposed by the available language and concepts. In the final stages, several Dharma Publishing editors offered valuable technical assistance in clarifying the presentation, which had become fairly complex. Anyone who finds *Love of Knowledge* helpful to their own understanding owes thanks to each of these individuals, and to all at Dharma Publishing and Dharma Press who contributed to the production of this book.

In exploring the TSK vision, I have been keenly aware of my own limited knowledge. The vision has no established lineage or acknowledged masters, and I have had to make my way slowly, searching vigorously and in new ways. As a student of Time, Space, and Knowledge, I have very few answers — only questions. Still, my reflection on human history and human realities has convinced me that my questions are shared by others, even if these questions have not been framed in the same ways. For that reason, I have not hesitated to present here a record of my own process of learning.

Love of Knowledge proceeds by returning to a point 'before the beginning' of *Time, Space, and Knowledge* — tracing out links between space, time, and knowledge and our ordinary understanding. The presentation inquires primarily into the structures of conventional, 'first-level' thought. Only when these structures have been identified and analyzed does the focus shift to a 'higher' level of knowledge. Of course, distinctions such as 'higher' and 'lower' are themselves conventional; in terms of a more encompassing knowledge they might have to be completely re-examined.

One of the most interesting consequences of this course of inquiry is the recognition that knowledge is not a matter of content, but of an active knowing expressed in inquiry itself. Every effort has thus been made to keep the presentation neutral and open, so that the reader can participate directly in the unfolding of a vigorous and dynamic knowledge.

Open inquiry can penetrate directly to the energy of time and the depth of space, allowing new insight and appreciation. Such knowledge can be readily shared, and my hope is that in the future students of TSK will make use of the insights they gain to present the vision in new and more fruitful ways.

In considering this prospect, I sense that others have much more to contribute to the TSK vision than I do. A dynamic of great potential is waiting to be activated. By focusing on time and space and on their interaction with knowledge, it may be possible to unify fields of learning that are now separate, and to bring together concerns that now seem opposed. For myself, I hope to have the opportunity in the future to explore several topics, including the complexities of field theory and the behavior of matter. I would also like to pursue a more experiential approach, looking more deeply into the love of knowledge as it unfolds into a knowledge of love.

When I was a young man, I studied for many years the rich and complex teachings of the Buddhist tradition and the Nyingma school, and I have continued to explore those teachings ever since. Thus, when *Time, Space, and Knowledge* was published, there were those who concluded that it must be based on esoteric Buddhist teachings. A few readers even wondered whether it might be harmful to study the TSK vision without first receiving adequate preparation based on the Buddhist tradition.

To the best of my knowledge, such a connection between Buddhism and the TSK vision simply does not exist. In presenting the vision, I have not attempted to draw on or reinterpret any tradition of knowledge or line of teaching. By the same token, I have not considered the vision to constitute a break with existing traditions. The vision is independent, fully capable of standing on its own without reference to other teachings. Undoubtedly my style of inquiry and expression has been influenced by my training in Buddhist philosophy and practice, even when I cannot directly trace this influence. However, I do not consider the TSK vision to be specifically Buddhist or even religious.

A reader interested in Buddhism, or in some other tradition of inquiry — whether religious, scientific, or philosophical — might find in the TSK vision a source of inspiration and new insight. To my understanding, this would not be 'evidence' that the vision is 'only' a 'restatement' of another tradition. On the contrary, I would consider it a welcome sign that the vision was being effectively communicated.

The interest in making connections between the TSK vision and other paths of inquiry, though natural, is evidence that a 'lower' form of knowledge is in operation. Knowledge is naturally free, but when it is claimed on behalf of a particular doctrine this unlimited freedom is easily lost. Labeling ideas and then comparing those labels does little to further a deeper knowing. In contrast, when inquiry 'takes place' *within* Space, Time, and Knowledge, it does not require adopting one position or rejecting another. As the activity of Knowledge itself, it reveals 'knowingness' and celebrates the independence of the human mind.

A number of my good friends may find it strange that I continue to give my energy to a way of thinking so different from the tradition of thought and practice in which I have been trained. I hope that they will be patient with me, even if they do not share my interest in this new vision. My own conviction is that the way of inquiry and insight presented here may prove deeply beneficial to the modern world. At the least, I am confident that it cannot lead to harm.

The Time, Space, and Knowledge vision will be activated only as it becomes accessible to others. Whether the present work succeeds in advancing that goal will be up to each reader to decide. For myself, I can testify that the exploration undertaken here has contributed to my own understanding. I hope that others may find it useful as well.

Tarthang Tulku
Berkeley, CA
May 1987

HOW TO READ
THIS BOOK

For readers well-acquainted with *Time, Space, and Knowledge*, the present work can serve as a catalyst to activate new ways of knowing. For those unfamiliar with the TSK vision, this book offers a way to review and deepen conventional modes of knowledge and to open an alternative vision, which could then be further explored through the careful study of *Time, Space, and Knowledge*. In either case, the two books are complementary, though each also stands alone.

Love of Knowledge is first and foremost an inquiry, and it is important to give attention to the way in which this inquiry is conducted. Investigations usually rely on a pre-existing understanding, which may or may not be formalized as a working 'philosophy'. Though useful as a tool, such *pre*-established understanding tends to be lifeless. It accumulates outward forms that weigh inquiry down and rob it of flexibility.

As an example of this difficulty, consider the view that reading this book or practicing the exercises contained in it will 'lead to' insight. This way of talking is almost inescapable, but the sense of 'process' it invokes is deeply bound up with conventional ways of being and understanding. A 'process' is initiated when something 'goes into action', and this means that time unfolds in the ordinary way. Once we step onto the wheel of time, there is no way to get off again: We are like passengers on a runaway train.

Few things seem as self-evident as the notion that knowledge arises as the result of a process — whether initiated internally or externally — that 'leads to' understanding. But this very self-evidence is grounds for suspicion. The more clear and distinct conventional ideas appear to be, the less new knowledge they can 'hold'. Once the 'process-oriented' model is accepted, related concepts such as 'experience' and 'experiencer' prove impenetrable to inquiry. For that matter, the basic nature of inquiry itself becomes a mystery.

Inquiry shaped in advance by specific structures or concepts can still expand the range of insight and understanding and restore greater balance to human life. In the end, though, such understanding will fall short of true *intimacy* with Time, Space, and Knowledge. Behind the barricades of pre-established structures, the foxes of the intellect may engage in clever reasoning, but the lion of Being continues to roar outside the gate.

Space, Time, and Knowledge are available for investigation directly, without our having to measure or observe them with the tools 'at hand', including the understandings we take for granted. An inseparable intimacy links the 'quality' of our lives and the active presentations of time in space. We are partners with space through physical existence, partners with time through actions, and partners with knowledge through awareness. Though these three facets of being may be neither 'absolute' nor 'ultimate', they constitute the 'stuff' of our lives — starting points for an inquiry that can transform our being.

Such an inquiry requires no special belief and establishes no fixed path. It can develop along the lines of philosophy, religion, or science, finding significance in every field of human activity. The forms that appear 'in the world' and the activity of the mind become gateways for a knowledge that lets us participate fully in our own lives. Inquiry becomes an adventure — a boundless field of action with no fixed starting point or goal.

Exploring Time, Space, and Knowledge

To explore the TSK vision directly, *Love of Knowledge* could be read three times — once from a Space perspective, once from a Time perspective, and once from a Knowledge perspective — paying special attention to the ways these three approaches interlock. Another approach is to seek out those parts of the book that deal specifically with space, time, and knowledge and use them as keys for investigating the presentation as a whole.

Because each individual expresses in his or her own being the interplay of Time, Space, and Knowledge, each reader will respond to the material in *Love of Knowledge* in a different manner. Certain individuals may readily contact through their reading an open, spacious quality within experience, but be unable to focus on specific arguments or generate the energy that can penetrate established patterns of being. Others may have no difficulty with intensive study of the points in the text, but be repeatedly frustrated in their 'efforts' to relax and appreciate the presentations of a deeper knowing.

☆ Readers who have difficulty appreciating Time but find Space comfortable and even familiar can direct their major efforts to the study of Knowledge.

☆ Readers drawn to Time who have difficulties with Space can look within discussions on Time for a Space component. A good initial focus in working with Space would be the space within the body.

☆ Readers perplexed by Knowledge can trace the origin and unfolding of human consciousness, starting with the development of knowledge in the course of history. *On this basis* it is possible to investigate the relationship between name and form, and then to move to knowledge as it arises through the human senses and through the interplay of psychological functions. The meaning of the terms being used in the book will become increasingly clear, and the concepts applied in analyzing knowledge will take on new significance.

Another, complementary way to read *Love of Knowledge* is in light of the TSK vision's presentation of three levels of Time, Space, and Knowledge. 'Levels of reality' are commonplaces of philosophy and religion, and even play a role in science. In the TSK vision, however, these levels are presented as directly accessible to knowledge: first in the experience of the senses and then in the interplay of the senses with the mind.

If *Love of Knowledge* is read as proceeding on three levels at once, the limitations of linear exposition are confronted directly, and the reader gains confidence in the simultaneous accessibility of knowledge. The three levels of Space, Time, and Knowledge will be found to support one another: A second level of knowledge can express more of the second level of time, while the second level of time can point towards a third level of time that can then make available a third level of space and of knowledge. Since Time, Space, and Knowledge can each be investigated in this way, there will be nine levels in all. As investigation deepens, these nine levels can each be understood as embracing nine more levels, and so forth. The reader can work out such connections, looking for their interplay from chapter to chapter and section to section — even within each paragraph.

It is also possible to proceed by asking the purpose for which each sentence has been written, and how it relates to the presentation as a whole. When discussions of specific topics leave issues open, the reader can try to work through the presentation for himself. If there seem to be gaps in the discussion or unexamined assumptions, the reader should inquire whether they mask flaws in reasoning, or whether they can become openings to further insight or new questions.

A presentation that operates at different levels simultaneously, returns repeatedly to consider the same topics from different perspectives, and offers only a few hints on how to understand several key points is certainly non-standard. However, this approach invites an active participation in unfolding the meaning of what is said. It has the further advantage of keeping the scope of the presentation within reasonable bounds, for otherwise it would be easy to expand almost every point presented here into a separate chapter or even book.

Methods of Inquiry

Love of Knowledge attempts to communicate the vision of Time, Space, and Knowledge in several different ways. First is the text itself, which varies in style but in general invites the reader to make use of the analytic powers of the mind. Rigorous in places, the text requires careful attention and thoughtful inquiry and observation.

Complementing the text but addressed to different faculties of the mind are illustrations that appear at the opening of each new chapter. The illustrations invoke multiple levels of meaning, and can suggest new ways of reading the text they accompany. The captions for the illustrations point toward this multi-layered significance; they can be approached in an open and playful way, as though standard rules of grammar and syntax had been temporarily suspended.

Finally, exercises related to the themes of the book have been placed at the end of each chapter. As invitations to inquiry, the ideas presented in *Love of Knowledge* could themselves be considered 'exercises' for the mind and spirit; however, these more formal exercises may help readers engage the experiential significance of the vision in its unfolding. I discuss below ways for working with these exercises for those who wish to make them a central element in their study.

These various forms of presentation can be freely combined, each serving to illuminate the others. When one approach no longer seems fruitful, another may lead to new insights or suggest a different perspective. Each reader can work out a unique way of engaging the vision.

Whatever methods of investigation are chosen, it will help to be sensitive to the circumstances that surround the course of inquiry, for the deep interconnection of Time, Space, and Knowledge means that our understanding may be affected in unexpected ways. For example, autumn and winter seem more conducive to the study of Space, while spring and summer are more in harmony with Time. The reader may discover other, more subtle interrelationships linked to environment, climate, prevailing moods, and so on.

As investigation continues and positions fall away, a sense of confusion may arise. This can actually be a healthy sign: an indication that inquiry is truly under way. On a deeper level, confusion can be understood as an *expression* of knowledge — an echo of conventional understanding that engages inquiry at a new level. If this shift does not occur and confusion about the meaning of what is being said persists, it may help to reread a difficult passage or chapter several times, slowly and thoughtfully. Meanings and connections that seemed obscure initially may then become clear.

To be truly effective, the study of Time, Space, and Knowledge cannot be burdened by a sense of obligation or frustration. If serious inquiry and study lead only to deepening confusion, it might be best to work with the ideas presented more 'lightly'; for example, by keeping a key idea in the back of the mind and bringing it to the fore from time to time to observe its effect. Maintaining a journal will assure that insights and understandings that arise in such moments are not lost.

Style of Investigation

Although we value freedom of thought highly, we seldom acknowledge that this freedom can be undermined from within as well as from outside. Lack of awareness and knowledge constrain the freedom to think in truly creative ways far more effectively than any dictatorial regime. The true safeguard for freedom of thought is an active, open inquiry that stimulates the mind and encourages creative intelligence.

Following the path of open inquiry means treating *Love of Knowledge* as a companion in investigation rather than as an authority. Throughout *Love of Knowledge*, there is an emphasis on questioning all beliefs and doctrines, and this applies with full force to all that is said here. Even statements that seem to be presented as principles or axioms are better understood as suggestive ways of looking at the evidence that thoughts and experience provide.

Although the vision presented here could be understood as a new and more incisive 'read-out' of what time presents, to stop at this level would 'reduce' the vision. Replacing one set of views with another brings only limited benefit, even when the new views allow for alternatives that the old views exclude. Instead, the TSK vision is best understood as a symbol for creative freedom — a symbol *activated* through an inquiry that sets no limits in advance.

Such an approach might be understood as 'skeptical' in the classical sense, but this does not mean adopting the stance of a 'non-believer'. While the 'believer' may not recognize his belief as 'just a presentation', the 'non-believer' does not recognize his 'non-belief' as a form of belief. Neither 'position' is true to the full potential of knowledge; both tend to reduce inquiry to a conceptual attitude or activity.

More generally, little purpose will be served by categorizing this presentation according to conventional models or fields of knowledge. The inquiry here investigates the fundamental process by which human beings turn perceptions into judgments, judgments into patterns, and patterns into fixed positions. It resonates with the central issues of philosophy, psychology, religion, education, and every other field of knowledge that takes the human situation as central. Anyone from any background can study and benefit from the TSK vision, without undergoing special training, adopting a fixed perspective, engaging in particular practices, or making implicit commitments. There is no specific program or methodology of inquiry to follow. Even the reader who proceeds casually on the basis of simple curiosity may discover interesting insights.

To insist on *defining* the knowledge that inquiry discovers and placing it into categories is considered a 'professional' approach to knowledge. 'Professionals' trained in this approach, such as psychologists and philosophers, have been among the most enthusiastic readers of *Time, Space, and Knowledge.* Yet this kind of enthusiasm is often confined to the level of ideas, and ideas, no matter how 'interesting', do not lead to change at the deepest level. If knowledge is pursued in this way — *within* a conventional framework — the point may be missed and the vision dismissed.

In investigating knowledge, it can be advantageous to proceed as an 'amateur', not bound by 'professional training'. It is possible to read, think, reflect, and observe without structuring these activities into an orderly progression that moves from a specified starting point to a specified goal by means of an approved methodology. Freed from such presuppositions, knowledge becomes available as a basic 'knowingness', unaffected by limits and boundaries.

The full implications of the *Time, Space, and Knowledge* vision will reveal themselves most clearly through a focus on experience that calls the *framework* of experience into question. Time, Space, and Knowledge are active components of our own being. Space is not only the empty container for objects, or the distance that separates one thing from another — it is the 'background' or even the 'substance' for everything that appears 'within' it. Time is not only the measure for what happens, but the active intensity within experience, which manifests equally in anxiety, fascination, or sharp awareness. Knowledge is not simply the accumulation of facts and methodologies, but a creative engaging that offers the potential for deep appreciation and flowing enjoyment.

One way to investigate the *human significance* of Time, Space, and Knowledge is through an inquiry into balance. As individuals, we are often out of balance, whether on the psychological level, the physical level, or in our relationship with external circumstances. An experiential inquiry can open Space, energize Time, and make Knowledge available, restoring a balance that brings harmony to the way we live our lives.

From within the TSK vision, however, this view is only a first-level approximation of the true potential for balance. The language we use inevitably directs us toward the individual actor at the center of any experience, but the balance attained by the 'actor-self' is a 'personalized' version of the interplay among Space, Time, and Knowledge. The self singles out as *its possessions* emotions, self-image, attachments, relationships, and a sense of personal freedom. It sets in motion a momentum that heads at once toward imbalance.

The style of inquiry introduced here counteracts the tendency toward 'singling out', thus signaling a return to balance. With no positions or possessions, such inquiry is committed only to knowledge, and this commitment, *because it remains available as a subject for inquiry*, is in an important sense self-correcting.

Complete commitment to inquiry can be maintained only through the activation of a subtle, probing intelligence. The self tends to *adopt* a position that it describes to itself as being *free from* positions. The resulting confusion and self-deception are similar to a drunkard's conviction that the most ordinary thoughts are profound and revolutionary insights.

Inquiry best suited to activating a more subtle intelligence is one that goes beyond words and concepts, judgments and distinctions, and the sense that the self 'gains' knowledge. Investigation can certainly make use of such basic concepts as 'higher', 'lower', 'process', 'path', 'progress', 'transformation', etc. But if the words take on a reality of their own, the pursuit of knowledge degenerates into word games.

The TSK vision offers a highly practical, 'realistic' understanding of the way things are, producing a direct and immediate effect on the ways we act and the satisfaction available to us. Yet if inquiry succeeds in activating 'knowingness', a new and complementary perspective arises, in which the vision itself can be explored as a fiction to be enjoyed, a story that the reader can join in creating.

WORKING WITH
THE EXERCISES

T he exercises in *Love of Knowledge* evoke a more
global knowing, a more active temporality, and a
more accommodating space. They can help to heal the
frustration and pain that arise through our ordinary ways
of being and knowing. Varied in content and approach,
they can be explored in different ways.

The early exercises are intended primarily to initiate
a process of opening to the possibilities implicit within
Time, Space, and Knowledge. Later exercises tend to
complement the reading more closely. Although the
exercises do build on one another, they need not be
practiced in the order they are presented. Each exercise is
assigned to a series, and could also be practiced effectively in conjunction with others in the series. Working
out the interrelationships between text and exercises
and among exercises would be one way to engage text
and exercises alike.

It is generally best at the start to practice in tranquil
settings situated higher than their surroundings. Spring
and autumn, or other times of the year when the weather

is mild, offer good opportunities for extended practice. Once a firm basis in the practice of an exercise has been established, it can be illuminating to experiment with carrying out the same exercise in crowded, noisy, distracted environments. With heightened sensitivity, the insights and ways of seeing stimulated by the exercise can be available under any circumstances.

A good approach is to set aside a two-hour period in which to practice an exercise, and to practice at least twice a week. If it seems too difficult to sustain attention for this length of time, other alternatives would be to practice several related exercises in one two-hour session, or to combine practice with reading and reflection, or with the keeping of a journal. Another approach is to resolve to set aside time at regular intervals, without making a commitment to specific periods of time. The exercises can also be dealt with more casually, though their benefit may be reduced accordingly.

Keeping a journal can be a valuable adjunct to reflecting on the ideas and exercises presented in *Love of Knowledge*. Insights can be shared with others who are engaged with the TSK vision, and journal entries can also offer useful personal feedback. Comparing entries over time may reveal signs of 'progress' in understanding that can encourage continuing inquiry and also suggest new avenues for exploration.

Some of the exercises that call for visualization or intense imaginative activity depend on first developing strong concentration. A good preparation, which could be used at the start of each period of practice, would be to relax the body and mind. The exercises in *Kum Nye*

Relaxation, available through Dharma Publishing, can lead to a deep and also energizing relaxation; other well-known relaxation techniques could serve a similar purpose. Once a basic relaxation has stabilized, three factors should be synchronized: alertness, calm, and deepening. When these factors have all been activated, visualization and imagination can quickly lead to clarity and insight.

The exercises offered here may help give access to the TSK vision for those studying it independently. Other exercises require personal supervision, as well as strong personal interest on the part of the student, and I have chosen not to present them here. Topics explored in such exercises include the unity of space without borders or edges, order and the open mind, the direct understanding of time, integrating levels of knowledge, knowledge without objects, 'knowingness' without subject-object polarity, and opening emotional blockages.

The basis for this decision perhaps requires further comment. In writing this book, I have been keenly aware that language is an imperfect tool for instruction, and in its written form in particular offers endless opportunities for miscommunication. Though the voice may be ready to speak, it is the mind that determines what will be said and what will be heard. If the mind is bound by specific identities and definitions operating 'beneath' the conscious level, communication will be intrinsically limited. In writing, there is no opportunity to counteract such tendencies through more immediate contact.

The exercises in *Love of Knowledge* can help clarify the structures that shape inquiry, but there are other aspects of the search for knowledge that cannot be as readily presented through the medium of words and concepts. If more is to be communicated through language, it is better done in a setting where communication need not rely on words alone.

None of this means that the insight available through careful, independent study and investigation of the TSK vision is in some way intrinsically limited, whether or not the exercises are practiced. There is nothing about the 'process' of insight initiated through investigation that sets any limits whatsoever. The reader who engages the vision carefully, reflecting, observing, and questioning, will find that understanding deepens in accord with a momentum of its own. The text has been written in such a way that the reader can structure his or her own inquiry, finding new connections and deeper meanings. Not every topic will appeal to everyone, but each reader can find aspects of the vision that inspire inquiry.

Love of Knowledge can be understood as an invitation to know presented by knowledge itself. Yet this invitation can only be communicated in ways that perpetuate subtle limitations. When these limitations come to the fore, leaving the reader discouraged or frustrated, it may be useful to recall that it is the nature of this presentation that is limited, not access to knowledge itself. What can be placed within the pages of a book does not fully reflect the intimacy of Being.

Guide to the Exercises

SERIES A

Manifesting Space, Time, and Knowledge	81
Situational Positioning	87
Patterns in Space and Time	95

SERIES B

Calming Body, Mind, and Senses	167
Field of Space	229
Sound Within Sound	237
Observing Hearing	255
Resonating Sound	261
Founding Receptivity	311

SERIES C

Drawing on the Past	9
Inventing the Past	107
Projecting the Future	153
Building the Past	209

SERIES D

Layers of Mind	15
Feeling Thoughts	31
Thoughts in Conflict	49
Background of Thoughts	55
Gravity of Thinking	65
Expanding and Contracting Thought	73

Protecting and Projecting   177

Sameness in Difference   327

Space of Mind   335

Essence of Thought   355

Mind Without Images   369

SERIES E

Dissolving Tension in Time   23

Disowning Tension   41

Locating Tension in Space   199

Embodied Energy   317

SERIES F

Object of Desire   161

Inviting Awareness   247

Inviting Being   285

SERIES G

Field of Awareness   145

Exchanging Feelings   295

Visualizing Feelings   303

Accumulating Feelings   361

SERIES H

Moments Between Moments   119

Cloud of Knowing   135

Point of Transition   183

Observing Without Owning   191

SERIES I

Reversing Time   127

Reversing Momentum   221

Playing with Momentum   267

Glowing Journey in Time   277

SERIES J

Field of Feeling   341

'Ness' of 'Ness'   349

SERIES K

Alternatives to Mind   377

Symbolic Interplay of Action   385

Exploring Space, Time, and Knowledge   393

Symbols of Being   401

Adventure of Being   411

INTRODUCTION

The freedom to know is our greatest treasure. The transmission of realization in spiritual disciplines, the painstaking refinement of scientific methodology, the careful formulations of logic, and the revelations of art or mathematics all express a freely active knowledge. To awaken appreciation for such knowing at work in our awareness is to let the love of knowledge enter our lives.

Human knowledge has attained great heights, establishing a body of known facts far beyond the capacity of any one person to master. Yet our own active knowing remains undeveloped. How often do we truly realize that we are each unique human beings, alive in a world of constantly shifting forms, sensitively attuned to the universe that we experience? Without such appreciation for our situation and prospects, knowledge cannot easily come alive within our intelligence.

When we activate knowledge, we find wonder in the simple circumstance that our body is embodied in space, our experience unfolds in time, and our mind expresses ever-expanding 'knowingness'. We discover how to look beyond the standard modalities of knowledge and investigate at a more basic level the origins of the human capacity to perceive and to reason, and the purposes which those capacities might serve. Knowledge becomes more effective, communicating on all levels simultaneously, so that we can directly touch the heart of knowledge as an all-pervasive quality of being. As such knowing is distributed throughout the range of our personal experience, a healing process is activated that can profoundly affect the self and others.

Whatever the restrictions on our knowledge, *we are already engaged in knowing.* Inquiry and observation bring to that knowing clarity, appreciation, and intelligence. We find that we know more than we realize, and develop the strength to act on what we know, so that our actions bring benefit to ourselves and to the world. With greater appreciation for the riches that experience presents, time deepens and expands, allowing a further maturation of knowledge and promoting harmony of thought, word, and deed. Commitment to the welfare of others arises spontaneously: a direct response to the unfolding of a new vision.

As human beings, we can embrace the time and space out of which we arise and within which knowledge unfolds. Acting with vigor, letting the love of knowledge be our guide, we can become masters of our own space, commanding our own time. We can respond to knowledge by activating more knowledge, so that knowledge unfolds 'beyond' and 'within' all limitations.

This book responds to the unfolding of Knowledge by giving expression to the Time, Space, and Knowledge interplay. Since it communicates Time, Space, and Knowledge, whatever understanding results through the act of reading and reflecting on it will express Time, Space, and Knowledge as well. The vision evokes itself, active in all communications and in each act of inquiry.

This evocative quality of the vision distinguishes it from more standard forms of inquiry. Analytic modes of thought and investigation make knowledge into a possession acquired only with difficulty. The great insights of human beings throughout history, however, depend on a different, more spontaneous way of knowing, one which supports and draws on analysis, but also goes beyond it into the more mysterious realm of genius and inspiration. The TSK vision taps this 'other' way of knowing directly.

The standard view of knowledge relies strongly on the self as knower. Analysis can challenge this understanding, but only by confronting the self 'head-on', with conflict, defensiveness, and confusion the likely result. The analysis and exploration undertaken here, however, do not call for this kind of confrontation. Instead, they loosen the hold that the self has on knowledge by offering the self a new kind of freedom, based on the love of knowledge and the joy that comes through inquiry. *The knowledge evoked in this way does not depend on taking one position or rejecting another.*

Conventionally understood, knowledge takes form by moving through the stages of observation, experience, interpretation, understanding, and actualization. This step by step process widens the separation between knower and known, and easily turns knowledge in the direction of an intellectual process far removed from direct experience. The bond linking past and future to the present is severed, converting history into a lifeless abstraction and turning what has not yet happened into fantasy. The linear link between subject and object confines knowledge to a two-dimensional plane, leaving the depths of knowing unexplored. Even when experience seems direct, these same patterns may continue to operate on a more subtle level.

When knowledge is more inclusive and evocative, it embraces the activities of knowing and seeing, strengthening their power. Instead of the linear relationship of 'subject knowing object', there is the 'experience' of 'knowing' the experience of knowing. The *relationship between* subject and object becomes accessible directly, with the consequence that subject and object alike are transformed: The 'object' becomes knowledge itself, while the 'subject' becomes experience.

Once this transformation has been activated, Time, Space, and Knowledge can be acknowledged as vibrant facets of human being. As actors in this unfolding drama, human beings are 'in' Space, 'on' Time, and 'of' Knowledge. Philosophy is not confined to making sense of what has happened in the past, and 'doing' philosophy is not an activity undertaken to gain future understanding or to arrive at a valid proof of an abstract logical proposition. The history of knowledge and the future projections of the knowable come alive with a knowledge based directly on an ever-present 'knowingness'.

For first-time readers of *Love of Knowledge*, these prospects may seem abstract. As individuals whose lives are played out in a specific setting and sequence, we arrive at knowledge through a *process* of inquiry. A perspective that sets aside or challenges the conventional, linear understanding of 'process' remains largely inaccessible. It may therefore be of some benefit if I take a more conventional approach at the outset, describing the way in which the vision that guides this presentation emerged into being.

An Emerging Vision

The ideas that eventually led to the *Time, Space, and Knowledge* vision first appeared in my mind in somewhat the same way that forms might appear floating in empty space. These unexpected thoughts led me to investigate concepts and patterns that I had tended to disregard in the past.

Observing my experience in light of these new ideas, I began to notice that there were different 'levels' of existence, and that these were linked with different mental 'objects'. Little by little, I came to some understanding of how these shapes and forms arose and how they took on meaning and value. This process of investigation circled back on itself, and my senses and my observation on every level became more clear. I learned to see on more than just one 'level' — not in any esoteric sense, but simply in letting the mind look more directly at its own operation.

The changes that came with this new way of investigating brought with them a remarkable sense of freedom. Externally, events continued to unfold much as they had before, subject to their own momentum. But 'internally', I understood and experienced for myself how thought imposed patterns and limits. Once I saw these limits *in the act of being set up*, I found that I was no longer subject to them. At the same time, it was not 'I' who was gaining freedom or discovering new insights. Instead, knowledge seemed to be active in a new way.

In exploring these issues and insights, I made a distinction between the 'external' world of objects and the 'internal' world of sensory experience. In looking at the 'objective world' I could focus my understanding in terms of 'space', while in looking at the operation of the senses, I had to introduce 'time' as a factor in understanding. This in turn led me to look at 'experience', which seemed to be given by time directly, and to inquire into the connection between experience and the activity of the mind. The interactions among time, space, and knowledge engaged my attention more fully, gradually unfolding into an encompassing vision.

The course of investigation and research that I was carrying out seemed to me rather unusual. Although I had been raised in a tradition where inquiry into the workings of mind was an integral part of education, the specific approach I now found myself adopting had no direct connection to this tradition, or to any other path of inquiry that I was familiar with. I saw the clear potential for tracing such connections, or for exploring possible links between what I was discovering and the views of science. While this approach would have been interesting, it would also have led away from the immediacy of inquiry into a realm where identities, orientations, definitions, and descriptions played a large role. Instead,

I simply continued to observe myself and my experience in light of time, space, and knowledge, content to let the new vision develop naturally.

The unfolding vision allowed a more multidimensional understanding, as though I were being guided simultaneously by several compasses, each pointing in a different direction, yet each somehow accurate. The conventional limitation that confines observation to a single 'point of view' situated in space and time had less hold. Knowledge itself seemed to be opening, like a light that had previously been obscured but now was radiating from all directions. This knowledge was freely available: less a possession to be obtained than a luminous, transparent 'attribute' of experience and mental activity.

In tapping this powerful and liberating vision, I never had the sense that I had discovered an esoteric, hidden knowledge. Instead, it seemed to me that the TSK vision gave access to a knowing integral to all knowledge, potentially available within all times and in all circumstances. Observation and inquiry allowed anyone to become a 'witness' for the 'self-evidence' of knowledge. The inner strength and certainty released by the vision, the dynamic activity of the mind that knew, and the physical embodiment in space that made this knowing possible were all expressions of knowledge.

From this new perspective, there was no 'higher' knowledge; only different forms of 'knowingness', like the different levels of meaning in a richly symbolic work of art or philosophy. The varying manifestations of mind — in thought, in consciousness, in awareness —

could be understood as responses by 'knowingness' to changing circumstances and connections.

I found it helpful to think of conventional knowledge as being like a fabric, woven through the activity of the knowing 'subject' in its interaction with the known 'object'. This fabric served to veil the natural light of Knowledge 'within' being. But contacting 'knowingness' through observation and inquiry 'loosened' the fabric's weave, allowing a luminous knowing to shine through.

At first, this luminous knowing seemed quite separate from 'knowledge' of the ordinary 'objects' and the 'events' that time presented. Gradually, however, I began to see the 'fabric' of temporal subject-object interactions as a direct expression of knowledge, and the 'weaving' of the fabric as the active temporal manifestation of 'luminosity'. Only because conventional knowledge interpreted the 'temporal fabric' as an obscuring, 'solid' reality did experience so often have the flavor of stagnation, conditioning, and bondage. Emotionality, confusion, and not-knowing were 'postures'—the outcomes of 'positions' adopted by the 'subject' as specific interpretations of the subject-object interaction posited by conventional knowledge. By interpreting the positions themselves as being 'real', conventional knowledge assured that the postures adopted by the self would be frozen and inflexible.

A commitment to open observation appeared to reverse this well-established tendency, restoring balance and new potential to experience. I became increasingly aware of the artificial limits we place on observation, focusing on the world around us while ignoring our own minds and the operation of the knowing faculty. Observation can 'know' mental events such as feelings and emotions, and on that basis we assert that we 'know' how to use the mind in specific ways. Such 'knowing', however, is painfully restricted. We do not 'know' how to 'touch' the mind directly, or how to observe the interaction of 'subject' and 'object', 'self' and 'world'. We remain oblivious to the subtle constructs that shape both our understanding and the world that we experience.

Instead of challenging these restrictions, I let 'observation' expand to include them. Just as the mind knows 'events' and 'things' in a particular way, so it knows 'mind' in a particular way. But this 'minding' of the mind — the capacity for knowing and for constructing models that shape the scope of our knowing — can be observed directly in action. When I followed this course, conventional patterns and structures and the models or 'programs' that generate them began to seem transparent. Whether the new pictures and thoughts that formed as the old ones lost their hold were 'accurate' did not seem of primary concern; what truly mattered was the openness that allowed such new content to appear.

As this capacity for knowing and exercising the mind expanded, I tasted a deep and nourishing enjoyment. From enjoyment came clarity, and from clarity a sense of appreciation for the brilliant and powerful dynamic of knowledge. Eventually, I touched an awareness that seemed to 'embody' both clarity and appreciation, 'understanding' and 'feeling', but to go beyond them as well. I realized that this awareness could best be described as the love of knowledge.

The Value of Knowledge

Love of knowledge could be said to be the inspiration for the *Time, Space, and Knowledge* vision. The wonder that it fosters safeguards the impulse toward awareness and intelligence and counteracts the subtle inclination to accept as true presumptions, beliefs, and presuppositions. Guided by wonder, we remain free to look *within* our presuppositions and beliefs to the knowledge they contain. We participate in Knowledge directly.

Once love of knowledge is active, Knowledge itself supports the further deepening of knowledge. Full knowledge dissolves the 'distance' between knower and known that characterizes conventional not-knowing. With no distance, an intimacy of knowing emerges, and knowledge becomes inseparable from love.

Under such circumstances, there are no limits on the forms that knowledge can take. Common sense, rational inquiry, and logic can all be accepted as valid ways of exercising knowledge, without rejecting the insights of the great mystical traditions, the fruits of investigations into the paranormal, or the path of 'magic' and 'mystery'. Nor does this 'acceptance' place the TSK vision in the position of 'encompassing' such forms of knowledge, for the vision itself is not 'situated' in a way that sets it 'apart from' knowledge itself.

An inquiry open to all forms of knowledge is the heart of what I hope to share in this book. I have no wish to trace the TSK vision to a particular lineage of ideas, nor do I want to see it established as the basis for a new dogma or model. I have simply tried to report the results of my own investigations and thoughts, giving the reader a basis to build on that allows but does not determine.

Some people are suspicious of questioning, for they fear that it will promote confusion and contribute to human suffering. But based on my own experience, I would say that we do not need to fear confusion unduly. If confusion does come, it may only be a passing phase in the search for knowledge, a sign that new knowing has begun to operate. As we continue investigation into the unfolding of experience, allowing love of knowledge to take root and to flourish, more knowledge may appear spontaneously, almost 'accidentally'.

Love and caring are faculties active in each human being, even if they manifest only as greed or selfishness, or even as self-hatred. Despite the difficulties and deceptions to which human beings are prone, devotion and loyalty are native to the human spirit. But when knowledge is limited, love and devotion are easily distorted. When observation is confined to the 'objective' realm, individuals tend to submit their sense of worth and well-being to the 'objects' they encounter, looking to possessions, power, and circumstances for meaning and fulfillment. Unaccustomed to investigating the workings of the mind, the operation of the self, or the potential range of knowledge, they lose sight of ways of being that can be deeply healing and nourishing.

This pattern — love led by limited knowledge into fruitless ways of being — affirms the value of the love of knowledge. Awakening the innate human capacity for devotion and appreciation, love of knowledge can transform our lives. When appreciation and awareness are active, even the limits on what we know, even our lack of caring, express a deeper 'knowingness'.

Love of knowledge strengthens and encourages observation and inquiry, making knowledge available 'from within'. Subjective 'not-knowing' is no longer accepted as 'definitive'; instead, it is 'incorporated' into a more fundamental knowing. The fixation on the 'objective' realm that operates so powerfully in this culture is loosened. Relying neither on 'the facts' nor on feelings and emotions as the source of truth or happiness, we are no longer caught up in appearances, nor are we subject to the painful necessity of accumulating the knowledge we need. With knowledge directly available we gain new power over space and time — a 'first-level' indication that higher levels of Space and Time have become accessible.

The problems of human being ultimately trace to a lack of knowledge, or else to a lack of ability to apply the knowledge we already have. Having recognized that this is so, we have a clear choice. We can accept this lack of knowledge as inevitable, or we can commit ourselves to the pursuit of more fruitful ways of knowing.

Throughout history there have been those who have chosen the 'path' of knowledge. Within this very moment we are free to join in their lineage. Open to the gracious, entrancing play of 'knowingness', we can discover a world alive with significance. Pledging our efforts and intelligence to the course of inquiry, we can contribute to the manifestation of knowledge in time and space and claim our precious heritage as human beings.

Dedicated as an expression of Knowledge
to all who wish to explore
the Time, Space, and Knowledge vision,
wherever and whenever they may be.

PART ONE

Patterns
and
Possibilities

Unfolding Revealing

Inquiry unfolds
Directions and distances
Into dimensions of space
Revealing the dynamic
Of the measured flow of time
Knowledge of object
Points to knowledge of subject
Invites the subject of knowledge

THE PROMISE
OF KNOWLEDGE

No matter who we are or how we live, our lives are shaped by what we know. Knowledge determines what we hold true, what we stand for, and how we act; what we can be, experience, and accomplish. Knowledge has the power to change our lives and to change reality; indeed, new knowledge has often transformed whole societies, even whole civilizations.

Knowledge as such (as opposed to knowledge of this or that field) has long been considered a subject for specialists: philosophers, theologians, and perhaps a few theoretical scientists whose insights into the fundamentals of the physical universe have earned them the right to reflect on the nature of reality.

But knowledge is not an abstract field of inquiry for specialists — *it stands at the center of our being, the birthright of all humanity.* To see how a situation arises; to see what is likely to develop in the future; to see connections and possibilities: these and other, more subtle, aspects of knowing have a direct impact on the way we live and the satisfaction we enjoy. When we ask

3

questions about the nature of reality and the meaning and possibilities of human being, we are acknowledging our fundamental capacity to know, unrestrained by the content and assumptions of what is already known.

Appreciation for this fundamental capacity to know awakens a love of knowledge. It encourages us to discover new significance in our thoughts and our actions, the presuppositions we make, and the ways we interact with others. It reveals knowledge actively at work throughout space and time.

In every time and every culture, there have been individuals who have broken away from the accepted forms and predetermined limits of conventional knowledge to explore new ways of thinking and being. Disregarding the definitions that partition knowledge into standard fields of inquiry, they have probed the boundaries of the known, reaching out toward a broader vision. They have discovered the deep sense of meaning and profound satisfaction that come with a wholehearted commitment to inquiry.

The path that these pioneers have taken is open to everyone. We too can learn to ask fundamental questions with all the resources of our mind, heart, and body. The resulting understanding may allow us to manifest a new and higher knowing in our own lives, and to add to the store of collective human knowledge as well.

The insights of the great thinkers of the past quickly turn into the accepted truths and indispensable tools of later generations. As they evolve into routine formulas, the knowledge they express loses its capacity to inspire the further growth of knowing. But love of knowledge, which produces such insights, never loses its power to transform what is accepted and awaken what has lain dormant. Guided by the love of knowledge, we can open to new vision and commit ourselves fully to action that transforms and enriches our lives.

Signs of a Higher Knowledge

Most of us experience times when our awareness seems more powerful than usual, our experience more vivid. Beauty or love, flashes of insight, or subtle, unexpected sights and sounds can suddenly transform the mind. For a few moments, before old patterns of knowing set in, we feel more alive. In those rare and precious moments, we recognize that experience can be richer and more expansive than we usually imagine.

Such experiences may involve an element of wishful thinking or deception, and yet in a certain sense they are their own witness. Even if we do not understand fully what they have to tell us, they hint at alternatives to ordinary knowledge and invite us to seek them out by cultivating an active intelligence.

Moments of special clarity suggest that with a different understanding, our notion of knowledge itself could change. Step by step, knowledge could teach us knowledge. We could pursue questions in a new way: not just to accumulate information and ideas, but to learn who we really are and what we can do with our lives.

Testing Our Knowledge

To test the depth of our present knowledge, we can look at what is happening in our lives. Do we understand our circumstances and capacities in ways that let us act creatively and with inner freedom? Does our conduct conform to our values and our intentions? Are we satisfied with where we are heading — with our accomplishments and our prospects? Are we contributing to the world in which we live? Honestly seeking answers to such questions lets us determine whether knowledge is lacking. If we find that our achievements fall short of our goals, discover that our sense of vision loses its power to inspire, or recognize that our lives are out of balance, we can ask whether the knowledge we now possess will support our potential.

Even if we feel satisfied with our accomplishments, we are forced to acknowledge that much of what happens in our lives seems completely beyond our control. In the world around us, peace and prosperity reign for a time, only to give way to war, poverty, and malaise. While some people live fortunate lives, others seem born to suffering. Moments of satisfaction pass by too quickly, while restlessness, pain, boredom, and anxiety recur again and again, in cycles that we seem powerless to affect. Even the mind operates independent of our intentions, wandering here and there, dwelling on past regrets and future concerns or fantasies.

In the face of our inability to live as we would wish, the inadequacy of our knowledge stands out clearly. Our visions and ideals, our methods and explanations seem incapable of offering consistently effective guidance.

Choosing Knowledge

How do we reconcile moments of a finer, more subtle awareness with the knowledge that operates in our ordinary lives? Unless we learn more about knowledge itself, we cannot say. It may be that the limits on human understanding trace to immutable structures of reality, but we cannot know for certain without investigating further. Knowledge may have potential that goes unacknowledged by conventional understanding.

Even the most independent thinkers accept without question much of the understanding current within the culture. But relying on information and assumptions communicated to us by others establishes us in the habit of not exercising our own intelligence. Our capacity to know weakens in ways we do not even notice.

Once we have learned to accept the 'knowledge' that comes to us from outside, we may find it difficult to question and think carefully on our own. When we first try to do so, our inner resources seem limited, and we may grow discouraged. If we persist in exercising knowledge, however, new strength develops, and with it comes new confidence in our ability to know what goes beyond the range of the familiar.

As inquiry opens knowledge, freedom to know in new ways emerges. Going beyond what everyone 'knows' to be true gives us access to a world where knowledge can work its wonder. Even as we recognize that our past, our training, and our circumstances have conditioned us to limit knowledge in pre-established ways, we see that these limits need not bind us. Aware that our thinking is guided by models, we realize that we can create new and more powerful models. Sensitive to the knowledge embodied in vision and ideals, we can discover new ideals and explore beyond the farthest reaches of our own most cherished visions.

Perhaps we have had faith that a knowledge more encompassing than our own was active in the universe; now we may find that such a knowledge activates itself in our own understanding as well. Perhaps we have instead been skeptical of the human capacity to know; now we may find that knowledge can be self-sufficient and self-encouraging, dealing with obstacles directly through a more comprehensive knowing.

This natural development of knowledge is based on inquiry. Putting established truths to the test, letting knowledge lead to unexplored realms, inquiry opens to an understanding and intelligence that allow us to choose for ourselves how to think and act.

Chapter One

Knowledge at work throughout space and time;
path taken by great thinkers; appreciation and love
of knowledge; higher knowledge; acknowledging
not-knowing; new knowledge through inquiry.

Drawing on the Past

Take time over several sessions to list and to describe for yourself the patterns of your life, whether internal or external, recording the results in a journal. Choose particular patterns and trace them back into the past, recalling instances in which they manifested, not stopping with the usual memories or the usual boundaries. Identify and investigate standard interpretations associated with these patterns, and allow yourself to entertain a wide range of alternative interpretations. Look for interconnections, associations, and well-worn ways of understanding that seem self-evident.

Exercise One

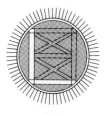

Being of Knowledge

Disclosures of Knowledge

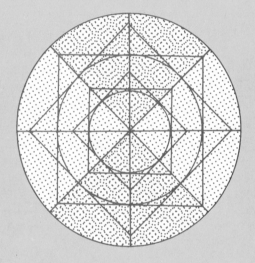

Kaleidoscope of Knowledge
Facets shift through time
Form and structure emerge
Given shape by Knowledge
Patterns preserve the rhythm
Potential of the point

KNOWLEDGE
ALIVE IN HISTORY

The lessons of history offer a good starting point for deepening and expanding knowledge. Knowledge presents itself in history in ways that extend well beyond the realm of the purely cognitive. The knowing in operation at a particular time and place profoundly affects the way people live their lives. It shapes their circumstances, their interests and values, the styles they adopt and then abandon, their concerns, and the outcome of their efforts.

Studying the forms and ways of knowledge through history gives perspective on our own time and our own 'self-evident' truths. The fundamental patterns of culturally transmitted knowledge operate in different ways across time, yet they reveal a sameness as well. Balancing this sameness and difference, we can learn to see the possibilities for knowledge in a new light.

The history of human knowledge extends back far beyond the beginnings of the early civilizations some four to five thousand years ago. Imagine how it must have been to be the first to build a fire! In the initial instant that a flame burst into life by human design, the range of the knowable was transformed, and human knowledge entered a new dimension. For those earliest builders of fire, it must have seemed that human beings had become godlike in their understanding. Gaining access to such miraculous knowledge may have transformed consciousness forever.

In the hundreds of millennia that followed, knowledge must have expanded in similar ways countless times. The knowledge once discovered but now lost would surely match in scope the knowledge that crowds our libraries today. How much of that knowledge, formerly so important to human beings, would be incomprehensible to the modern mind?

In the historical era, knowledge has taken new forms in each of countless cultures, creating a vast spectrum of knowledge beyond imagining. Common understanding and 'self-evident' assumptions differ from place to place and time to time. Within each culture, great artists and thinkers have their own unique ways of knowing.

Developments in knowledge transform a people's understanding on several levels at once. The invention of the spindle gave the Greeks a powerful metaphor for knowledge spinning out human destiny; the spread of mechanical timepieces transformed understanding of the way in which knowledge could shape the world; the use of the compass gave human beings a sense of mastery over place and a new understanding of directionality. Through such transformations, conventional understandings of time, space, and knowledge have taken on new dimensions of meaning.

The shifting flow of knowledge throughout history attracts little interest in contemporary culture, where the rapid rate of change makes past knowledge seem outdated and irrelevant. The resulting lack of historical perspective exacts a price. A narrow view of the past limits our understanding of the present and restricts our ability to foresee the future. Tied to ways of seeing and thinking for which we know no alternatives, we develop short-range solutions for our problems and discount the effects of our actions on future generations. Heedless of trends that have been gathering momentum over time, we are caught unaware by 'sudden' changes.

Knowledge of the past — of how patterns have developed and how they are likely to unfold in the future — can help correct this short-sightedness and give added depth to our own knowledge. History's patterns are a record of the rich and varied creativity of the human mind and spirit; in studying history we are learning to recognize the mind at work in time. Reflecting on the vast array of knowledge that has already unfolded in history awakens an appreciation for what knowledge has to offer humanity. Our current way of knowing, rich and vivid as it is, may reflect only a single narrow wavelength in the full spectrum of knowledge.

Knowing Through Appreciation

Appreciation for knowledge is itself a form of knowing. Once we are sensitive to the forms that knowledge takes, we can learn to recognize its manifestations. Each individual embodies a different way of knowing, contributing to patterns that reflect the capacity for knowledge in an ever-changing light. The great diversity of needs and interests, values and character, heredity and training all affect the ways that knowledge operates. Even this variety may present only a single band in the spectrum of knowledge — for all we know, other beings may fill realms unknown to us, embodying knowledge in ways we cannot begin to imagine.

Although the potential range of knowledge thus remains mysterious, we do understand something about the ways that knowledge develops in time, both collectively and individually. The interplay of observation, experience, and intelligence sustains the expansion of knowledge, leading to the acquisition of values and information and the adoption of standards of truth.

An appreciation for the different ways of knowing revealed by history awakens us to the presence of knowledge where we might never have thought to look. Acknowledging conceptually the diversity of knowledge through time can be the first step in loosening the bonds on our own ways of knowing. As we learn how to take knowledge itself as the topic, inquiry and wonder give rise to the love of knowledge. The source of our knowing merges with the subject under investigation, and knowledge becomes an ever-present companion and guide.

Chapter Two

History of knowledge; contemporary disregard for history; history as mind at work in time; appreciation for embodiments of knowledge.

Layers of Mind

Note the kinds of mental events that come up in the mind and their relationship: images and feelings, intentions, thoughts, judgments, etc. Which elements are dominant and which supportive? How do states such as tension, conflict, boredom, calm, clarity, or appreciation arise? Keep a journal in which you record your discoveries: an annotated catalogue or inventory of the contents of your mind.

Exercise Two

Open Space Dimension

Knowledge Taking Form

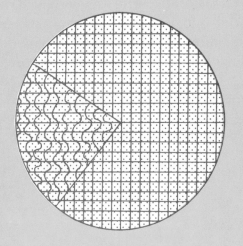

Knowledge perpetuates Knowledge
Building toward diversity and balance
Replicating limits and boundaries
Territories expand and contract
Within a field open to discovery
Pointing toward encompassing knowledge

FACES OF KNOWLEDGE

M odern knowledge reflects the accelerating pace of change that pervades our societies. The historical evidence suggests that transformations in the patterns of knowledge can now take place in the course of a decade or less, while in the past they might easily have taken a century or more. In the last century, one new field of knowledge after another has developed — from atomic energy and astrophysics to molecular biology and computer science. If the rate of change in knowledge can be loosely linked to the rate of population growth, present trends indicate that it will double in each generation. In just a few centuries, new knowledge and its consequences will create a world almost beyond recognition.

Even this speculation may be too conservative. The unparalleled change we have seen in the past century may only now be gaining its full momentum. Modern technology moves steadily toward higher velocities. Today it bases itself largely on the nearly instantaneous rhythms of electrons in motion rather than the measured, mechanical movements of earlier times. As this change affects ever more areas of life, the slower, more stable rhythms of older ways of life are overpowered by the spread of a global technological culture.

The Emerging Role of Technology

In the past, when cultures often had little contact with one another, different values and ways of life could easily co-exist in different parts of the world. Different ways of seeing and knowing might prevail from one valley to the next. In periods of increased cultural contact, those differences could stimulate new developments or lead to conflict. When cultures with different systems of knowledge met, their ideas and values, means of production and methods of inquiry, forms of government, and politics all came under intensified scrutiny. Each culture held out its own model of what was true or real or good; each asserted that it provided the best or most satisfying answers or experiences or products. Educational systems promoted one model over another, as did cultural institutions and even different forms of entertainment.

As such interactions have proliferated over the past decades, science and technology have emerged as the single most dominant model. The steady gains in technological knowledge over the past few centuries, and especially in recent decades, are indisputable, and give to technology a momentum that seems almost unstoppable. The result has been to bring new forms of culture and new prospects for human being to the fore. Just as new civilizations four to five thousand years ago broke decisively with old ways of knowing, so we in turn seem to have worked a revolution in human knowledge.

The success of this style of knowledge has had an unanticipated consequence: increasing uniformity of thought and understanding. Today ideas and values are in constant contact, and the patterns of history seem to be tending toward convergence. People throughout the world have begun to behave in similar ways, and to share the same values and understanding as well. As knowledge becomes more homogeneous, the same models for what counts as acceptable knowledge are taught around the world, with little variation.

In the perspective that arises from such homogeneous knowledge, science and technology are considered the culmination of human knowledge, but it has not always been so. In the distant past, shamanism was the highest form of knowledge, and at different times religion, philosophy, statecraft, and poetry have all been ascendant. History is like a tumbler in which different ideas and values are tossed and turned, with now one coming to the top, and then another. Changes in knowledge through time and space have a rhythm and quality of their own.

Most of us would probably consider it self-evident that the scientific view, which sees science as the culmination of a steady growth in knowledge over time, is more accurate than alternative views that understand the state of human knowledge as static, or even in decline. But this judgment depends completely on the measure of progress applied. As citizens of modern society, we follow a trend toward measuring success and achievement in materialistic terms, according to which this society's knowledge is the most advanced the world has ever known. This trend, which first began gaining momentum some two centuries ago, is now so firmly established that it is almost irresistible.

With the universal adoption of such standards, countries are commonly separated into two groups (currently designated as the 'developed' and the 'less developed'). Differences in their cultures are set aside: The sole issue is how fully they have been able to put into effect the norms of conduct, life style, and methodology specified by the prevailing model of technological knowledge.

Ironically, however, in countries where development has been underway for a century or more, there has also 'developed' a keen sense that technological knowledge has its limitations. We have learned that knowledge of how to accomplish specific ends does not necessarily prevent conflict or confusion; instead it may actually promote certain kinds of dislocation and danger. The power of technology magnifies the potential for destruction and harm in ways that have led in past decades to a widespread and deepening concern.

The problems that confront us — whether actual, predictable, or as yet unforeseen — are simply too major to be ignored. We have begun to wonder whether the growth in technological knowledge may not conceal the absence of other kinds of knowing. There has been a growing recognition that if material progress is not understood as the highest value, science will not necessarily be seen as the ultimate arbiter of knowledge.

While evidence of such dangers and difficulties is available for all to witness, the less developed countries tend to discount it in favor of a wholehearted commitment to the positive side of development. Flooded with reminders that people elsewhere enjoy an affluence and ease lacking in their own lives, inhabitants of 'underdeveloped' countries find it difficult to believe that confusion and suffering go on as before in the midst of prosperity. When they do hear of difficulties, they are more likely to blame them on political or social systems than on the commitment to technology. Occasionally some may wonder aloud whether the price of technology might not be too high, but such concerns seem powerless to affect the basic trend. If anything, they contribute to a sense of anxiety and nervousness, as though a secret best left unspoken were being named in public.

Assessing Technological Knowledge

The technological model for knowledge is at its most effective in showing us ways to attain desired ends within the material realm. Yet new possessions, advances in science, or even better health and longer lives may mean little if we lack the knowledge to choose our actions wisely, with a full understanding of their consequences. For all of its accomplishments, technological knowledge seems unable to meet this need. Wherever the knowledge embodied in technology is leading, it remains unclear whether it is bringing us any closer to understanding the purpose of human activity or to the goal of perfecting our capacities as human beings.

In the 'developed' countries, there are many who have been led by such reflections to look back at traditional ways of life with regret. They find there a stability and rootedness, a healthy absence of anxiety and neurosis, a simple ability to communicate directly and honestly with others and to enjoy life to the fullest. Yet even if this is so, nostalgia for a vanished past does nothing to change the present. There is no turning back to the earlier ways, which in any case are quickly disappearing. Nor would we really want to give up the benefits that modern knowledge has brought.

Moreover, on the most basic level, the limitations of technological knowledge only perpetuate a limitation that has endured through the millennia, transcending all cultural distinctions. Despite the wholehearted efforts of every human being who has ever lived, the collective, transmitted knowledge of humanity has left most individuals unable to be happy more than a small percentage of the time. From this perspective, technological knowledge is neither good nor bad. Like all conventional ways of knowing, it simply lacks the capacity to offer human beings complete fulfillment.

Chapter Three

Accelerating pace of change; emergence of technological knowledge; global uniformity based on science and technology; the loss of alternatives; awareness of limitations.

Dissolving Tension in Time

Tension has a temporal structure linked to patterns centered on the concerns and desires of the
self. Explore this structure as separate from the
content of the narratives it sustains. Look for
similar patterns in different situations, expanding your inquiry to include situations where
there is no obvious tension. This exercise can
also be practiced by taking postures that stimulate physical tension. Several exercises in *Kum
Nye Relaxation* could serve this purpose.

Exercise Three

Momentum of Time

Seed of Fulfillment

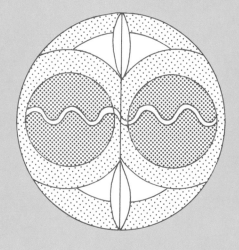

Ancient symbol of growth
Evocation of Knowledge
Distant from division
Prior to discourse
Two from One
Zero into Zero
Rhythms of nature
Seeds of knowing
Boundless yield

NO DIRECTION

The commitment to the onrushing technological wave has affected our understanding of knowledge in ways that are difficult to assess. For example, technology promotes the adoption of global standards that make communication easier. It has initiated a trend toward shared language, standards, and values that increasingly allows human beings to pool their knowledge and promotes global harmony.

Yet this same trend toward homogeneity may lead to the loss of a precious heritage of cultural diversity that in the past sustained a wide variety of ways of knowing. And adopting uniform standards may have the effect of allowing well-established techniques and understandings to prevail over innovative alternatives.

Similarly, the power and global impact of technology has a two-sided effect. On the one hand, innovators and creative thinkers can have an almost immediate influence on tens of millions of people. New ideas can quickly be acted on, contributing to an array of products and accomplishments that would have seemed miraculous in an earlier age. On the other hand, the forces of technology can be usurped by leaders whose vision distorts human values. History gives numerous examples of cultures led by faulty knowledge into mass delusion and deception, and we cannot assume that we have become immune to such developments.

With remarkable efficiency, technology replicates a particular understanding of knowledge. A distinctive technological language and way of thought result in a technological 'style' for managing the economy, making use of time, enjoying the benefits of leisure, and educating each generation for its place within society. 'Cost-benefit analysis' and other forms of utilitarian thought increasingly form the basis for human actions and interactions, even when they remain wholly unarticulated. Yet these manifestations of the technological modality are only instances of a more fundamental understanding that technology communicates — a way of making sense of knowledge itself.

Knowledge Technology

As technology has grown, it has generated whole new forms of knowledge. For decades, information has been broadcast through space to be reassembled into new forms; escaping the confines of the earth, it has traveled outward into the universe at the speed of light. In recent times, technology has made knowledge itself an object of innovation; examples include correlating trends and making predictions based on statistical analysis or computer simulations. The knowing capacity has been investigated through simulated intelligence in computers and other electronic devices, through genetic engineering that draws on the 'knowing' embodied in the genes, and in other ways that are only beginning to bear fruit.

'Knowledge technology' presents a tremendous potential for the extension of human intelligence, perhaps as significant in its impact as the earliest technology of hand axes and cutting stones. Such technology has a remarkable capacity to feed back on itself, so that great change is possible in a short time. The field of 'artificial intelligence', though still in its infancy, offers a striking example: Eventually computers programmed to emulate the mind may be able to open unexpected avenues for the human capacity to know.

As technology explores knowledge in this way, it challenges human beings to develop new ways of knowing. Already we compete with machines that could be said to 'know' far more efficiently than we do. If we cannot advance our own knowledge to match the achievements of technology, we may one day be incidental participants in a world that has escaped from our control.

Benefiting from technology requires matching the growth in 'knowledge technology' with a growth in the knowledge that guides this technology. But the steadily accelerating momentum of change subordinates more reflective ways of knowing to the simple need to cope with what is happening, leaving little opportunity for new forms of knowledge to develop. Modern life is increasingly complicated, crowded mentally as well as physically. Most of us go about our daily business preoccupied by countless details and concerns that leave no room for new ways of knowing. Simply dealing with stress, anxiety, and the loss of identity and values symptomatic of our times is enough of a challenge. The 'relaxation technologies' that go in and out of style seldom take deeper knowledge as one of their goals. At the same time, the technological 'model' for knowledge itself places limits on knowledge. Because 'progress', 'modernization', and change have become good in themselves, the possibility for new ways of knowing is assigned to the future. Technology promotes a fascination with 'what will come next', turning new knowledge into a product to be acquired rather than a faculty to be exercised and developed.

Perhaps it is due to these tendencies, which limit the kinds of knowledge available to us, that modern systems of education and learning seem increasingly unable to prepare young people for pursuing meaningful activities or making value-oriented decisions. Questions about the purpose of our lives and the meaning of our actions cannot be answered by innovations in 'knowledge technology'; in fact, such technology tends to lead inquiry in a direction that leaves the fundamental questions unresolved and even unacknowledged.

Choosing the Future

Technological knowledge leaves its own way of knowing outside the scope of its inquiry. The consequence is that knowledge itself develops 'unknowingly', tracing with an ever-accelerating momentum outlines whose larger patterns remain unknown. The future remains unpredictable, and we as individuals and as a society are left subject to an uncertain destiny.

Coming generations will almost certainly accept as commonplace conduct and circumstances unimaginable today. We cannot say whether we would regard such changes as beneficial or not, any more than we could predict whether a visitor from the past would find our world a heaven or a hell. But based on the forms of knowledge in operation today, one fact seems predictable: The course of future development will continue to operate largely out of our control.

If we hope to affect the future rather than simply be subject to it, we must start now to gain a more comprehensive knowledge of knowledge itself. We can do this by investigating the model of knowledge that technology itself puts forward. Despite proclaiming itself 'value-neutral', technology inevitably provides a set of standards and values. The technological model gives subtle support to specific ways of acting and being over others, contributing to *unacknowledged limitations* in human knowledge and being. Unless we take the model itself as a subject for investigation, these limitations will continue to operate.

As a vehicle for inquiry, technology has made it possible to ask new and dynamic questions that have led to remarkable discoveries, expanding incalculably the scope of what is known. But as a model for what knowledge is and what can potentially be known, technology tends toward a too ready acceptance of its own presuppositions. In suggesting that the technological way of knowing is uniquely competent to advance our knowledge, it confines the range of the knowable and the capacities of human intelligence.

Rather than accepting as absolute the model of knowledge that technology advances, we can recognize in the ever-changing face of technological knowledge a witness to the possibility that knowledge can be transformed at a deep level. Having learned from technology that knowledge itself can change, we can apply this lesson to investigate new prospects for knowing.

Chapter Four

Impact of technology; need for guiding knowledge; new knowledge assigned to the future; no knowledge of knowledge; potential for new knowledge.

Feeling Thoughts

Trace the link between thoughts and the positive, negative, or neutral feelings that accompany them. Note how your observation affects both feelings and thoughts. Do feelings precede thoughts, or vice-versa? Is one the basis for the other? Does one dominate or encompass the other? When you can observe without comment or judgment, a stable calm will form, allowing a more precise investigation.

Exercise Four

Knowing Through Space

Secret Interplay

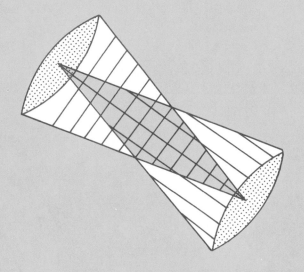

Within subject
Within object
Before meaning
Beneath intention
Center to center
Point to point
Hidden rhythm
Secret interplay
of Knowledge

BINDING
THROUGH IDENTITY

Technology affects knowledge on a level so fundamental we may not easily notice it. The technological model proclaims that knowledge is about *ways to
obtain results*. How those results are to be applied is
a matter for personal belief or conviction. The value
or benefit of the results — their meaning in a larger
context — is *not presented as a question for knowledge*.

The technological model thus affirms the existence
of two separate realms: the 'objective' world of results
and the 'subjective' world of personal conviction and
concern. Knowledge is understood to apply only in the
objective realm; in the subjective realm of desires and
feelings, knowledge has no role to play. Since issues of
value and meaning fit into the subjective realm, they
recede from view as possible subjects of knowledge or
topics of public discourse. In such circumstances, what
is meaningless comes to the fore by default.

In the technological model, all knowledge is 'for'
a purpose. Ultimately it becomes the *property of the
self*, which decides what use to make of it. Yet the self

as such is centered in the subjective realm, and thus in its fundamental identity it remains inaccessible to knowledge. The technological model accepts the claims of the self to stand at the center of the world that it knows, 'owning' all experience, but it has no way of investigating those claims directly. While the cultural conditioning of the self, the modification of the self's identity over time, and similar issues are all open to inquiry, the 'fact' of identity itself, *to which all knowledge is subordinated*, is inaccessible to knowledge.

With the self established at the center of experience, a dichotomy at once emerges. The self finds itself to be separated from the objects that it needs to satisfy its wants. From this basic situation arises desire — a momentum directed outward toward possession of what is desired — and from desire comes action.

Bound up in these subjective patterns, the self works to acquire specific goods available only in the objective realm, using up its mental and physical energy in doing so. As the method for doing this, technology receives special emphasis. And since the technological model for knowledge supports the claims of the self, a cyclical dynamic comes into being, stimulating the ever-increasing production and consumption of goods to satisfy the needs of the self. A constant 'busy-ness' makes it unlikely that other forms of knowing can arise.

The subjective structures of desire help shape cognition in accord with the technological model. Based on memories and imaginings, the self projects an image of what is desired, and at once the projected image puts knowledge into its service. Fully occupied with the concerns brought forward by emotions, fantasies, and desires, the self subordinates awareness, concentration, and active intelligence to the push and pull of wants, fears, and needs. The division between the subjective and objective is constantly reinforced and applied in new domains. Because the mind is operating without a more comprehensive knowledge, there is little opportunity to disengage from the ways of being already set in motion.

Since the object of 'knowledge' understood 'technologically' is the 'objective' realm, the activity of the self — which consists of a process rather than the outcome of that process — is knowable only indirectly. Intelligence and will are put under the control of feelings and emotions; the self is guided not by awareness, but by the need to gain power over its circumstances so that it can obtain what it wants. In place of the light of knowledge, the thick darkness of wanting and the seductive images of desire determine how the self shall act. The patterns of action follow well-established ways of being, in which the self can only acquiesce.

As long as the 'subjective' self is cut off from the 'objective' world, such limitations on knowing seem almost inevitable. The split between the two realms places the self in a position where its time and space are confined and its knowledge fallible. The body, which seems somehow to straddle the subjective and objective realms, continues to assert its demands for pleasure, happiness, or comfort, leaving the self no choice but to respond. A pattern of want and need, punctuated by episodes of fulfillment, establishes the fundamental order within which knowledge can arise. Only a few alternatives for knowledge seem allowable: Knowledge that allows the self to identify and distinguish what is desired from what is not; knowledge of technological knowledge; and knowledge as a possible object of desire. The list does not seem to extend any farther.

Knowledge Without Power

With knowledge confined in this way, the self finds itself situated in a world given in advance. The role of cognition is to describe or 'make use of' this 'given' world. For the most part, this will take place through thinking, as knowledge offers 'models' of what is 'real' and 'true'. Certain information is provided or a certain logic is worked out, and then a rule is established. Following thinking's lead means *conforming to this rule or model.*

Once knowledge is identified with the structures established by thought, it becomes a second-class citizen in the self's subjective world, wholly subordinate to the structures of desire. Unlike desire, in which the momentum that leads toward action is intrinsic to the desire itself, thinking lacks the energy that flows directly into doing. Encoded in the rules and interpretations imposed by thought as a way of linking subjective and objective, 'knowing' loses its intimate connection to 'being'.

Divorced from penetrating intelligence and direct experience alike, and untested in action, knowledge based on thinking and models may gain substantial influence despite its flaws. The consequences can be deeply destructive across a broad reach of space and time. Since it is subject to manipulation by the dominant force of desire and emotions, such knowledge is also readily transformed into belief, rationale, or ideology, lending a cloak of intellectual respectability to patterns of action based on desire and need.

When new knowledge does arise, it is understood as being bound to the 'objective' realm, which is *not the realm of the self*. Thus, such knowledge does not directly affect the self in its being. Though conceptual models, new scientific theories, or new ideologies may seem inspiring, the response they evoke fails to bridge the gap between the being of the self and the being of the world that the self somehow 'inhabits'.

The direct consequence of this pattern is that the impact of even the most powerful insights quickly fades. As we discover that the knowledge we attain seems incapable of transforming our being, we may lose confidence in the value of knowledge to affect our lives. We are left torn and frustrated, knowing that we 'know', but witnesses to the inability of our knowledge to affect us at the most fundamental level.

Territory and Identity

The restrictions on technological knowledge not only undermine the search for 'knowledge alternatives', but also establish as beyond the range of knowledge the most basic structures within which human beings operate. When we *use* knowledge as a means for attaining pre-established ends, not only the ends themselves, but also the claims of identity and territory on the basis of which desired ends are *defined* are placed outside the domain of inquiry. The bonds of country and place, family and class, the circles of friendship, profession, ideology, and lifestyle can be identified and studied from outside, 'technologically', but they apparently cannot be 'known' directly from within.

Thus, though it may seem clear enough that we 'know' what we desire or how we feel, this 'knowledge' makes sense only by being referred back to the pre-established domain of subjective identity and the values and attitudes that identity sustains. And this domain remains inaccessible to knowledge.

The technological way of knowing is aware of this limitation on the knowledge it presents, and tries to counteract it. However, it does so not by expanding the domain of knowledge to include the basic identity of the self, but by adopting measures to *cordon off* technological knowledge from the bias that unexamined claims of identity and territory would otherwise introduce. The scientific method, which insists on elaborate safeguards against 'subjectivity' in its attempts to arrive at the 'objective' truth, is perhaps the fullest expression of this concern with the inaccessibility of the subjective realm to knowledge and the resulting potential for error.

Valuable as the scientific methodology is within its own sphere, it accepts as a given the domain of not-knowing that technological knowledge posits at the outset. The structures of identity, value, and meaning remain beyond the scope of inquiry. So well-established is this way of thinking that the limits on the scope of knowledge introduced in this way go largely unnoticed.

Private and Public Knowledge

At the other pole of contemporary understanding are the fields of knowledge that seem to go beyond the technological model. Where technology leaves questions of value and meaning to one side, psychology, religion, philosophy, art, and similar forms of inquiry all could be said to take as central the need to investigate (in their own ways) the meaning and nature of human being and the quality and the capacities of the mind. Instead of looking only at externals, they explore questions of motivation and inspiration and may even ask directly how the objective and subjective realms interact.

Nonetheless, such forms of inquiry as they are practiced today continue to share the technological, 'self-centered' model of knowledge, in which the subjective and objective realms are opposed to each other and 'being' is split uneasily between them. They pursue a knowledge understood as being available through a turn 'inward', toward the subjective realm.

Since this approach leaves the technological model intact, the result is to undermine the validity of the 'deeper' knowing that 'private' knowledge professes. Without agreed upon 'objective standards', such knowledge (as opposed to the judgments it leads to or the explanations it spawns) cannot readily be a topic for public discourse. It tends to occupy a shadow world, easily overlooked or ignored on the one hand, or confused with fantasies and daydreams on the other. With 'objective' modes of knowing active in the foreground, knowledge that is considered 'only' subjective is denied any ultimate significance.

So long as the technological model for knowledge governs our understanding, the conventional response to such alternative forms of knowing will be distrust or skepticism, or else misinterpretation of their message as consisting of another 'model'. Indeed, with knowledge fragmented into the 'subjective' knowing of individuals, there is little alternative. Even if a new, more 'comprehensive' way of knowing did somehow 'arrive', there would be no way to communicate it, no way to transmit such 'personal' knowledge into the shared domain of public discourse and 'objective' knowledge.

Chapter Five

Knowledge as a means and as property; knowledge subordinated to identity; the structure of separation and desire; knowledge through 'self-centered' models; knowledge as powerless; private and public knowledge; new knowledge unavailable.

Disowning Tension

The temporality associated with tension and fixed patterns (see Exercise 3) depends on a sense of the self who organizes, interprets, and 'owns' the situation. To experiment with this orientation, focus instead on the self as part of the 'given' content of the situation. Watch loosely but alertly, using this expanded view to shift awareness from the content of the situation. You may touch more directly the energy of time.

Exercise Five

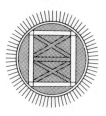

Opening Time

Senses Consensus

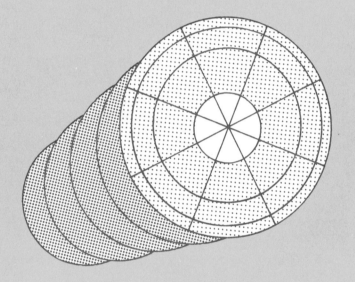

Concentric momentum into time
Limit knowing without knowing
Backward tracing forward
Known as known as unknown
Freedom from knowledge
Light from dark
Point of origin

THE KNOWN

Technological knowledge, with its emphasis on the objective realm, assigns primacy to knowledge of the 'already known'. The rule is put forward that knowledge must be based on the familiar: on labels, descriptions, and categories that are given in advance and serve as finite, discrete, and isolated 'counters' available for knowledge to manipulate.

In this way, knowledge is linked to judgments that classify what is 'known'. Judgments as such, however, do not further communication and the growth of understanding; instead, they restrict intelligence and limit the possibilities for knowledge. Acts of discrimination that place what is 'known' into familiar categories cut us off from experience. Once labeled, the experience has been 'spoken for' in advance and is no longer available to be known. Entities become available to knowledge only *after* they have already been 'manufactured' and have entered the 'distribution system'.

The consequences of such knowing are twofold. First of all, whatever nourishment or energy might have become available through a more direct knowing is lost. The resulting limitation in knowledge could be understood as a 'not-knowing', but because we are accustomed to it, we are more likely to notice it as a characteristic lack of vitality within experience. We may feel as though time and space themselves are ill-suited to our needs — too crowded or too empty, too vast or too limiting.

Second, when our knowing leaves us without direct knowledge of 'the known', we lose the chance to see how the already 'distributed' object of knowledge has been put into operation. The influence and interplay of contributing factors (such as previous, collectively determined judgments and understandings, the supporting environment, the temporal sequence of cause and effect, the accumulated historical momentum, the tools we use to label and identify, and our own lack of knowledge) remain beyond the reach of our knowing.

Due to the limitations of knowledge based on the familiar, we find ourselves adopting positions and taking actions with little sense of the likely consequences, even when those consequences are potentially far-reaching. Although we can assign reasons to account for what happens, the reasons we give may be only a part of the 'product' being distributed, like 'packaging' added to protect the product or make it more saleable. They do not necessarily offer additional knowledge.

When knowledge arrives in an 'already distributed' format, everything is established 'beyond questioning'. What appears within this 'pre-established' domain is then judged in terms of oppositions such as good and bad, right and wrong. The judgments in turn find expression in words and labels, and from this foundation come doctrines, traditions, customs, styles, and ideologies. In this way systems are instituted that profess to 'embody' knowledge, but that actually force on us the conviction that as individuals we lack the capacity to know. We learn that we are dependent on a knowledge that comes from 'outside' — transmitted through structures based on past conditioning or memory rather than the immediate encounter with the present situation.

Without such direct knowing, the knowledge available to us lacks stability, and we fall easily out of balance. For example, fascination with a desired object may give way to a loss of interest once it is obtained. Is this because we do not know our mind in the first place? Is it because the mind has inexplicably changed? Without direct knowledge, there is no basis for an answer.

A Rush to Judgment

The tendency away from direct knowing and toward judgments and labeling is fostered by the tremendous pace of modern life. Events unfold too quickly to be comprehended, encouraging us simply to sort them into categories instead. Our focus on what is new and exciting pitches the activity of the mind at a high level, so that we can make up in restless intensity what we lack in depth. Even our judgments thus take into account only the most superficial features of a situation. We take extreme measures, hurrying through our experience so quickly that sensation and enjoyment are dulled. Since such experience gives little satisfaction, we redouble our efforts, perhaps eventually becoming nervous, almost panicky. Like someone on a roller coaster, we rush forward with our eyes fixed straight ahead, instead of on what is happening now.

So long as our knowledge is based wholly on pre-established standards, this pattern can only continue. Although we are spared responsibility for the knowledge we claim to possess, we lose the opportunity to develop new intelligence. New ways of knowing seem out of reach, as though they required from us some organic change, like growing eyes in the back of our heads.

Despite what we have been taught, going beyond the known may not be so very difficult; in fact, we may not have to 'go' anywhere at all. A starting point would be to let go of our usual preoccupations and presuppositions, looking with fresh vision upon our 'familiar' world.

Challenging the Familiar

Although we live our lives based on certain patterns and principles, on ways of knowing and values that we hold to be fundamental, the knowledge that establishes these patterns and principles and the limits it presupposes are seldom called into question. Lacking a clear knowledge of how our understanding is structured, we acquiesce in the truths handed down to us and the situation in which we find ourselves. Circumstances condition our lives, and freedom remains beyond our reach.

The technological model of knowledge might well acknowledge that we are conditioned by history and circumstances, but propose that we remain free to shape the vision, the values, and the aspirations that guide our lives. Can this distinction be maintained? When we act on the basis of our desires and emotions are we really choosing our own path? Where do desires come from, and what momentum do they reflect? If dreams and fantasies shape our actions and our lives, can we truly say that we ourselves are responsible for the constructs we rely on to define our potential?

Conventional knowledge defines 'freedom' as the absence of external coercion and the right to act on 'subjective' impulse. But such 'freedom' leaves us confined by the rules, restrictions, meanings, and interpretations of what is already known. Freedom understood in this light depends on the sense of self, but how well established is the self? Is the 'self-evidence' of the self perhaps the outcome of biological, cultural, and socially patterned programming? Even at this most fundamental level, history and circumstance may invade our knowledge, catching us up unwillingly in unacknowledged structures that define our being in limited ways.

When we look at human being with open eyes, how can we escape the conclusion that the way in which we see and understand the world is largely a product of resources, methodologies, and conceptual structures transmitted to us by our culture? Whether we want to or not, we receive, preserve, act out, and faithfully transmit our cultural heritage. Technological knowledge depends on inherited constructs, and so do our standards for determining what is true and what has value. Even in pursuing our own aims, even in our self-understanding as 'I am', we seem to be working out variations in history's story, taking up and then passing on to future generations the structures of our own conditioning.

Acknowledging our dependence on the past at the deepest levels may undermine our sense of freedom and autonomy. But if we respond with denial or seek escape, the forms that our denial takes will emerge from this same conditioning, in accord with the times: a hunger for daydreams, entertainments, and fantasies; an immersion in well-worn and widely shared illusions; apathy disguised as stoic acceptance; or perhaps an angry rebellion that mirrors the structures it seeks to overthrow.

There is another alternative. We can acknowledge the limits imposed on us by inherited structures and models, and then go on to challenge the familiar, asking how the accepted understanding comes to play such a dominant role in our lives. By what vehicle is conventional understanding transmitted, and how does it maintain itself? What mechanism at work in our own minds leads us to embrace it?

Chapter Six

Knowledge based on the familiar; lack of vitality; judgments and labels; no time for knowledge; no freedom through relying on constructs; self-understanding as historically conditioned; investigating the mechanisms of limitation.

Thoughts in Conflict

Bring a positive or negative thought or judgment into the mind and while maintaining it look for its accompanying opposite. Let the two opposed thoughts do battle with each other, while you observe the conflict. At first the two thoughts will likely alternate, but later they can both be present at once, carrying equal significance. You can maintain this balance through a focus on the feeling of disagreement, conflict, etc.

Exercise Six

Concepts of Knowledge

Angles on Knowing

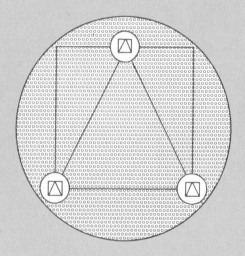

Belief confining knowledge
Pointing toward the known
Shaping and defining
Belief disclosed in closing
Known in not-knowing
Act of knowledge activated

REPLACING KNOWLEDGE
WITH BELIEF

W henever we need or desire knowledge, we are free to investigate for ourselves the limits of what is already known. Most often, however, we do not choose this course. Instead, we turn to an established authority, adopting the content of a knowing made available in advance. Whether we look to tradition, the instruction of parents, the advice of friends or experts, the guidance of a supernatural power, or perhaps simply the accumulated memories of prior acts of knowing, the outcome is the same: the substitution of a belief for knowledge.

Once adopted, a belief operates in a characteristic way. The mind classifies or labels experience in conformity with the belief and draws conclusions accordingly, perhaps 're-presenting' the result as potential content for a new belief. The structure so determined screens out direct knowledge of experience itself.

In establishing this structure, the key step is the acceptance of the content of the belief as trustworthy. Although we 'know' the content of the belief as content, we adopt the belief not because we know its content to be true, but because we accept the authority of its source. It is this acceptance that makes the belief a belief.

The accepting of a higher authority entails no knowledge, only the hope or conviction that the transmitted belief has been safely captured and that it 'encloses' accurate knowledge. What then is the basis for yielding to the authority of a source whose knowledge we cannot directly verify? We might reply to such a question with specific explanations and arguments intended to establish the 'trustworthiness' of this or that specific authority. More fundamental than any such explanations, however, is another belief: the implicit notion that we ourselves *lack knowledge*, that someone or something else has greater access to the knowledge we need.

Perhaps it seems that *this* belief, at least, can be traced to a more direct knowing, for daily experience confirms at every turn that we lack access to the knowledge we need or want. But this lack may *reflect* the basic belief in our own not-knowing, rather than *confirming* it. Perhaps we do not know simply because we have forgotten how to make contact with knowledge, or else because we do not make the effort to do so. Perhaps we originally accepted a belief in our own not-knowing for reasons that suited our needs at the time, or have carried it forward unthinkingly from the original state of not-knowing that characterized the first years of our lives.

Present knowledge insists that there are fixed limits on our ability to know, such as the physical limits that situate the self in space and limit it in time, or endow the body with specific attributes. Would such fixed limits operate in the same way if conventional belief structures were not in effect? For example, if our belief in the self shifted, would new possibilities for knowledge open?

Beliefs as Carriers of Knowledge

If beliefs could truly communicate knowledge, the only thing standing between us and knowing would be correct judgments as to which beliefs were trustworthy. This state of affairs, however, does not seem to apply. Even assuming that beliefs were 'carriers' for the knowledge we are lacking, there seems to be no way that we could benefit fully from that knowledge.

In the first place, the communication of knowledge through the transfer of beliefs will succeed only to the extent that we have the capacity to understand what is being communicated. Qualities of perception or awareness implicit in the belief will be lost in the course of transmission if they lie beyond the range of our own experience. We will receive from beliefs a knowing that has been leveled down to conform to our own lack of knowledge. In this sense, the belief as we receive it is a projection of the activity of our own mind.

Second, when we rely on beliefs we are accepting a structure that posits our own lack of knowledge and confirms our needs and wants as the basis for all action. The limitations that these presuppositions establish will continue to operate, no matter how subtle and refined the system of beliefs to which we give our allegiance.

Third, beliefs interpose themselves between our own experience and our knowledge of that experience. No matter how comprehensive the belief, it will leave the experience itself unknown.

Finally, even if a belief contains 'true' knowledge, we have no way of knowing whether that knowledge is complete. We could only determine this on the basis of another belief. As long as we 'import' knowledge from outside our own knowing, we will lack the capacity to determine the depth and the scope of what we know.

In relying on beliefs, we are accepting an imperfect *substitute* for knowledge. Perhaps this seems necessary if we are to gain access to a vast range of knowledge outside our direct experience, but the result is just the opposite. We choke off knowledge that we might develop on our own, without escaping the limitations of the knowledge we have already adopted.

When beliefs replace knowledge, vision is foreclosed, leading to stagnation. Beliefs may be accurate in their content and useful in their operation, but in being passed from one person to another, they bypass our most fundamental concerns. We touch the true significance of a belief only by discovering for ourselves *the knowledge it embodies*.

Chapter Seven

Belief in place of knowledge; accepting authority; belief in the lack of knowledge; inability to benefit from the knowledge contained within beliefs.

Background of Thoughts

The interaction of thoughts seems to depend on a temporal rhythm that allows the mind to move from subject to subject and from form to form. Observe how a thought arises and how it disappears: the conditions, accompanying feelings, and the relation between thought and feeling. Where does the thought go? What 'happens' in the interval between one thought and the next?

Exercise Seven

Knowledge of Being

Inner Circle

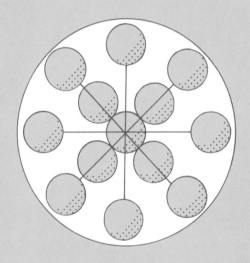

Circle of knowing
Momentum of frustration
Waxing and waning
Knowledge always distant

Knowing the circle
Knowing belief
Open centerless
Transition to Knowledge

QUESTIONING LIMITS

W hen the knowledge that guides us is transmitted through the form of beliefs, we are left in a condition of not-knowing. Choosing our course on the basis of 'external' sources of understanding, we follow pre-established patterns and routines, and soon find ourselves caught up in their momentum.

The consequence is a sense of individual helplessness in the face of history. The ceaseless and overwhelming display of events in time unfolds in rhythms that seem to repeat without end. Our efforts and concerns have no effect on these unfolding rhythms; instead, they can be seen as simply another expression of the same dynamic.

The patterns that apply in our own lives are duplicated in the larger sweep of affairs. Caught up in a momentum that no one seems able fully to comprehend, society's leaders take power and rule for a time, only to leave office or be deposed. On a larger scale, empires and nations rise and fall; powerful cultures that dominate their place and time are replaced by others that undo their works and reject their values. Great thinkers and artists may create a few precious works that extend the domain of knowledge, but not all of these endure; of those passed on to future generations, some are rejected or fall out of favor, while others exert varying influence from one decade to the next.

The unending flow of events and their underlying sameness call into question the ultimate significance of any human activity. Whatever the specific sequences and transitions that the events of our lives reveal, a fundamental mechanism based on not-knowing has already been set in motion. Misunderstanding, frustration, and confusion are fixed and indisputable parts of our lives.

An Imperfect Knowing

The knowledge that might change such patterns seems inaccessible. Ways of understanding as taught in our schools or exchanged in our dealings with others simply perpetuate the old conditioning. Even when we make use of technological knowledge to solve difficult and challenging problems, or share our deepest feelings and emotions, we are staying strictly within the limits of the known. We may learn new facts or 'interesting' and 'useful' information, but all the time we are leaving unexplored the possibility that a deeper knowing could transform our lives.

If we let the dissatisfaction we feel in the face of such limitations emerge into our awareness, we can use it as *a warning sign that the knowledge we rely on is incomplete.* Perhaps this incompleteness seems inevitable — after all, it is part of human knowledge to be imperfect —

but the conclusion that this is so is based on assumptions rather than inquiry. Would our conclusion change in any way if we took our wants and desires, the obstacles and resistance we encounter, and our not-knowing itself as subjects of inquiry? Have we ever really tried to understand these basic structures of experience?

Guided by our own sense of dissatisfaction, we can see directly how little room conventional knowledge allows for awareness and for appreciation. Our ability to share in the dynamic presentation of appearance is limited in ways we have come to take for granted; our consciousness is bound by patterns that seem to close off the prospect for change. Seeing these limits in action, however, creates a dynamic that can lead to new forms of knowledge. The possibility emerges that knowledge can go *behind and beyond itself*, allowing a deeper knowing to be embodied in the domain of our being.

Unacknowledged Knowledge

Within the ordinary, limited, and limiting knowledge of everyday awareness, an unacknowledged knowledge is already at work. The circumstances of human being are *known* to all of us, but because they are so deeply humbling, we tend to look past them. Born into a specific time and place, we are bound to live out a life that moves from ignorance and immaturity toward decay, loss of powers, and death. Our attributes and faculties, perhaps even certain of our attitudes and predispositions, are imprinted on us from birth. Chance encounters and accidental events determine the range of our actions and opportunities. We acquire knowledge only with difficulty, and fall short of our goals and aspirations.

In the face of such limitations, it seems natural to try to carve out a domain where we can be the masters of our circumstances — a territory within which to assert the claims of identity and sovereignty. But we choose this course at a cost, building confidence in our faculties and understanding by turning our backs on the knowledge we already have. We subordinate the possibilities of knowledge to the need of the self to exercise dominion.

It is this concern for dominion that leads us to insist that the 'knowledge' we have access to through belief can offer firm guidance. We know that our views and opinions are in constant flux, and that they have brought us little closer to satisfaction and fulfillment. Yet we discount this evidence, continuing to hope that one day soon we will win for ourselves the happiness we seek. In the meantime, the push and pull of desires continues to shape our conduct.

Just as we rationalize or look past the evidence of the past, we turn away from what we know of the future. Our time on earth is running out: Each day that passes is gone forever, and an opportunity lost seldom returns. Yet we act as though the supply of days were endless. Our impending death is virtually the only certain knowledge of the future that we have, yet we usually regard death as a remote and unreal eventuality, confining it to the category of things that do not affect the self directly. If we really *knew* that we would die, our knowledge would hold us accountable, and would find expression in our actions and intentions. But such knowledge is 'beyond us': Because it conflicts with the self's identity and self-understanding, it remains 'unknown'.

Nor are we usually willing to face what we know of our own physical circumstances and the threats to our person. Each day people are disabled, fall sick, lose their sight or hearing, contract fatal diseases. They are robbed of their possessions, their honor, their sense of inner worth. They sink into depression and grow mentally unbalanced. Any of these calamities might befall us too, without prior warning. Our bodies and spirits decay with the passing years; our strength fades and our vision alters. Even now just a few hours of illness or a passing problem sap our energy and leave us without the will or the resources to act. Yet we maintain to ourselves that we will be prepared when we encounter real adversity.

Most of us cherish a self-image that elevates fantasy and wishful thinking over what we know to be the case. On some levels we may be honest with ourselves, or even unduly critical, but at the same time we hold on to a secret picture of who we really are. We see ourselves as brave, beautiful, successful, wise, compassionate, humanitarian; we dream about what we will accomplish and the acclaim we will reap. We admit freely that we fall somewhat short of our own ideals, but despite our past failures and compromises, we continue to plan for our future successes and cherish our hopes for attainment.

We are equally obstinate about our own fallibility. Again and again the choices that we make, collectively and individually, breed difficulties and dangers, yet we continue to believe that the old ways of acting will let us choose wisely in the future.

Despite a constant flux in the *contents* of our experience, the *patterns* that have caused us so much pain and difficulty continue as before. What happened in the past is happening today and will happen in the future. We break our vows and resolutions, tire of our pleasures, and watch our dreams of transformation go unfulfilled.

Looking for Another Way

Building on the basis of what we already know, and newly aware as well of the limitations on our knowledge, we may feel ready to set out in search of a new knowledge. But if we try to do so, we will soon realize that the old patterns are firmly established. The education we receive during the first twenty years of our lives chiefly serves to confirm us in the understanding accepted by others. If we do try to break the bonds of conventional wisdom to question the accepted understanding, we are likely to come away confused, or else prematurely convinced that we have found answers to our questions.

As we reach maturity, we may begin to gain a certain clarity regarding the weary routines and limited knowledge that govern our experience, but at the same time there is a growing feeling that our lives have begun winding down. Our habit patterns are firmly established, our vitality is beginning to lessen, and our obligations have increased. As the years go by, the sense of our own mortality weighs heavily, and we cling to the positions we have already established.

Nor is it clear that we have the power to break through our conditioning. If dismay or discouragement are the motives for our quest for knowledge, we have reason to be suspicious. Perhaps this pattern of neediness and disappointment is itself symptomatic of an underlying lack of knowledge. In the same way, the styles of knowing that we try to adopt in order to penetrate the limits of the familiar may only reflect on an increasingly subtle level the impact of accustomed ways of thought and judgment. We may be trapped without realizing it in a vicious circle of not-knowing.

If we do break through the standard limits, so that we find ourselves standing outside the circle of the known, we will have to face the frustration of trying to communicate with those who have not made the same move. If the sense of isolation becomes too great, it may be tempting to recast our new understanding to conform with the old. In that case, whatever new knowledge may have emerged will quickly be lost from sight.

Signs of an Alternative

Despite such difficulties, there are clear indications that we do have a choice. Through the centuries new forms of understanding, new instruments for perception, and new ways of acting have emerged, witness to the creative power of human knowledge. Individual achievements and discoveries demonstrate that human awareness is not static and human prospects not closed off in advance. Even if the need we feel for change reflects old patterns in operation, it can still play an important role in stimulating new inquiry. And though the patterns of history may have shaped our knowledge at a deep level, once we are aware of those patterns *in operation*, we are free to turn our intelligence on them, investigating for ourselves to see how the values, rules, and interpretations that shape our world come into being.

It may be that this 'turn' itself is just a modification of the same patterns. Yet this need not mean that our inquiry will be fruitless. Knowledge has an intrinsic clarity that may operate even within old ways of knowing. Once we have made the commitment to knowledge, we may discover that our conditioning, though comprehensive, does not foreclose knowledge in quite the way we had imagined.

Chapter Eight

Momentum of pre-established patterns leading to frustration; no room for awareness and appreciation; unacknowledged knowledge within ordinary knowing; concern for dominion; turning from knowledge of patterns; power of conditioning; history as witness to a creative alternative.

Gravity of Thinking

In the movement from one thought to the next, a force of attraction emanates from specific thoughts, creating a momentum that 'pulls' thought forward. Some thoughts loom large and others small, exerting a different 'gravitational' pull accordingly. Observe this gravity of thinking in operation. Can it be experienced directly 'within' the thought, or only through its effects?

Exercise Eight

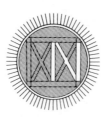

Time As Self

Interlocking

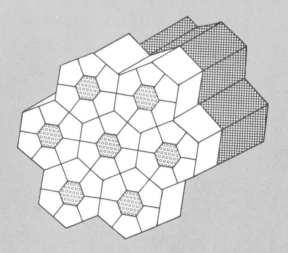

Space Time Knowledge
Knowledge transitions Time
Time dimensions Space
Space commands Knowledge
Unlock Love of Knowledge

THE RANGE
OF THE KNOWABLE

Although we have learned to regard some kinds of knowledge as immutable, even the most fundamental elements of the knowable are bound to a specific time and place. For example, cosmologists agree that during the first few moments of the universe, time and space themselves may well have 'acted' in unimaginable ways. On a more immediate level, the objects of our 'known' world, whose attributes our knowledge spells out in such detail, had not yet come into being in an earlier age. Today's accustomed ways of thinking and seeing — the basis of conventional knowledge — are still more transitory.

On the far smaller scale of a human lifetime, the styles of thought and action we follow and the customs we take for granted change from year to year and decade to decade. Ideas that once seemed self-evident have fallen out of favor, and today strike us as deeply misguided, or possibly laughable. Similarly, the ingrained assumptions and understandings of our time may be incomprehensible to future generations.

If time and space might not always have been as they are, and if the contents of our knowledge are accurate only within a specific setting, how firmly established can we consider conventional knowledge? The forces that have shaped us lie largely outside the domain of our understanding, and the road leading from the moment of our conception to the present is shrouded in mystery. In the face of such ignorance, can we be certain of even the most basic elements of our understanding? Can we justify speaking of 'then' and 'now', 'before' and 'after'? Can we affirm that we are inevitably bound by the past, or that we are moving inexorably toward the future?

Unlimited Presentations

Our lives unfold in terms of hours, days, and weeks. The prospect of even five minutes of pain or great joy can affect our actions and inspire us to special efforts. Yet global history spans millions and billions of years — unimaginable lengths of time 'filled' with a range of events beyond the power of any individual to grasp.

If we could keep alive within our awareness the sense of this far more encompassing time-frame, the knowledge on which we have learned to rely and the concerns that shape it would lose their self-evident nature. For example, we could reflect on the billions of people who will live and die in the course of just the next century. Toward what goal will they have lived their lives? Do they exist in time and space just so that their bones can be added to the graveyard of history?

If we imagine the remains of six billion people piled on top of one another—a thousand times a thousand times a thousand skeletons, doubled and then tripled—how big a mountain would they form? Will all these people have emerged into time just for the pleasure or experience they can gather before vanishing completely? Do the 'answers' to such questions fall within the range of what we conventionally consider knowable?

The potential depth within experience is another source of knowledge that falls outside the conventional range of the knowable. In times of beauty, the world can appear like a celestial garden, shimmering with treasures awaiting discovery. In times of leisure, the abundance of the senses delights us. Nature and our own capacities bring us great pleasure. If our minds are active and our hearts open, we can discover the riches of joy, romance, fantasy, and love. Art, music, and ideas can reveal a realm in which the power of creativity expresses and ennobles inner knowledge. Spiritual insight can lead to a tranquility that nourishes and heals. Free from our usual concerns, we can know wholeness, fullness, and well-being that take us far beyond our usual ways of knowing.

We can also expand our vision of the knowable by acknowledging the enormous outpouring of activity within the flow of time. A handful of dirt from alongside a country road swarms with life; a single drop of pond-water viewed under a microscope reveals a whole world of beings living out their lives at what to us would seem a frenzied pace. Beneath the surface of the oceans or the surface of earth, life abounds in a profusion of forms, and deep in outer space there may be countless planets no less prolific than our own. Does our knowledge explain the point of all this activity or the purpose that it serves?

A glance at any book of statistical data reveals a world in dynamic flux on a scale that cannot be comprehended. Americans jog almost thirty million miles a day, and drive more than three billion miles. They spend almost a billion dollars a day on recreation, make 800 million telephone calls, and buy about five million books. They use 250,000 tons of steel, produce over 100,000 tons of salt, use 450 billion gallons of water, eat fifty million pounds of sugar, slaughter 100,000 cattle, and consume thirty million sleeping pills.

In just a single hour, the hearts of human beings around the world pump some 400 billion gallons of blood. Countless trillions of cells die and are replaced, and incalculable numbers of chemical and electrical reactions take place within the nervous systems of innumerable beings. In that same span of time, how much energy do human beings invest in emotional reactions to situations — in anger and pain, guilt and regret, desire and frustration, fantasy and illusion? In just one hour, how many words are spoken without real purpose; how many thoughts repeat with slight variations what has already been thought? If each person has ten thoughts in a minute, this would mean six hundred thoughts in an hour; collectively, this would amount to several *trillion* thoughts. What does this enormous output of mental energy accomplish? At the close of each hour's thinking, has human understanding increased? Has the world advanced in any way?

An Invitation to Inquiry

The unlimited activity that courses all around us responds to a momentum of its own, about which conventional knowledge has little to say. Nonetheless, we remain committed to that knowledge, even when it is called into question. For example, modern physics proposes a new view of space and time at the subatomic level, in which all locations are indeterminate, all sequences relative, all knowledge uncertain. It suggests that structures we regard as solid vibrate with a constant motion that makes even their boundaries a matter of arbitrary assignment. Though grounded in the methodology that conventional knowledge appeals to as its ultimate authority, the new physics calls into question the most fundamental aspects of that knowledge. Yet human beings continue on as they have for millennia, pursuing the same concerns, bound by the same conception of what is knowable, largely unaffected by the revolution in what is 'scientifically' known.

Backed by the unrelenting momentum of the long-established, the dominance of conventional knowledge calls the value of inquiry into question. Why probe too deeply, when the old patterns will continue in effect no matter what we find? Caught up by standard ways of knowing in our immediate concerns and positions, we may tell ourselves that our knowledge works 'well enough', and that our lives are comfortable. Tacitly we accept the conviction that mysterious and uncontrollable forces operate behind the scenes to direct the patterns of our lives and our world. Since such forces are beyond the range of what is knowledge, knowledge itself is denied the power to open new ways of being.

If we are *willing* to question this conviction we see at once how little we understand about our situation as 'knowledgeable' human beings. This need not mean our knowledge is necessarily incomplete; instead, it suggests that much remains to be known.

If we can question the pervasive 'not-knowing' that underlies conventional knowledge, we may find a more embracing knowledge. New questions and perspectives loosen old limits, calling attention to structures so well-entrenched that they have become invisible. Starting with what we already know, and acknowledging the potential range of the knowable, we can recognize that there are levels of knowledge, and that even within not-knowing a fundamental clarity and awareness is at work.

Open inquiry takes us naturally beyond the concerns of the self and the structures of knowing such concern sustains. It allows us to 'embody' a more fundamental knowing. At present, this potential may seem remote and unrealistic, but we must be ready to investigate more closely. The prospect for transforming human destiny may already be implicit in the first real question we ask.

Chapter Nine

Questioning conventional knowledge; awareness of vital presentations; clarity in not-knowing; embracing and embodying through questions.

Expanding and Contracting Thought

Practice 'expanding' and 'contracting' thoughts. Consider as aspects of the thought the surrounding feeling, the sense of the one who thinks, etc. Investigate whether you can expand one aspect of this complex while condensing another. How does expanding and contracting affect the gravitational pull of thoughts (see Exercise 8)?

Exercise Nine

Knowing Space

To Be

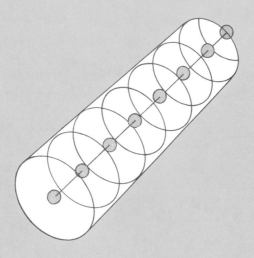

Deepening dimension response
Opening line of rhythm
Freely available to be
Accommodating all points
In Space Time Knowledge

ADVENTURE
OF KNOWLEDGE

Tuning in to the rhythm of open questioning reveals the prospect of a new way of knowing. Once old labels and judgments begin to lose their force, more subtle shapes, flavors, and textures appear within the flow of events. 'Difficulties' can yield a special knowledge that makes them a vital source of strength, and 'negativity' can become a potential reservoir of energy. 'Fantasies' that we use to escape unwanted knowledge can point toward the spark of creativity within, while 'obstacles' can become tools for realization.

This revolution in knowledge has its origins in simple observation. The ordinary understanding that views observation as bound within the conventional structure of subject-object interaction is incomplete, for observation can encompass equally what appears 'before us', the one who observes, and the structures of knowing and interpretation built into the observing process. Thus enriched in character and capacity, observation sustains the growth of intelligence and allows new kinds of knowing to come into play.

Once active observation is initiated, a wide range of questions present themselves. For example, we could focus on the self — the one who observes, and who also judges, interprets, and acts. What is the nature of the self, and how does that nature emerge and present itself in different moments? Are the self's wants and judgments clear and consistent? To what extent are they shaped by circumstance or by inherited judgments?

New angles of observation can be opened up with each new question. Is the self solid and well-established, or does it seem to grope for definition, a sense of worth, and self-understanding? In what ways does the intrinsic awareness of the mind relate to the self? Does our knowledge of the self show us how sense impressions, labels, and thoughts are integrated? Could we observe the self in operation before the standard structures of wanting and judging are in place?

Observation remains limited as long as it is understood as a *means* for attaining the personal goals we adopt on the basis of the knowledge we already 'possess'. This approach restricts the potential for new knowledge and encourages us to hoard the knowledge we gain lest we fail to fulfill our desires or maintain our positions. A more encompassing observation reflects a discriminating awareness — *not bound by positions, but simply aware whenever positions are in operation.*

An observation free from positions retains an immediacy that fosters awareness, undermining any tendency toward stagnation or dogmatism. Instead of being ruled by the need-centered concerns that are served by technological knowledge, open observation responds to a more fundamental concern. It asks what is valuable and meaningful in our lives and in the unfolding of events in time and space, refusing to accept in advance the claim of technological knowledge that such questions can be 'answered' only in the private realm of the individual conscience. Foreclosing no options, it restores the potential for a new way of knowing.

Individual Responsibility

Knowledge that arises through the discipline of a non-positioned observation expands the limits of the knowledge available to all humanity. In pursuing a deeper knowledge, we are fulfilling a responsibility to our fellow human beings.

Our intrinsic engagement in knowledge supports and extends this responsibility. All that humanity has been able to accomplish has been the outcome of knowledge, and the search for more knowledge is a natural way to express our appreciation for the opportunity we enjoy in having been born as human beings. Knowledge and human destiny are interwoven.

At one time the knowledge traditions of the past seemed to offer guidance to those who hoped to deepen and to transform knowledge, but today the message of these traditions has been muted. Perhaps some teachings are no longer appropriate, or perhaps the initial impetus and awareness they expressed has been lost. Perhaps we simply lack the understanding that would allow alternative ways of knowing to be communicated. In any case, the apparent lack of such guidance places responsibility squarely on the individual. Only when individuals act to embody knowledge directly does the possibility arise that the suffering and frustration of human beings could come to an end.

We may not feel ready to assume this kind of obligation. Living in a crowded, busy world, we tend to regard the time we have available for ourselves as a hard-earned luxury. Even if we are idealistic and energetic, we may not want to take the time to evaluate the meaning of our lives or the power and depth of our knowledge.

If we let this initial response determine our course of action, the opportunity for new knowledge will likely slip away. The awareness that change is needed begins to fade, and the dominant styles of knowing assert themselves. Proceeding from what is already established, knowledge falls into confusion, mistaking belief for knowing and affirmation of the known for inquiry. Words no longer hold their meaning, or else the meaning is lost or distorted. The world becomes cluttered with familiar structures, so that the clear light of knowing is blocked and the energy of an active intelligence cannot flow freely. The power of active knowledge to sweep all obstacles before it is drained away, and even true dedication and effort may fail to produce results.

Personal commitment to knowledge can clear away such confusion. On the surface, such commitment may look like a return to the 'privatism' characteristic of the technological model for knowledge. But technology positions the self very specifically with respect to the possibilities for knowledge, whereas active questioning takes responsibility for knowledge without deciding in advance who owns it or what its limits shall be. The structures of the self, the distinction between subjective and objective, and the goals we pursue are all available for investigation.

The technological model confines any potential for deeper knowing to the realm of private insight, from which it can be shared only as ideas and information: the content of a prospective belief. But the commitment to an active knowledge arising through questioning and observation can readily and spontaneously be communicated to others. Because knowledge does not belong to us as individuals and is not confined to the private sphere, it is freely available. *When we communicate the free availability of knowledge, we fulfill our responsibility to knowledge and to our fellow human beings.*

Like a good friend, the knowledge that arises in questioning responds to our concerns while also drawing us beyond our usual view. It is not just conceptual, nor does it focus on solving problems identified in advance. Revealing the patterns at work in established knowing, it allows clarity to emerge from within what is already known. It teaches us how to become knowledgeable and how to bring knowledge into the world, transforming responsibility from a duty to an opportunity.

It is easy to forget that we participate in knowledge simply in being human beings, alive and active in space and time. Accepting the limits of a pre-established knowing, we lose sight of intrinsic human awareness. But questioning based on observation brings the quality of knowledge into each activity, so that our participation in knowledge becomes open and direct. Questioning invites knowledge to inspire our thoughts and awaken deeper understanding from within. Responsibility for knowledge is the natural response to such participation.

Questioning that goes beyond the familiar can lead to profound transformation. It awakens an intelligence that encourages direct communication between mind and body, nourishing a satisfaction that can deepen into a new understanding of both matter and spirit. Even the sense of physical embodiment may shift, suggesting that our bodies themselves could be transformed. Suffused with knowing, they could become bodies of light, alive with intelligence and awareness.

An inquiry that offers such prospects can awaken a deep delight, like the eager joy an explorer feels at the outset of a journey. This joy reminds us that knowledge is not a matter for the head alone, but for the heart and spirit, the body and mind—an adventure for the whole of our human being.

How truly wonderful that we need not accept what is already known! How marvelous that awareness lets us explore the secret store of knowing within us! If we allow appreciation for this opportunity to build within us, deepening into love, we will be preparing to follow in the path of knowledge explored by all the great thinkers and leaders of human history.

Chapter Ten

Knowledge through observation; focus on the self; immediacy, engagement, and responsibility; inspiration; adventure of knowledge.

Manifesting Space, Time, and Knowledge

Investigate the ways in which space, time, and knowledge appear individually in the moods and attributes of human beings. Include in your inquiry the mental, physical, emotional, and energy realms. You can observe this in others and in yourself, looking for characteristic orientations and at how they change over time or in specific situations.

Exercise Ten

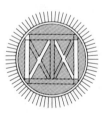

Being and Time

Dynamic Models

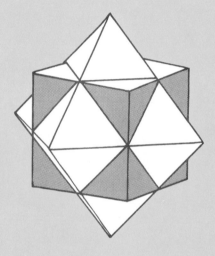

Interpenetrating order in Space
Self-regarding echo of Knowledge
Sustaining retaining remaining
Gateway dimensioned through
Propagation in Time
Opening toward opening

DISCLOSING
NEW POTENTIAL

Inquiry and observation are free to make new knowledge available so long as they are not limited by the terms of a particular understanding. For example, conventional knowledge interprets 'objective' observation in terms of particular assumptions about 'subject' and 'object'. But these assumptions are themselves based on labels and presuppositions that specify the nature of knowledge and 'distribute' knowledge in advance. To confine observation to such a 'pre-established' model may place important areas of inquiry 'out of bounds'.

In contrast, the freedom that comes with questioning protects observation from proceeding in the familiar ways. As observation expands in range and depth, it is always ready to look again and to look anew, not resting with established positions.

For inquiry and observation to make available a new *way* of knowing, they must challenge prevailing views of how knowledge can arise. Although we may not acknowledge it specifically, this view is shaped by a model that accounts for the emergence of knowledge, and it is this model that must be investigated.

However, it is not sufficient to question this model in relation to other possible models. To refine the model, develop additional models, or even substitute a new model in place of the old will not necessarily lead to a new way of knowing. Instead, the view that our *knowledge of knowledge itself* depends on the application of a model must also be subject to vigorous challenge.

The prevailing model of conventional knowledge allows for a certain rhythm to knowing. As this rhythm propagates itself forward into the future, it sustains the old order and limits the prospects for new understanding. Even when the model tells us we are 'free' to explore, it limits that freedom within pre-established boundaries. What we find in our explorations may be only the echo of what was 'available' to be known at the outset.

Nor do such limitations apply only on the cognitive level. The prevailing model supports the role of the self as central to knowing, and thus puts forward as fundamental to the knowing activity the concerns of the self. The regard for comfort or pleasure, for security or recognition sustains old styles of knowing, allowing knowledge few means to go beyond itself.

As long as such concerns remain foremost, the prospect for transformation suggested by the rapid change characteristic of today's world will go unrealized, and the basic model of knowledge will continue in effect. The alternative is clear: We can take responsibility for knowledge. Once this happens, the concerns of the self no longer dominate. The potential range for change itself changes, transforming not only the contents and the positions that knowledge supports, but also the way in which knowledge functions. We can investigate how knowledge arises and penetrate more deeply the nature of human knowing.

Wealth of Knowledge Through Inquiry

Inquiry lets us step away from the stream of patterns and structures that are the manifestation of a *particular* knowledge in operation, so that a deeper knowledge can come forth. Whatever appears or has appeared in the past is available as an expression of knowledge. We can see how knowledge has developed and what it has produced; we can bear witness to the power of knowledge in operation. Our capacity to know is strengthened, reinforcing a way of being in which our commitment to knowledge becomes unshakable.

The wealth of knowledge available to inquiry, which in itself goes far beyond the conventional range of understanding, makes it possible to acknowledge knowledge as the birthright of human beings. Inquiry reveals that human beings are in partnership with knowledge. It discloses a natural abundance of knowing as an ever present opportunity.

Without commitments to particular ways of knowing, knowledge itself becomes newly available — not as the outcome of a structured activity to which a particular model can be applied, but as an uncontrived, natural capacity within being. Space and time themselves are transformed through the infusion of knowledge into all appearance. All presentations are understood as dynamic and alive — friends to human being.

The prevailing tendency in modern knowledge has moved away from the possibility that appearance could be the friend of human being. Space is understood as a chilling void and time as a relentlessly unfolding force. Human aspirations confront the emptiness of space and the power of time with a wary apprehension. Individuals struggle to use what appears for their own purposes, knowing at a deep level that at any moment appearance might present obstacles to their goals and desires. At bottom space and time are understood as indifferent, almost hostile. Is this hostility intrinsic to the relationship between space, time, and human being, or does it reflect a specific pattern of knowing that assigns characteristics and establishes obstacles?

Asking such questions honestly and openly offers a tool for refining and reshaping our knowledge. Space and time appear in a different light; obstacles and frustrations lose their fixed quality. New prospects come to light: the first manifestations of a remarkable vision.

Chapter Eleven

Limits within the prevailing model of knowledge; turning from self-concern; knowledge as a capacity within being; presentations in space and time as friends to human being; manifestations of vision.

Situational Positioning

We all connect to present time and place in terms of variables such as openness and freedom, perspectives, wants and needs, security, and identity. Color and form, taste and sound, thoughts, attitudes, and other forms of mental activity both contribute and respond to this positioning. Investigate in yourself and others typical patterns for making contact with a situation as it appears in time and space, as well as methods for trying to change that situation. How consistent are these patterns over time?

Exercise Eleven

Knowing Itself Being

Star Vision

Inner spark outer radiance
Quality of being transformed
Elements of Knowledge
Alchemy of Time and Space

TRANSFORMING
TIME AND SPACE

As long as we lack a deeper knowledge, time will unfold in a way that leaves us powerless in the face of its onrushing momentum; space will be partitioned into territories and identities, assuring conflict and establishing barriers to understanding; knowledge will fail to provide the insight that would let us transform our lives. Whatever the shifting circumstances of our lives may bring, we will remain bound by inherited patterns of knowing. Even if we live in accord with the highest moral code, devote ourselves to profound spiritual practice, or dedicate our energy to strict mental or physical discipline that challenges our resources and commitment to the fullest, these limits will persist.

If deeper knowledge does become available, however, the potential for transformation appears *within* our present situation, not as a future possibility but as a present actuality of immediate significance. If we learn to see more, new vision will arise. Engaging the mind actively allows this vision to expand, so that the imagination 'learns' to imagine the unimaginable.

Apart from exploration through observation, analysis, and inquiry, we can cultivate a deeper knowledge through respect for the possibilities of our own intelligence, and through a willingness to explore in all directions. This may require developing new symbols and a new language—metaphors and concepts that can do justice to all the circumstances and possibilities that inquiry discloses. But however we proceed, knowledge is more likely to make itself known when we do not judge in advance what is worthwhile and what not, or close off inquiry by relying on conventional views of what is advantageous to the self in satisfying its projects and needs. Being 'open-minded' in this way does not mistake openness for uncritical acceptance, but it does allow whatever appears to present itself fully for investigation by the inquiring mind.

Perhaps the best way to stimulate knowledge, however, is just to acknowledge what we do not know. A healthy regard for not-knowing marks the emergence of knowledge in the midst of the unknown. Learning to recognize the signs that *we do not know that we do not know*, we know where to direct our inquiry so that knowledge can emerge.

Signs of a New Knowledge

Knowledge that knows in these ways acts as its own support. When we have access to such knowledge, we can learn from whatever happens. We find knowledge less in the content of what we know and more in the activity of knowing itself. Even though we are still operating on a conventional level of understanding, we have the opportunity to transmute all situations directly into knowledge, participating in a fundamental alchemy of knowing.

Among the indications that a vision born of new knowledge is in operation is a tolerance for ourselves and others, born of the global perspective that comes with a more comprehensive knowing. We understand more clearly how to deal with different people; we have more patience with our situation. Praise and blame, pleasure and pain, and the other concerns of the self lose some of their importance. There is a sense of being more at ease within our situation: a foretaste of real freedom. Openness to different kinds of knowledge brings with it the energy and skill to accomplish more.

If we learn to evaluate the *quality* of our knowledge in light of these possibilities, looking at the net result of our actions and our understanding, our awareness will deepen naturally, awakening a dedication to knowledge. Now we can investigate our situation at a more fundamental level, exploring all that appears within time and space, together with the nature of time and space as such. We can kindle a love of knowledge, *allowing* knowledge to make itself known.

Knowledge Knowing Time and Space

Although a fundamental change in knowledge may seem unlikely, this view is the product of a particular way of understanding. For example, it presupposes that changes in knowledge would unfold in a linear way in time. A deepened or expanded knowing might present time in a wholly different way. The possibilities that time now situates in 'the future' might become directly available 'now', illuminated by a knowledge active 'beyond' present knowing.

Again, it seems that a change in knowledge depends on being able to break through the barriers to knowing established by the territories and identities we adopt. But we adopt such positions based on a certain understanding of space, in which the self demands space in which to exist. Deeper knowledge might reveal space to be more accommodating than this picture suggests. The protective barriers that we have taken such pains to establish might suddenly dissolve, because they were no longer needed. We would have space enough, whatever our circumstances, and time enough, whatever our obligations. With no barriers or positions, the possibility would be open for still more knowledge to arise, free from every impediment and obstacle.

Such possibilities suggest that knowledge has as its domain a world we have not yet begun to explore. When we awaken our imagination and give power to our visions, we see that what knowledge knows is time and space. We discover for ourselves that this relationship is reciprocal: The unfolding of time and the accommodating power of space are what allow knowledge, knower, and known to appear.

New knowledge allows space to open in new ways and time to present a different dynamic. In turn, space and time themselves support the further growth of knowledge. In the system of positive feedback that results, each new situation tends to reveal unbounded space, unlimited time, and perfect knowledge. In this creative new realm, we may find the answers to questions we did not even know we had, and learn to penetrate barriers that were previously hidden. We may gain access to a new way of being.

Ownership of Knowledge

Knowledge becomes available when we trace out our own understanding. When we pursue this inquiry far enough, we begin to question whether such understanding is really ours, or whether it can even be owned. We begin to see that the patterns that shape our being reflect a specific understanding of time and space.

Perhaps knowledge at a deeper level responds to a time and space that extend beyond the specific positioning of an individual knower. As human beings sharing the same physical universe, we may share in universal ways of knowing as well. Each 'mind' may be connected with every 'body', and each 'body' with every other 'body'. The whole of creation in time and space may participate in a most remarkable intimacy, with wisdom, compassion, and moral conduct of the highest order its spontaneous expression.

These ideas, emotionally satisfying or intriguing as they may be, do not yet embody knowledge. Nor will knowledge come from 'proving' such ideas true (or false) through any conventional sort of logic, though such a proof might form a valuable part of a more thorough and multidimensional inquiry.

Beyond the logic of models and reasons, however, knowledge can make itself available directly within our knowing. Free from the concerns and structures within which we confine it, it can disclose a 'knowingness' that goes beyond anything we might have anticipated or predicted. Investigating without demands or expectations — not for the sake of the answers we may find, but for the sake of the understanding that comes with inquiry itself — we can invite such knowledge to come forward, disclosing itself in space and time. If we can *let knowledge be*, transformation and achievement of the most significant kind can become a reality within the structures of daily life and conventional knowing.

Chapter Twelve

Acknowledging not-knowing; alchemy of knowledge; signs of new knowing; knowledge of time and space; accommodation; interaction of time, space, knowledge; no ownership of knowledge.

Patterns in Space and Time

Observe the links between the patterns investigated in Exercises 10 and 11 and space, time, and
knowledge. For example, space relates to color,
shape, form, and texture, and time to sound,
rhythm, aesthetic appreciation, and feelings. As
such links become more clear, chart the interplay of time, space, and knowledge unfolding
from morning to night and month to month.
Look for recurring patterns related to time of
day or year. Investigate this interplay within
different domains: energy, intellectual activity,
accomplishment, feelings, senses, emotions.

Exercise Twelve

Space of Knowing

PART TWO

Models
of
Knowledge

Distant Parting

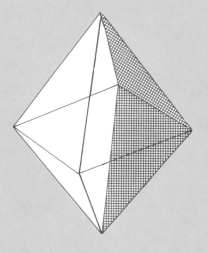

Time of now then
Space of here there
Knowledge penetrates excavates
Bearing within divisions
Without knowing
Carving space and time
Diamond transparent partitions

KNOWING
THROUGH POLARITY

The model we use to account for how we know is fairly well-established, even if we seldom reflect on its details. Wholly apart from what the latest scientific findings or contemporary philosophical theory might suggest, we operate with a basic model of how knowledge arises, drawing on analogies from the physical world, well-known scientific principles, and the 'evidence' presented by shared experiences. Examining this model (without concern for establishing or disputing its accuracy in each detail) allows us to see how far our *knowledge of knowledge* can take us and how bound we are by its conclusions.

The world we know is made up of objects appearing in space and events occurring in time. To understand the structure of conventional knowledge, space and time themselves will make a good starting point, for the structures that space allows and the patterns that time presents appear to be decisive for all knowing.

Physical objects appear in space, and it seems that without space they could neither appear nor exist. As the absence of what 'exists', space might be considered 'non-existent', and yet if space did not exist in some sense, objects could not exist either. This paradox, however, is not an issue for conventional understanding, for from the ordinary perspective space is simply irrelevant, and so 'disappears' from view.

Just as space is the empty container for what is real, so time is the domain within which events occur. 'Time' 'measures out' or 'distributes', separating one event from another and making it possible to establish order.

For human being, which establishes itself as real through occupying space and taking up time, knowledge is based on the senses. It arises as the sensory faculties make contact with the things that appear in space and the events that occur in time. The resulting sensory data provide the basis upon which interpretation and other forms of knowing can then be constructed.

The individual relying on sense knowledge can know only the exterior surfaces of objects present before him, and only as observed from a specific perspective. His knowledge will be 'temporal' — linked to a specific time and place and to his 'position' as an observer — and thus also temporary, for it arises under specific conditions that are constantly shifting. Common sense insists on the reliability of such temporarily valid knowledge, asserting that what is true now was (in the vast majority of cases) also true in the immediate past and will remain true in the immediate future. But only inference and assumptions based on previous experience support this seemingly self-evident conclusion.

Knowing Through Polarity

In the act of observing on which temporally situated knowledge depends, the possible modes of being appear to be divided into two aspects or poles. At one pole is the 'perceiver', who has the capacity for knowing and experiencing. At the other pole is 'objective reality', which has the capacity for being known 'as an object'. Since the 'perceiver' can know only 'objects' and 'objects' can appear only to a 'perceiver', the two poles are linked, yet each remains separate and distinct. *The knowledge afforded by the interaction of these two poles can be called 'polar knowledge'.*

The structure of division and polarity that operates in polar knowledge means that for the perceiver, 'isolation' and 'no-knowledge' take priority over knowing. *At the outset, nothing is known.* A 'knowledge gap' separates 'subject' and 'object', 'perceiver' and 'perceived'. Knowing arises when knowledge is somehow transported across this 'gap', ending the original isolation of the two poles.

The dualistic structure of observation inherent in 'subject' and 'object' finds further expression in the distinction between 'here' and 'there'. The knowing capacity resides 'here'; the known content resides 'there'. (The more inclusive 'here' sometimes used in speech or thought is not the kind of 'here' that makes the knowing activity an issue.)

In the same way, *the perceiver appears 'now', in the present, whereas the content of perception manifests 'then', in the past.* This distinction is often overlooked, but it follows naturally from the recognition that perception is not instantaneous. (At the most the content of perception is communicated from 'there' to 'here' at the speed of light, so that it will take a discrete amount of time to arrive.) Thus, what is perceived is *at best* the object as it was in the previous moment. The 'then' of a more distant past or a hypothetical future figures only indirectly in this more immediate knowing.

The polarities 'here/there' and 'now/then' are basic to standard observation. The separation between here and there — the expression of the 'knowledge gap' in conventional, extended space — exhibits itself as distance. The separation between 'now' and 'then' — the expression in conventional, linear time of the primacy of 'no-knowledge' — presents itself as the distinction separating 'perceived' past from 'experienced' present.

The Self and the World

There remain some underlying questions. Why is there a temporal movement toward knowing at all, instead of the unchanging, static condition of not-knowing? What motivates the act of knowing — the drive to bridge the 'knowledge gap'? How does the perceiver arise as perceiver, and the perceived as perceived?

The source of this movement lies in another fundamental polarity: that between 'self' and 'world'. The self 'knows' a world that takes shape around the self *in the act of being known*. Only by moving out from the central 'here/now' to incorporate as known the content of 'there/then' can the self determine the identities and assign the meanings that together make up this 'known world'. Knowledge in this sense is the outcome of the self's response to its original isolation. This response can be described as 'temporal knowing': action to establish a structure (the known world) within which the self can assign meanings and make sense of its own being. *The resulting knowledge, bound to the structure of self and world and to the temporal order within which that structure unfolds, is 'temporal knowledge'.*

Temporal knowledge brings to polar knowledge a dimension that makes the world of conventional reality possible. In the act of polar observation carried out by a 'perceiver', knowledge is absolutely momentary. The 'object' of observation is simply 'raw data', somewhat like the configurations of light and dark that might register on a light-sensitive screen. The knowledge that results, however, gives no access to enduring entities such as trees or human beings. Confined always to the moment, without prior referents, polar knowledge takes as its content a meaningless blur. If this were the only form of knowledge on which they could draw, human beings would be perpetually as innocent of understanding as new-born children, and the identity of the self as the owner of experience would have no chance to form.

We are 'saved' from such a perpetual innocence through the link that the self maintains between present and past. As the content of each sensory observation appears in the present, the self identifies it in terms of its previous experience. It looks back in time, making judgments and associations, comparing and contrasting characteristics established through earlier interactions and culturally transmitted constructs. This is not the movement into the just preceding moment entailed in any act of polar knowing (even including, for example, the recording of data by machine). *The turn toward the past to identify and label a known world — a distinctive aspect of temporal knowledge — is unique to the self.*

Although the role played by the self in establishing the 'time-centered' understanding upon which conventional knowledge depends is readily understood, the nature of the self remains problematic. For conventional knowledge understands 'the real' as being what appears in space. In this 'space-centered' view, there is no 'room' for the self, which does not seem to occupy space in the usual way, and thus cannot be considered an ordinary object. It has been argued that the self is identical with its embodiment, which does occupy space. But there are facets of the self that do not seem capable of being adequately described in terms of the body. We shall return to this problematic nature of the self below.

A World Described

The turn toward the past characteristic of the 'self/world polarity' is a fundamental aspect of temporal knowledge. We can call it 'descriptive knowledge' to distinguish it from the polar knowledge of 'here/now' observation. *Descriptive knowledge draws on the past to bring essential coherence and order to the direct experience to which polar knowledge gives access.* Through reference to established structures, it allows distinction-making and the assigning of meanings. Only through descriptive knowledge can the self know its world as specific objects and events, each with its own distinguishing qualities and characteristics that persist over time.

Yet descriptive knowledge also places severe restrictions on what can be known. The self understands the content given in each new moment of polar knowledge in light of available concepts, prior descriptions, and fixed definitions. Each succeeding definition or description sets in place a 'fixed perspective' with its own 'focal setting', limiting what can be understood. *To define is to be confined within the definition's narrow range.*

Because the self perceives by reference to the past, it is invariably drawn outside experience, which occurs only in the present. For example, if the eye sees the moon reflected in the waters of a river, the 'present' experience is the continuously changing flow of water illuminated by the light of the moon. Descriptive knowing, however, leads the self to identify the content of the experience, naming it 'the reflection of the moon'. That definition is then verified in succeeding moments (aided by a characteristic shortcut that 'makes sense' of each new moment by assimilating it to the previous one except for specifically noted differences). Repeatedly confirming the echo of its initial perception, the self perceives a steady image of the moon, while the 'present' play of light on water recedes from view.

Although the move toward descriptive knowing is necessary to give form to the content of polar knowledge, something vital is lost in the move away from immediate experience. In seeing something for the first time, before 'accustomed' ways of knowing have a chance to form, there is often an intensity and intimacy that later vanishes. Such 'first moments' draw on other, prior experiences, yet they hint at what descriptive knowing 'un-knows'. This original intensity may at times spontaneously reappear, but descriptive knowledge as such cannot recapture the 'first-moment experience', which is accessible only as a memory.

The implicit model we have for how knowledge arises thus proves rather complex. To summarize, it appears that the direct content of experience is given through a polar knowledge confined to a particular location in time and space. The polarities of 'perceiver/ perceived', 'here/there', and 'now/then' mark the various aspects of this 'micro-level' knowing, which seems to have special reference to the sensory realm.

In themselves, however, these polarities are inadequate to account for conventional 'objective' reality. This 'reality' forms the basis of descriptive temporal knowledge, which is referred to a 'self existing over time', whose 'nature' is unclear. But descriptive knowledge directs the self away from what it seeks to know. It assures that the unknown will remain unknown even while it is being defined, classified, and positioned. *It is a knowing that is equally a not-knowing.*

Chapter Thirteen

Polarity in space and time and knowledge; distance and the knowledge gap; polarity of self and world; the self's motive for knowing; confining structure of descriptive knowledge.

Inventing the Past

Focus on the memory of a specific event, either 'routine' or emotionally charged. Trace the future that developed out of that remembered event. Experiment with ways to 'strip away' this future, for example, by 'transporting yourself' directly to the past event, or by making the same journey sequentially, 'dropping' subsequent memories as you go. In doing the exercise, also pay attention to the evidence meant to validate the accuracy of what is remembered.

Exercise Thirteen

Matter of Time

Space Complex

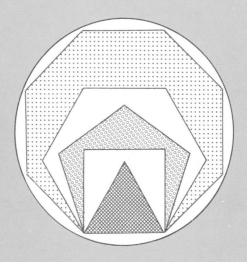

Building on building on
Perpetuating replicating
Time in moments bridging
Space to space contriving
Play of Knowledge elaborates
Amplifies Space of not-knowing

PROBLEMATICS
OF POLARITY

Descriptive knowledge as a fundamental constituting element of the self's 'known world' entails as its consequence a continuing isolation from direct experience. If we are unwilling to accept this consequence as final, we must find a way to trace out and investigate the authority of descriptive knowledge, and to determine whether its structures can truly be considered binding on knowledge as such.

Based on the analysis in the last chapter, the claim by descriptive knowledge to reveal what is true depends in the end on the more immediate 'here and now' of polar knowledge. The perceiver's momentary contact with the perceived, distributed across past and present, is in some way made accessible to the self, which in turn makes use of it to structure a world of identities, interpretations, meanings, and values.

For polar knowledge to play this founding role successfully, three sorts of connections must hold. First, descriptive knowledge must have access to and must accurately reflect the contents of polar knowledge, as that content unfolds across 'moments' of time. Second, the 'perceiver' in polar knowledge must gain accurate information about the 'perceived'. Third, the 'known content' of polar knowledge must 'correspond' to an underlying reality. Though we normally take these connections for granted, each of them raises significant topics for further inquiry, and each will be explored in this and succeeding chapters.

Polar Knowledge: Unfounded Limits

In daily life, polar knowledge appears to operate without our conscious attention, in much the same way that the nervous system coordinates the underlying motor skills that allow basic activities such as walking or speaking. Satisfied with our ability to accomplish what we want, we have no motive for calling into question the base-level knowledge that makes our actions possible.

In accepting the functioning of polar knowledge as the source of what we know, we start from the model (advanced most strongly by science) that only that which can be precisely measured, strictly specified, and consistently replicated counts as knowable. However, this model operates in the realm of descriptive knowledge. Because the 'raw data' of polar observation are prior to *all* definition and interpretation, it seems questionable that they can be directly measured at all, while replication already calls for the kind of comparative operation that the momentary structure of polar knowledge does not seem to allow for.

Instead, polar knowledge plays the vital role of offering a support for the 'scientific model': a basis that guarantees 'objective validity' for the data that science investigates through measurement, specification, and replication. It functions in the way that subatomic particles function in theoretical physics — on the one hand 'most real', with all other phenomena built up out of them; on the other hand, a hypothetical construct put forward to make convincing sense of conventional reality and the way in which the phenomena of direct experience unfold.

If polar knowledge is not directly accessible to our ordinary understanding, the basis for that understanding, as expressed in the scientific model, can no longer be considered self-evident. It may seem that this need not concern us unduly. Granted that the senses can be mistaken or deceived in the information they offer, due to careless observation, faulty assumptions, or unconscious impulses toward distortion. Even so, the information that the senses provide seems to meet our basic needs. We can walk from here to there, reasonably confident that we will not stumble on some invisible obstacle along the way. We can drive cars, build houses, use telephones, and recognize friends. When more precision is needed, science has developed a careful methodology to control the magnitude of error and guarantee predictable results. In short, the senses function well enough to let us make our way in the world.

This 'common sense' view may be proceeding at the wrong level of concern. The known world that polar knowledge appears to found is one in which we are subject to a reality we cannot change. Accepting the world of sense experience and descriptive knowledge means accepting a lineage of constructs and interpretations that results in the 'no-choice' realm of historical conditioning, predetermined patterns of thought, and limited understanding.

If the world that polar knowledge founds limits our visions and aspirations, are we right to say that polar knowledge works 'well enough'? Are we 'making our way' when we are headed nowhere, traveling only in the well-worn circles of past conditioning? Even if polar knowledge gives reliable information, can we 'trust' it to guide our lives in accord with our own values?

The issue is fundamental. If the structures of polar knowledge are the basis for conventional understanding, and if the claim made by polar knowledge to present an 'objective' reality can be sustained, then no matter how the content of descriptive knowledge may change, the choices available to us in living our lives and pursuing knowledge will ultimately come up against certain 'hard facts' that set final limits. On the other hand, if the world based on polar observation proves to be less firmly founded, the seemingly solid limits on our way of being might suddenly dissolve. *Investigating polar knowledge means asking whether we are free.*

Disconnected Knowledge

An act of polar knowing depends on transporting information through space and time, from 'there and then' to 'here and now'. For example, a simple model of visual perception might describe light as reflecting off an object and entering the eye, where it then excites a cascading sequence of processes that are in some way converted into a datum of knowledge. But is the knowledge gained in this way accurate? What guarantees that the object has remained unchanged in the interval between 'then' and 'now', or that the image formed 'here' is a true likeness of an object 'there'?

Let us look at this from the point of view of the 'perceiver'. Having directed attention toward an object, the 'perceiver' sets out to journey from 'here' to 'there' and from 'now' to 'then'. But when it arrives at its destination, it finds that 'there' has become 'here' and 'then' has become 'now'. The original object of inquiry will always be situated in a time and place that remain wholly inaccessible. The difficulty is twofold: knowledge is possible only in the 'future', when the 'perceiver' makes 'contact' with the 'perceived'; yet what can be known is only the object as it was in the 'past'.

A similar problem with 'connections' arises with respect to the momentary structure of polar knowing. In conventional understanding, a 'moment' is the span of time necessary to 'hold' a single discrete event. (If this were not so, and a moment could hold more than one event, it would be difficult to maintain that those events were separate from each other.) Thus, it seems that the 'perceiver' must 'know' in a single moment of time. This is so even if from another perspective that moment is the 'outcome' of previous moments in which information is collected, received, etc.

Based on this view, the momentary act of perceiving uses up its moment with no remainder (since whatever 'remained' would be another moment). But even if moments seem best understood as complete in themselves, knowing cannot be solely a momentary operation. The meaning-giving constructs of the human world depend on moments being linked together to establish descriptive knowledge. Our lives unfold in time in a 'from/to' structure that imparts significance in the same way that a melody brings coherence to musical notes. Thoughts, intentions, and emotions all depend on the connection between moments.

Linking Moments of Knowledge

Consider what 'takes place' when an object first appears within the 'perceiver's' field of vision. This sudden 'presence' of the object can be established only by being linked to the 'non-presence' of the same object in the previous moment. If the object is still present in the next moment, this 'continuing presence' must likewise be linked to the previous moment of being present.

The structure of human experience depends fundamentally on just such linkages. Without them, there could be no knowledge that some 'thing' had appeared or was present. If moments remain irrevocably separated from one another, or if they all arise simultaneously, the world in which we live and act cannot possibly emerge into our awareness.

How is this vital link, which we normally take for granted, possible? Let us ask first with regard to the perceiver. For a link between moments of perception to take place there must be a way for the perceiver in one moment to know what has occurred in the previous moment. But the perceiver operates only 'now'. Knowledge obtained in an earlier moment, situated 'then', will be available, if at all, *only as an object for perception.* The perceiver must thus perceive or 'know' two things, seemingly at once: the immediate momentary object of knowledge (already situated in its own past 'then'), and the previous 'object' of knowledge (or rather, the content of the previous act of knowing).

There is another, equally universal kind of linking. Suppose that in one moment we recognize or observe an object. In the next moment, we may view what we consider to be 'the same' object, but now through a different lens or filter. For example, we may see a car and then hear it going by. Although we may merge these two acts of knowing in our awareness, it seems that each occurs independently, for the two sense fields are separate from each other. Even if we said that these two acts take place in the 'same' moment (for example, if they are processed simultaneously by different parts of the brain), in *referring* these two momentary knowledge-acts to 'the same' object, we somehow relate them.

This 'relating' is another distinct act. How does it take place? It cannot be an activity within each moment, for we have seen that activities such as seeing and hearing fully 'use up' their respective 'moments' without remainder. If we say that the 'relating' occupies a third, intermediate moment, this moment must in turn be related to those that come before and after, establishing an infinite regress. We seem able to escape this endless chain only by saying that there is a separate linking between moments that is not itself momentary, through which connection, meaning, and interpretation can emerge into being.

A Phantom Bridge

For the perceiver situated 'within' a particular moment in time, the link between moments and the linear progression from one moment to the next *cannot be directly observed*. From the perspective of such a perceiver, it might equally be true that time is random in occurrence. The conventional sense of specific occasions and sequences bound together in a definite order might be a construct superimposed by the observing mind. If we pursue these possibilities out far enough, even the idea that time 'proceeds in moments', whether linear or random, might have to be abandoned.

Although the sense that moments of time are linked together is basic to all our understanding, what do we know about such non-momentary linking? Considered as a kind of bridge, it must have a beginning and an ending — a way of spanning the gap between one moment and the next. But the mechanism of spanning or transition remains unknown, even when we succeed in contacting rather subtle levels of mental experience.

If the bridge between moments is a phenomenon different from moments, what is its nature? From within moment-to-moment polar knowledge, it makes sense only to describe it as a 'gap between'. If this gap is truly just empty, how can it serve as a bridge? If it is not empty, is it 'occupied' in some way? And is this occupant some different kind of 'perceiver'?

The problem arises with special force in reference to the initial moment of knowing in a series, which stands in an indeterminate relation to a previous moment of not-knowing. How can a moment of not-knowing be linked to a moment of knowing? For the link to be established, there must be some common ground between the first moment and the second. But how can an unknowing have anything in common with what it does not yet know?

A Widening Puzzle

Such difficulties have consequences beyond the scope of knowledge gained through observation. For example, deductive reasoning depends on logic rather than temporal observation. But logic itself rests on the fundamental principles of identity and contradiction. And these principles in turn depend on simultaneity: Two things cannot at the same time be both 'the same' and 'different'. When successive moments of knowing cannot be linked, however, simultaneity does not apply, and the logic of identity and contradiction falls away. What was impossible in one moment might be possible in the next; what was black then might now be white.

The entire moment-to-moment structure of time that polar knowledge presupposes seems subject to the same kind of difficulty. As a result, the world available through descriptive knowledge comes under question in a fundamental way. *Either the 'knowledge' that we have* learned to rely on has no real basis, or it has its basis in a source we do not know.

All such difficulties arise from the basic structure of polar knowledge. When knowing is limited to a single moment in time, how can what is known be transported from one moment to the next in a way that validates its authenticity? Where and when will the validation take place? When knowledge remains isolated from moment to moment, *can it qualify as knowledge at all?*

Chapter Fourteen

Polar knowledge as not directly accessible; consequences of accepting polar knowledge; missing temporal links; structure of moments; challenge to linear time; lack of foundation for the known.

Moments Between Moments

Observe in your own experience the flow of time from one moment to the next. If the mind is calm and alert, you may notice that between two initially observed moments A and B lie other, intermediate moments:

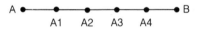

Practice observing from moment to moment in a way that makes available, on an ever 'smaller' scale, moments 'between' moments.

Exercise Fourteen

Fourth Time

Missing Links

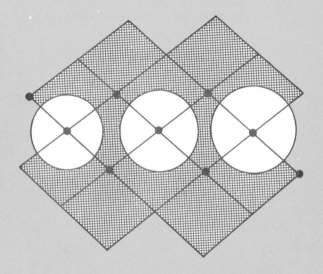

Coming from where
Depending on when
Transported through what
Connections which
Sequence how empowered

COMPELLING
FLOW OF TIME

The difficulties with the linear flow of time seem closely tied to the view that polar knowledge is momentary. Accordingly, it has sometimes been suggested that time is not momentary in structure; that the present is somehow broad enough to encompass more than one moment. But even assuming this approach does not create more problems than it solves, the movement of time from past to present to future remains a necessary prerequisite for the conventional order to establish itself. If we set aside for now the problems that arise in linking together separate moments, how does the more fundamental structure of a linear temporal flow from past to future fare under analysis?

A Linear Unfolding

When something appears, where does it come from? Conventional understanding, based on temporal knowledge, answers that present appearance depends on the past. Each moment (even in a broad sense, in which the moment encompasses more than an instant) arises from the preceding moment. Whatever exists now traces its origins to events occurring 'earlier in time'. Even a stable object, such as a mountain, exists on the basis of having been formed over millions of years; on a more tightly focused view, the mountain exists in this moment on the basis of having existed in the moment just before.

Yet how can the past hold such a wealth of possibilities? Does each earlier moment already encompass within it the potential for all succeeding moments of time? Did the first moment contain within it in some unexpressed form everything that has ever happened and will ever happen? Causal determinism of any kind seems to point in this direction.

If the first moment of time did contain all succeeding moments in some inchoate form, a whole series of fundamental questions would arise. What makes linear time unfold as it does? Why should there even be a first moment? And why should its potential contents — the entire range of events in time — come into being in sequence, rather than all at once, or in some different order? What brings the flow of time into being at all: What purpose does it satisfy; what motive does it fulfill? Does it make sense to speak of motives or purposes existing prior to time, or beyond it? Or do such notions only reveal the limits of time-bound linear thinking?

What can be said about the first moment of time? Did anything precede it? How could a first moment come into being without having a past of its own? If it had a beginning, did this originating act occur in another, more basic kind of time?

If the first moment did arise within a more basic, primordial time, how could it ever originate the flow of conventional time? Without standing in relation to a linear past, could it give rise to the linear future? What would it even mean to 'give rise' to the linear flow of time, when 'giving rise' seems to require the flow of time in order to occur?

Was the first moment caused? If it was not caused, did it just arise accidentally and from nowhere, without any cause? Did some power bring it into being in an unimaginable 'acausal' way? If we say the first moment originated in an unknown and perhaps unknowable source 'beyond' linear time, or suggest that an equally unknowable source establishes a time without beginning, are we referring to something possibly real, or have we just succeeded in finding a sophisticated way of acknowledging our not-knowing?

Would such a power or source 'beyond' time itself be timeless? Or is 'beyond time' just a pointless bit of talk, called into being by a trick of language? Does it refer to a time 'beyond' time in this universe? Then what if there were another universe, with a different 'kind' of time? Which time would be 'beyond' which?

The whole idea of 'prior to time' or 'outside of time' remains linked to time in a way that seems inescapable. Even the idea of 'timeless' must be related to the human sense of time. The standards for measurement and for structures of thought that we can bring to bear all relate to a human scale of comprehension and to the dimensions of human experience.

Outside of Time

Living within linear time, we may be unable to conceive of any other form of time, much as a fish cannot form any understanding of dry land. To speak of 'timeless' or 'before time' may be a faulty extrapolation from the world we know. It may be that our language, which has built-in assumptions about 'beginning' and 'before', leads us astray when we try to use it to encompass what goes beyond conventional experience.

The same difficulty, however, seems to apply even to the understanding of conventional temporality. For example, how can we measure out time? When we speak of moments of time, we apply a construct based on conventional experience and on descriptive temporal knowledge. How can we truly know that what is being measured has anything to do with time as such? As has sometimes been pointed out, the structure of temporal movement — back to the originating moment or forward to the end of time — may say more about the human mind and how it shapes experience than about 'time itself' (assuming that it is possible to make sense of such an unknowable construct as 'time itself').

Again, the common understanding accepts the idea of a sphere of mental activity that remains unconscious, in the sense that it is not normally accessible to the conscious mind. Suppose that time operated in a completely different way in such an unconscious realm than it does in the physical realm and in conscious experience. If this were so, we would seem to have no way of knowing it to be so. Yet if there is an unconscious realm, it might well be that conscious experience is vitally dependent on such unconscious patterns of time.

Even in conscious experience there is a subtle aspect to the temporality of sense awareness and thoughts — their arising and passing away, their inner dynamic and interconnections — that is not normally accessible to direct investigation. Is the structure of linear time 'adequate' for exploring such phenomena? Or does temporality instead hide them from view?

If the linear structure of time is open to question, the basis for the world known through descriptive knowledge collapses. For descriptive knowledge depends on the general validity of the premise that what was 'true' in the past (and is not specifically acknowledged to be subject to change) is true in the present as well. If the link between the past and present or even the 'existence' of past, present, and future as such is uncertain, there can be no relying on 'descriptions' at all.

Description and Memory

We have seen that if descriptive knowledge is to be accurate, there must be a link between the moment being described and the moment of description. This link proved on investigation to be difficult to establish. But even if linear time allowed for such a structure, the inherent logic of descriptive knowledge tends to undermine it. When we try to link together two moments, what we bring into contact are not the original moments at all, but our memories of those moments. Presupposed in the act of linking is the premise that what is remembered is related in some way to the original event.

Perhaps this premise can be accepted on practical grounds, since it seems to give us the information required to act in the world and can be verified by comparing our memory against the memories of other observers. But this justification, while roughly workable, collapses under investigation. A memory may be related to the event it purports to call to mind, but that relationship is not a perfect correspondence. The moment presented to memory reflects other structures and memories, assumptions and presuppositions. *The subject of memory depends on the memory of the subject.*

It seems that a 'filter' inevitably interposes itself between the event or experience and the memory of it. The past cannot be present, even in memory. The sound that we hear in memory is at best the echo of the sound that we heard originally, and it is only *by stipulation* that we can say the echo is an accurate one. Is there any other way to 'validate' what we call to mind? When we can rely only on memory, descriptive knowledge is suspect from the beginning. Is this in fact the case? Does conventional knowledge have no more substantial basis?

Chapter Fifteen

The linear unfolding of time; the first moment and its origin; source 'beyond' time; temporal flow as construct; possibility of unconscious time; link between moments and memories; memory in doubt.

Reversing Time

Review the events of the past few hours, starting with the present moment and proceeding *backwards*. Sights, sounds, and tastes, conversations, thoughts, judgments, and interpretations, even other memories, can be included as events for review. In what sense are you 'reliving' these memories? What is your vantage point? Can it be varied? You can also practice this exercise at the end of each day to cultivate clarity or defuse residues of tension. As an alternative, instead of starting your review from the present, review times 'situated' in the more distant past.

Exercise Fifteen

Space Between

Replication into Whole

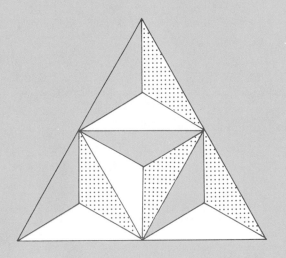

Constructs built to
Specification based on
Constructs placed aligned
Defined in mirror image
To built constructs

MODELING
SELF-CONSTRUCTS

The pattern that we observe in analyzing memory also operates on a level still more fundamental to the founding of descriptive knowledge. Descriptions are in essence constructs, arising in dependence on the categories and definitions supplied by language, collective knowledge, and personal experience. The 'original experience' to which constructs are applied — whether we understand it in terms of polar knowledge or not — remains inaccessible, as though we were trying to experience the feel of a fur coat by touching it with gloves on.

If the 'world' (understood as the 'underlying reality' regarding which we set out to obtain knowledge) is known only through constructs imposed on it, is this truly knowledge at all? How can we tell that what we 'know' is not simply the reflection of the constructs through which our knowing arises — that we are looking not through clear glass, but at a mirror?

Ordinary knowledge could be described as knowledge built up through 'models': explanations or descriptions of how things work within a specified domain.

These models provide the mental constructs that claim to represent with some accuracy the 'objective' reality that appears in conventional space and time.

Starting as children and continuing into adulthood, we follow a standard pattern for gaining knowledge. First we accept a basic model, then we gain sophistication in its use, possibly refining or modifying it in light of new facts, experience, or changed circumstances. We learn to work with models through other models that have as their content the valid ways of forming models and communicating knowledge. Our model of education accepts the idea that knowledge is transmitted through the imparting of models, while our model of science gives us ways to verify or disprove models. The presentation being made in these paragraphs is still another 'model about models'.

Certain kinds of models are frequently subject to questioning and revision; for example, those that present scientific explanations or formal philosophical positions. Other models, however, tend to go unquestioned. The model *that establishes models as a valid way to transmit new knowledge* is one such model. Another is the model linking knowledge to the senses. Still a third is the model that establishes the correlative existence of a 'knowing self' that endures over time on the one hand, and an 'objective world' populated by enduring 'objects' that are the 'carriers' of sensory data on the other.

Such models are so familiar to us that we may never reflect on them explicitly or notice them in operation. And because each model supports and draws support from countless others, a structure is created that is far too complex to be examined as a whole. As a result, we lose sight of the difficulties and contradictions that interacting models generate, and simply accept the 'knowledge' such models provide as 'the way things are'.

If we inquire into the reason for accepting such models, the basic answer would seem to be that they seem to 'fit' with our experience. But while this appeal to experience is powerful, its validity depends on another model — one that defines models as 'true' when they 'conform to experience' (or, alternatively, when they have predictive power, or meet certain criteria of elegance, simplicity, etc.).

It seems doubtful that authentication at this level can be successful — that a model can bear witness for another model. After all, our usual understanding might be reversed: The prevailing models might match our experience because we *shape experience to conform to the models*. Our 'real' reasons for accepting the validity of the prevailing models might be based on a different set of concerns entirely.

As long as models can be said to 'work', perhaps it does not matter very much if they remain unfounded. Even if in the end we can rely only on 'blind faith', our reliance may be justified in terms of what it accomplishes, or on the basis of other, less immediately obvious criteria. Whatever the specific reasons we advance, however, there are good grounds for investigating further, for it seems that reliance on models limits knowledge in fundamental ways.

What Models Leave Out

In the first place, *models tend to freeze out the possibility of fundamental change.* The model establishes a pattern that allows for only certain kinds of events and certain sequences in which events can unfold. Events that do not conform to such sequences may be flatly ruled out, or else placed outside the scope of possible knowing. If change unauthorized by the model occurs, it will be 'unlawful'. In certain kinds of models it might be considered 'miraculous'; in others it might be ascribed to a freakish set of circumstances, explained away, or simply ignored as beneath notice.

Because models restrict the kinds of change available to be known, they work against our ability to adapt to our surroundings. History offers frequent examples of individuals, social groups, and entire cultures that adhered to a way of life or a set of beliefs that restricted knowledge, rendering them unable to deal with new circumstances. Despite their usefulness, there are times when models can be destructive, even dangerous.

Second, *models tend to allow only knowledge that fits within the basic structure of polar and descriptive knowledge.* This structure works well as a basis for knowing only when applied to events that are rigidly and routinely repeated. Knowledge that does not accord with this pattern of mechanical repetition (which underlies the basic effectiveness of descriptive knowing) tends to be lost or overlooked. When we know through models, we 'know' that the same patterns recur over time, and it becomes 'natural', even 'inevitable', to say that progress comes only slowly, or that human nature cannot be changed, or that our destiny is in the hands of fate.

Third, *knowledge based on models is distanced from direct experience in favor of conceptual structures.* Since models are conceptual, the knowledge that they lead to will consist of a steady succession of thoughts and images. Though this flow in itself embodies a vital energy, the focus of the models is on the content of each thought in turn. As one fixed idea succeeds another, the vivid immediacy of experience is lost. Immediate experience may be the *source* of the knowledge that the model expresses, but when this knowledge is put in the form of a model and transmitted from person to person, this source is not directly communicated. Instead, knowledge is recast as technology or as belief, while other possibilities for knowing recede from view.

Finally, *models turn our attention away from a direct inquiry into the unfounded assumptions of the models themselves.* When we label something as 'good' or 'bad' in the terms that the model establishes, we tend not to ask why the good is good. If it can only be 'good' in relation to 'bad', then why is the bad bad? Knowing from within the model, we may find such questions as meaningless as the endlessly repeated 'whys' of a young child. But this sense of questions as being without meaning is based on the model's juxtaposing presuppositions to establish an order, complete with identified entities and excluded alternatives. Such juxtaposition stops inquiry before it has rightly begun. Because limitations on knowledge are a 'built-in' feature of the model, they become inevitable.

Once in operation, 'model-based' knowledge is self-perpetuating. If we try to ask why the assumptions of models are beyond questioning, the answer comes from within another model. For example, models of discourse or inquiry may define the scope of rationality in such a way that reliance on pre-established axioms is a logical necessity. A very different set of models may make certain kinds of knowledge accessible only to faith. But the invoking of such additional models only serves to underscore the lack of knowledge inherent in the models as such.

In each model, then, there is a 'place' that remains impenetrable. The limited knowledge allowed within the model is positioned in a specific way (for example, as wisdom, rationality, faith, empirical truth, etc.). A line is established beyond which knowledge cannot go.

Chapter Sixteen

Knowledge built up through models; the model for transmitting knowledge; the unfounded appeal to experience; models as freezing out change, knowledge, and direct experience; models as impenetrable to knowledge due to positioning.

Cloud of Knowing

Ordinarily, we look at objects, forms, shapes, and events from one perspective at a time: a simple linear relationship that can be understood either temporally or spatially:

Viewed more closely, observation does not follow this simple linear path. As we observe one thing, other thoughts, images, or judgments may come to mind:

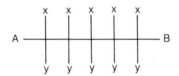

Again, the object we are observing may reveal new aspects or dimensions, or we may see it from different perspectives:

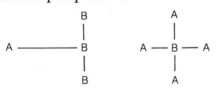

Observe perceptual situations with sensitivity toward this non-linear complexity.

Exercise Sixteen

Underlying Understanding

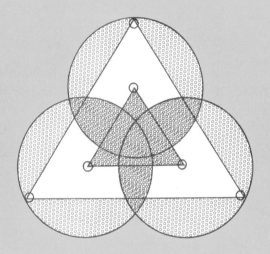

Concepts fundamental to themselves
Built of Space Time Knowledge
Building space time knowledge
Naming and proclaiming
More than names
Less than named
Meets the I

INTERPRETATION
AT THE CORE

To investigate why we follow models, the models themselves, including models for how to investigate, must be put aside as far as possible. Unless we turn directly to experience, we will continue to play one model off against another, trading in old belief structures for new ones. If we have no model for how to investigate without applying models for investigation, this is probably all to the good.

Conventional understanding asserts that a model (which might be expressed in the form of a statement, interpretation, theory, or story) is 'true' when it offers knowledge of 'the facts', or what is 'really so'. But this model of 'the truth' is not easily maintained, for it seems that 'facts' are nowhere to be found. In trying to contact an 'objective' world, we make use of a model and its constructs to do so. The world that we are accustomed to, even in its most 'direct' and 'immediate' manifestations, is an intricate and overlapping complex of models, built up out of interpretations, presuppositions, concepts, meanings, values, and memories.

Such constructs can be seen in operation in the shifting views of physical reality through history. Earlier cultures generally accepted earth, air, fire, and water as the basic qualities of all that was physically 'real'. A similar model was accepted by the Greeks, and was followed by Western culture until a few centuries ago. This picture offered more than just a theory; it described the way that 'reality' was actually experienced.

After the discovery of oxygen in the eighteenth century, modern science embarked on a course that led it to reject this view. The old 'elements' were set aside as faulty interpretations of reality, and a new set of elements, more directly tied to the idea of substance, was put in their place. However, the new model continued to accept the model of a physical world 'out there', built up out of fundamental elements that existed independent of human knowledge concerning them.

In this century, that model has changed once again. Elemental atoms were found to be composed of more fundamental particles, and these in turn were interpreted as fluctuations of energy or fields, or even as probabilities. It was also suggested for the first time that the exact nature of these particles might depend on how they were observed, thus linking knower and known in a way that goes against the grain of everyday understanding and the structures of temporal knowledge.

Through all these changes, however, scientists have continued to uphold the basic model that our interpretations apply to an 'underlying reality'. Thus, the physical sciences go to great lengths to eliminate from their data 'subjective' elements such as bias, faulty perception, or interpretive structures that might come between the observer and the 'hard data' that represent 'reality'.

It does not seem that this attempt can be successful. The drive for 'objectivity' still depends utterly on a model that gives meaning to such concepts as 'object', 'measurement', and 'replication', and on the collective understanding embodied in our models of 'science', 'scientist', and 'valid means of knowledge'. When the 'facts' of human experience are conditioned by such 'subjective' elements, how can they be 'objectively' true?

An Underlying Reality

Philosophers and students of knowledge have long been aware of such difficulties. Despite their persistent questions, however, common sense continues to maintain that a 'reality' more fundamental than models, constructs, and interpretations does exist. Some philosophers have sided with common sense, and the resulting debate has continued for millennia without resolution.

Let us explore this debate briefly, without trying to make any definitive contribution, in order to see the limits within which descriptive knowledge operates.

The most convincing evidence that models 'correspond' to an underlying 'reality' appears to be pragmatic. Some interpretive structures 'work' while others do not; therefore, some interpretations are true, others false.

'Truth' in this sense is understood to mean correspondence with the 'actual' facts. For example, if a hungry man imagines that he sees food before him and tries to eat it, he will not satisfy his hunger. Even if he is so deluded that he imagines in perfect detail the sensations of smelling, tasting, chewing, and swallowing, he will receive no actual nourishment. If he persists in eating such 'meals', he will soon starve to death.

This example seems to demonstrate what we already understand to be the case: that it would be foolish to deny the distinction between true and false as a working principle. But it is quite another matter to conclude that 'true statements' (or 'true' perceptions) are 'true' insofar as they 'correspond' to an independent reality. Without disputing the trustworthiness of the 'facts' that we rely on in our conduct, we can acknowledge that the *understanding of those facts as existing independently of our interpretations is itself an interpretation of what it means to label a statement as true.* Applying a pragmatic test to see whether a statement matches 'the facts' simply means looking to see whether one set of interpretations corresponds to another.

If we take the view that 'facts' are 'real', we only shift the interpretive dimension to the issue of what is 'real'. A novelist who gives his hero blue eyes in chapter one cannot give him brown eyes in chapter five. Does this mean that the hero's eyes are 'really' blue? Within the 'reality' of the novel, the answer is yes, but if we apply the quite different standards of conventional reality, we can only say that the hero himself is fictional, and that it makes no sense to speak of the 'real' color of his eyes.

When 'underlying reality' is itself a construct, it seems that we can never move beyond the descriptive realm of models and interpretation. Perhaps our interpretations can be more fully worked out and refined, so that they guide our actions more effectively; perhaps they can integrate other interpretive structures, so that they become more comprehensive and thus more accurate. But they cannot point to anything 'beyond' or 'under' interpretive structures.

When one construct matches another, does this prove that either is real? Suppose that what we understood to be fundamental elements of experience were simply interpretive projections onto a random matrix, with meanings, actions, and results all expressions of the original act of projection. If this 'act of projection' were 'fundamental' would our experience necessarily differ in any way from what it is right now?

Only Interpretations

Language, concepts, and reasoned arguments can all be understood as sets of interpretive structures, pointing only to more such structures. But if this is so, what 'solid' foundation is there for knowledge? When we have an experience 'within' time, who 'has' the experience and where? Does the mind 'receive' the content of knowing or 'create' it? When 'we' ask ourselves a question, is the answer an echo of the question? If there is confusion, who is confused? From where would clarity come, and how would it be communicated? By what measure will we know there has been 'real' understanding?

When we ask whether the domain of meanings and meaningful distinctions is meaningful, we 'receive' an answer in the terms that language makes available to us. What significance attaches to such linguistic constructs? The speaker finds meaning in each word, but a foreigner may hear every word as meaningless noise. Which understanding is 'really true'? How could the speaker convince the foreigner that his words had meaning? Language is a complex, self-referring system, a highly structured game. But can it be said to have any 'objective' significance?

Human experience testifies to what can be achieved through communication based on agreement that words refer to specified subjects of discourse. Yet 'achievement' and 'communication' are themselves concepts. If they were unavailable, there could be no 'meaningful distinction' between a random motion of the hand and the skillful actions that help construct a bridge, organize a meeting, or shape a sculpture. Could a foreigner who considered such distinctions meaningless be shown to be mistaken?

Suppose you dream you are dreaming. Within the dream, there would be no way to determine what was dream and what was reality. If you 'wake up', this awaking might still be part of the dream within a dream. Or it might be a waking up into the dream. Finally, it might be a 'real' awakening. How could you tell?

The Witness

Firmly trapped within interpretation, we face a fundamental 'not-knowing' that defies penetration. Analysis and questioning themselves arise within interpretive structures, so how can they illuminate those structures?

How can we counter a 'not-knowing' that throws into doubt each and every interpretive structure?

From within conventional experience, only one answer seems possible. Turning from logic and reasoning, we can point to an ever-present 'witness': the 'feeling' of reality, or the conviction that 'this is so'. Wholly apart from subtle philosophical investigation, it is this feeling we rely on in conducting the business of our lives. Thus, the difference between waking up into a dream and waking up into 'reality' is ultimately a matter of feeling tone and conviction: We simply 'know' what it is like to experience the real.

Imagine observing a cup on the table before you. Next, imagine that you have closed your eyes and are imagining the same cup as vividly as you can. There remains a difference in quality between these two experiences. *This 'quality' is the ultimate guarantor or 'witness' of the real.* What we perceive in the imagination lacks this quality, and that is why we consider it unreal; what we dream appears to possess this quality, but when we awaken from the dream we realize that the witness was only a 'dream witness'.

If the witness deceives us, so that we assert the reality of what is 'unreal', we speak of delusion, hallucination, and even psychosis. Such a description can be applied only from outside: Within the experience the testimony of the witness is conclusive. We may disregard what the witness tells us, because it conflicts with our beliefs or with conventional definitions of 'valid' experience; even so, we are applying external criteria to dismiss what we would otherwise 'know' to be true. In determining what is 'true' about the truth, the witness is more powerful than the content of what is witnessed.

Philosophers of several traditions have noted that the content of our experience may be doubted at the deepest level, but that the sense that 'I am experiencing' seems somehow beyond doubt. Reflection on the nature of the witness thus seems to lead in the end to the sense of self. It is the self, impelled by its own needs and intentions, that unites the momentary observations of the 'perceiver' into a coherent whole. This coherence is inseparable from the ineffable but seemingly undeniable quality of 'the real'. Temporal knowledge proclaims itself 'true' precisely because it is knowledge acquired by a self. The self stands squarely at the center of experience, the knower and doer, the measure of all things. *Because the self 'exists', the world is 'real'.*

To continue our inquiry into temporal knowledge, the self and the patterns of intentionality out of which the self emerges must come under investigation. But when we turn to initiate this inquiry, we find that the structures of space and time implicit in our investigations until now undergo a sharp and sudden shift. It is almost as though we were entering a different world.

Chapter Seventeen

Models based on constructs; basic model of an underlying reality; pragmatic argument for 'reality' based on constructs; language as self-referring; relying on the witness; self as guarantor of the real.

Field of Awareness

Investigate the 'background' aspect of feelings, linked more to mood or attitude than specific content. How do feelings relate to awareness as the 'field' for thought? Conduct this investigation both in the morning and the evening, noticing the differences. Continue with the practice even if you are not sure what you are looking for. Continued practice can contact the intuitive internal mind, bringing greater clarity and calm.

Exercise Seventeen

Being of Self-Knowledge

Self Center

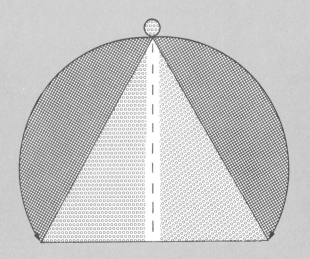

Witness persistent persisting
Presenting past present future
Here now now here emergent
Dispensation of the known
Willed to be toward
What will be

THE WORLD
OF THE SELF

The self as understood by conventional knowledge exists and acts across time. If we analyze this understanding (which in itself 'belongs' to the self), it appears that the self *establishes itself and the world that it knows* by moving off-center, 'beyond' the point-instant of temporal knowledge. In one unified action *it takes a position, posits a situation, and imposes meaning.* The self finds itself 'in the world'—its attention defines 'there' and 'then' and its vantage point locates 'here' and 'now'. Form and feeling, specific characteristics and qualities, knowing and being, and the entire realm of human values and meanings all arise as a direct consequence of the self's positionings.

In taking a position, the self remains bound by all the polarities of conventional observation: Without the structure of 'perceiver' and 'perceived', the self would be powerless to make knowledge its own. But while the self assumes the role of the 'perceiver', dwelling 'here' and 'now', it also views itself as *persisting 'over' time*, uniting the succession of 'nows' and able to move freely

147

from 'here' to 'there'. The difficulties that led us to wonder in an earlier chapter how moments of time could possibly be linked are of no concern to the self, which 'knows' that it has the capacity to establish the link.

The Self Traversing Time

Continuity over time is the hallmark of the self's identity. Although always 'present' (for only in the present can the self act, experience, and know), the self exists in the present by drawing on the past and shaping it into the future. Without a continuing relation to the past, the present self would just vanish, to be replaced in the next moment by something completely different; without a transitional relation to the future, the present self would endure forever, like a woman who was always pregnant. Neither possibility truly allows for a self to exist.

Unlike the 'perceiving subject', the self is a historical being, somehow 'extensively' situated 'within' the flow of linear time. Subordinating the perceiver's isolation in the 'here and now' to its own claim to be the owner of its experience, the self asserts that it 'wills' the successive acts of temporal knowing that give rise to the structures of its known world.

The persistence of the self over time might seem to parallel the persistence of what the self knows through descriptive knowledge. But there is an important difference. While the self's known world is salvaged from the past, the self that knows emerges from the future. For the self constructs its being through its desires and wants, and desire and want, though their contents are drawn from the past, are based in what has not yet come to be.

The self's fundamental desire is *the desire to know and establish a world into which the self can emerge.* Responding to this desire, the self appropriates the past through descriptive knowledge, structuring a present reality in which its own existence as knower of the known and meaning-giver is assured.

But desire takes more complex forms as well. In contrast to the pale and often disappointing world accessible to descriptive knowing, desire manifests an endless variety of moods and 'atmospheres', holding out the promise of infinite possibilities. In terms of content, the future seems likely to offer only variations on the rigid world of past definitions and structures. But on a deeper level, the future offers the momentum of an indeterminate becoming, alive with possibilities that fuel hope, fear, and longing.

Led on by such emotions and expectations, the self lives toward the future. Its actions 'now' are governed by a concern for the future's 'then'. Intent on what might be but is not yet, it shifts from mood to mood, reinterpreting the past, reassessing the present, responding more or less consciously to the rhythms of wanting. The self wants to become a certain way or attain a certain state. It wants to be happy, to be in possession of something, to be finished, or simply to endure. Cravings, wishes, and hopes induce a self-propelled acceleration that draws the self forward. *The force of the self's desire unfolds as the momentum of linear time.*

The Knowing Self in Time and Space

We can now see in a preliminary way the nature of space, time, and knowledge in the world that the self occupies and structures. First, whereas space is central to the world of objects, time is central to the world of the self. The time that unfolds with a dynamic momentum from past to present to future is the domain of the self—*whereas objects 'occupy' space, the self 'experiences' and 'owns' time.*

Space is likewise no longer an empty container for things; it too has become 'personalized' as the expanse separating the self from what is desired. The self's 'here' is no longer the isolated point occupied by the 'perceiver' engaged in polar knowing, but rather a specific position adopted by the self and maintained as separate from the object of desire, which is positioned 'there'. As structures of desire, 'here' and 'there' cut across the distinctions of object-centered space and time, for separation can be understood equally well in terms of space *or* time.

Finally, the knowledge particular to the world of the self is what might be called 'intentional' knowledge: *knowledge that arises with regard to the future, as the self determines its goals and decides what it intends to accomplish by its activity.* Through intentional knowledge, the self shapes its being over time, choosing a course of conduct and way of life, and defining itself and its world.

The dynamic, future-centered interplay of space, time, and knowledge in the world of the self thus differs in fundamental ways from the interaction of object-centered space and time and the corresponding, past-centered descriptive knowledge.

However, this is not the only way of looking at the self. It is one of the puzzling facts about the self that it also has object-like existence. Through 'its' body, the self interacts with other objects, in ways that seem better described by the 'space', 'time', and 'knowledge' of a 'space-centered' objective reality. We shall return to a consideration of this 'dual citizenship' of the self below.

The availability of two ways of understanding space, time, and knowledge may help explain why the critiques of polar knowledge carried out in earlier chapters do not in themselves seem convincing. Though the logic of polar knowledge cannot account for how anything is ever known, the self insists that it 'knows' nonetheless. Even the failure of descriptive knowledge to establish the 'truth' of any position, which relates more directly to the 'temporal knowing' of the self, leaves intentional knowledge unaffected. *In terms of the 'different' space, time, and knowledge within which the self appears to operate,* such difficulties play no role.

What is the relation between the space, time, and knowledge of the 'space-centered object realm' and the corresponding factors in the world of the self? An answer that drew on conventional understanding might suggest that the intentional structures that accord with the self's way of being are only 'interpretive overlays' on the more 'fundamental realities' of the object realm. But even if this suggestion could succeed in reducing the unique attributes of the knowing self to manifestations of object-centered reality (which does not appear likely), we have already found it ineffective to label one view of reality as 'real' while dismissing the other as 'interpretation'. *The distinction between reality and interpretation is itself an interpretation.*

The inevitability of interpretive structures — understood as the outcome of activity by a self — does not 'mean' that the 'self-centered' interpretation of space, time, and knowledge is 'the real' one. This conclusion attempts to escape the 'all-interpretations' view by positing 'interpretations' as a 'reality' underlying interpretations. But even this 'reality' can only be established on the basis of an interpretation.

A final alternative — that the 'different' space, time, and knowledge 'enjoyed' by the self are independent of the 'object-centered' space, time, and knowledge — also raises major difficulties. How could the two kinds of space and time be brought into contact? Would this require a third kind of 'time' or 'space' that encompassed both of the 'other' kinds?

To study these questions, the structures of intentional knowledge and the patterns that establish the self need clarification. Only then can we investigate with sufficient care the dimensions of space, time, and knowledge that a self-centered view begins to open.

Chapter Eighteen

Self as persistent; as directed toward the future, unfolding through desire the momentum of linear time; desire as founding intentional knowledge; self as occupying 'different' space and time.

Projecting the Future

Reflect on a specific memory as it relates to the future that has not yet come. How do hopes, fears, and anticipations color the past? Now reverse the exercise: Imagine events in the future — routine, fantastic, or wishful. What part of this imagined future is not based on memories of the past? Note: This exercise and Exercise 13 can be deepened through personal instruction.

Exercise Eighteen

Knowing Time

All Movement

Overlapping prospects rotate
Control out of control
Forward fragments taking shape
Intention momentum
Knowing less knowingness

THE REIGN OF
INTENTIONAL KNOWLEDGE

Intentional knowledge complements and completes the world revealed in descriptive knowledge, making that world meaningful to the self. Since the content of experience is described and identified in terms of the self's concerns, intentional knowledge could even be considered the more basic of the two.

Even so, intentional knowledge does not improve on descriptive knowledge in its capacity to give the self satisfaction. Because the force of desire and wanting thrusts the self ahead into what might be, the possibility of enjoying what is already present is blocked. Yet the anticipated joys of the future (as distinct from the double-edged pleasures of anticipation itself) are not yet available to be tasted and experienced. And when the guiding image of future satisfaction is at last obtained, the transplanting of the desired object from one aspect of time to another—from image to object—alters its makeup and destroys its allure. Just as a memory will always differ from the original experience, so whatever is attained departs from the once imagined goal.

Tightly bound by yesterday, swept along into tomorrow, *the self is cut off from its world*, stranded and isolated. Its ways of knowing foster not-knowing; its ways of fulfillment result in frustration. The self lives in the present like a traveler in an inhospitable foreign land: ill at ease, unsure of how to act, never really at home with its experience.

The Life of Feelings

When the world of attained objects proves unsatisfying, the self can turn 'inward' to the subjective realm of feelings and emotions. Whereas objects seem not to be *directly* knowable and goals seem not to be *directly* achievable, feelings and emotions do seem directly accessible. Rather than being bound to a vanished past or a future that remains out of reach, feelings are the immediate 'stuff' of experience, undeniably available in the present. There seems little doubt that feelings offer a kind of nourishment that would be difficult to obtain in any other way.

For all their immediacy, however, feelings and emotions remain bound to the future-centered structure of intentional knowledge. They are the subjective expression of the patterns of desire and longing, working themselves out through time. In fact, the turn toward feeling could be understood as the choice of intentional over descriptive knowledge — of what is felt over what is perceived. With this choice comes a shift in focus from *what* is desired to the longing or the satisfaction that desire brings in its wake.

The result is a knowing that can *hardly be said to know at all*. The self sucks on its feelings like a toothless old dog chewing on a sharp bone, mistaking the taste of its own blood for fresh, juicy meat. It judges good and bad, right and wrong by 'taste', and fights like a hungry beast for the objects that its desires single out. Understanding is filtered through the cyclic patterns of hope and fear; intelligence, reasoning, discrimination and language are reduced to a subordinate role, providing the attendant stories and rationales that serve to assure commitment to the reign of feeling. Reduced to this level, intentional knowledge comes close to abandoning what seems specifically human in the capacity to know.

When the 'gut-level knowledge' of feelings and emotions is installed as arbiter of truth, life becomes an emotional roller coaster. The self responds to patterns that constantly fluctuate, seeking out the highs, avoiding the lows, or resigned to the shadow-world of emotional indifference. Focused in on its own responses, the self lacks clarity about what is happening in its life. Passing desires are mistaken for heartfelt conviction; changing circumstances are easily overlooked and the lessons of past experience easily ignored. Disregard for key elements in new situations leads to increasingly distorted views over time.

In the end, the turn inward toward feelings turns the world upside down. Thinking that it is following a path based on immediate sensation, the self remains bound by the future-centered orientation of intentional knowledge, and so experiences continuing frustration. Yearning for an 'object-world' fulfillment that remains out of reach, the self finds that the patterns of its life bring stagnation and endless repetition. Yet if the commitment to feelings is complete, this stagnation is reinterpreted as the perpetual promise of the new.

Though a life based on feelings may seem rich in happenings, there is little sense of a knowledge that could give those happenings significance. There may be times of unexpected pleasures, when the range of experience exceeds the grasp of the imagination, suggesting rich new potential. But the special delight of such times only emphasizes how barren are the usual patterns.

Although aware that something is amiss, the self lacks recourse to a knowledge beyond feelings that could let it shape its life differently. Dreams and fantasies seem tightly bound to disappointment and frustration, or else to dullness, boredom, and anxiety. Unwanted changes are succeeded by feelings of repetition and sameness, in a never-ending cycle. The exhilaration of chasing after desires fails to conceal the underlying sense of a world stripped bare of significance and value, devoid of knowing, difficult to bear. A deep sense of loss prevails, and moments of real joy and openness are rare.

Strategies for Control

Instead of following the path of feelings and emotions, the self may try to reclaim a more meaningful knowledge by bringing its world under *control*. Feeling continues to determine values, but descriptive knowledge is reinstated, and given a new domain and a new task—the fulfilling of desires.

In this way, the turn toward intentional knowledge transforms descriptive knowledge into technology, as discussed in Part One. Intent on manipulating its world, the self relies on methods for knowing that promote a sense of mastery: logic, measurement, rhetoric, machinery. It establishes itself as arbiter of experience, separating the good times from the bad, judging and comparing. It asserts power where it can and builds defenses where it cannot.

Such strategies, however, do nothing to alter the basic intentional structure that allows fulfillment only in the future. No matter how far an 'object-centered' technological knowledge may extend its mastery, the objects of desire continue to remain out of reach.

Technological knowledge promises results, and the self may continue to believe in that promise despite repeated disappointments. Stubbornly it responds to frustration by seeking more of the same: more food, more sleep, more excitement, more oblivion. It runs its life as a foreman might run a factory that continued to produce with great efficiency a product for which the market had disappeared. Not recognizing that the cost of fuel and maintenance far outweighs the value of what it is producing, the self pours its limited capital into upkeep and new machinery, squandering its resources to no purpose, charting a course toward bankruptcy.

Technological knowledge places the objective realm in the service of intentional knowledge, but leaves intact the frustrations of the intentional mode. The endless segments of a technologically measured-out time seem to disperse and to diffuse the self's energy, while the endless complications of a technologically patterned life leave no room for change. Every situation is a problem, and every solution creates new difficulties. Space is filled up with the structures adopted by technological knowing; time is measured out in advance, like a desert tracked with endless footprints. There may be discipline, but it leads nowhere; there may be creativity, but it is channeled into rigid routines. Even when the promised results are attained, no satisfaction can be found.

Chapter Nineteen

Lack of satisfaction in intentional knowledge; the turn toward feelings; loss of knowledge; strategies for control; move toward technology; self's energy dispersed and diffused; no satisfaction.

Object of Desire

Imagine whatever object you desire most. Let this imagination build, intensifying the associated 'field' of energy until the mind almost *becomes* the image. Maintaining this energy, take the time to build up and enrich every aspect of the imagined perceptual situation, including form, shape, and qualities, as well as the attitude, intention, and feeling you bring to it. This exercise can also be combined with Exercise 8.

Exercise Nineteen

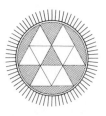

Knowledge to Know

All Sides

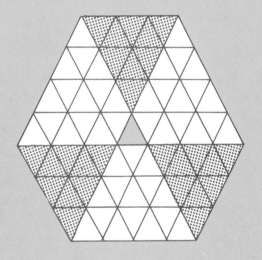

Before around surround
Define confine refine
Beyond respond
Inchoate genetic patterning
Knowledge before knowledge
Identity before identity
Questions for convention

GUIDANCE
AND DIRECTION

An intentional knowledge confined to the limited world of feeling and emotions threatens descent into anarchy, while technological knowledge offers order without meaning or satisfaction. Yet this is not the whole picture. Human society is structured in ways that inhibit the absolute reign of feelings and give coherence to the mechanisms of control. A source of guidance and direction is in operation. In their daily activities, human beings can turn for support to the culturally transmitted assembly of definitions and interpretations that constitute the fundamentals of being human — language, shared understandings and values, and the matrix for personal interaction. This system as a whole could be called 'collective knowledge'.

Collective knowledge balances the self's narrow preoccupation with its own desires and feelings and directs the efforts of technological knowing. It offers stability and security, together with a kind of routinized knowing that suggests appropriate responses in a variety of possible situations.

Collective knowledge itself is only the historical manifestation (or extension through time) of descriptive and intentional knowing. Each new generation is born into a world governed by such knowledge. It absorbs the complex understandings of those who have come before, and passes that knowledge on to future generations.

In this sense, collective knowledge is the 'field' of temporal knowing. Based on the same descriptive structures and intentional momentum that generate individual knowledge, it binds the awareness tightly to the identified structures of the past and intended prospects for the future. Abiding by its standards, each individual follows a way established by others.

The 'field' of collective knowledge has a structure and dynamic of its own. The transmission of collective knowledge allows 'new' knowledge to be 'manufactured' and 'distributed' like a product on an assembly line. There can be revisions and modifications in what is known, and established factors can recombine in various ways, but the underlying structures remain. If old standards break down, new ones quickly emerge to replace them, like new patterns taking shape in a kaleidoscope. Even such shifts are rare: For the most part fields of knowledge and the general culture faithfully replicate in different guises the prevailing views of self and world, objects and desires.

Collective knowledge thus supports the structures of observation and inference. Knowledge may increase in scope, but not in depth. Missing the dimension of depth, 'space' becomes simply 'volume' and begins to fill up.

The 'things' of the world grow dark and impenetrable, and experience untrustworthy.

To counter the proliferation of surfaces and mechanical interactions, collective knowledge turns to a more psychological understanding. But now emotions and feelings are put in control, and once more meaning and order slide toward chaos. Hope for finding a deeper significance in human actions fades.

Crowding and Tension

As collective knowledge duplicates itself, unchecked by alternatives, the proliferation of old patterns gives the sense that the space within the 'field' is being 'filled up'. Over time the products of accustomed knowledge — models, structures, and identities — multiply, confining active knowing to an ever smaller domain. The 'field' becomes increasingly crowded, like a warehouse filled to the rafters. All of space is occupied with self and structures . . . and still it fills up more.

With continued crowding, a kind of pollution clouds the atmosphere, and pressure builds, threatening to explode the boundaries of the 'known world'. A constant stream of new explanations, facts, and diversions fails to relieve the pressure; instead, it only adds to the crowding. With no other source of knowledge available, confusion is always close at hand. Simply coping with the situations of daily living drains off energy.

The momentum of crowding may engender a sense of intensity and high energy. On the cultural level there may be periods of rapid change, even revolution. Such upheavals may clear the air like a summer thunderstorm, but beneath the agitation, the knowing faculty remains confined. Space is full and time used up; history is an ever heavier burden. There is no room for inner freedom, open communication, or meaningful accomplishment.

Living in such a 'field', we are no longer the owners of our own experience. The past gives birth to the images and concepts we use to make sense of the world, and these become the parents of the future. New thoughts must conform to the structures of the old; a thought that goes off in another direction will no longer be 'thoughtful'. While patterns vary in ways that we may consider vitally important, sameness plays beneath the surface.

Whether we see this situation clearly or not, we feel a tightening grip that chokes off creativity and leaves no chance for autonomy. Lacking avenues of expression, our wants and desires build, adding their outward pressure to the inward pressure of the self's ever-narrowing horizons. We are like a people who have responded to the threat of anarchy by inviting in a foreign army to preserve order, and now find themselves the subjects of an invading force and its totalitarian regime.

Chapter Twenty

Stability through collective knowledge; support for temporal patterns; surfaces, crowding, and pressure; intensity without autonomy.

Calming Body, Mind, and Senses

Imagine a situation, either positive or negative, real or imagined, that evokes a powerful emotional response. Focus on the 'aliveness' of the response rather than the content of the situation or its tone; then practice maintaining this aliveness while allowing the emotional, agitated quality to subside, leaving clarity behind. Once you are familiar with this exercise, you can practice it in the midst of situations where there is agitation, stress, or high energy. Note: This exercise can be deepened through personal instruction.

Exercise Twenty

Memory of Knowledge

Owning One

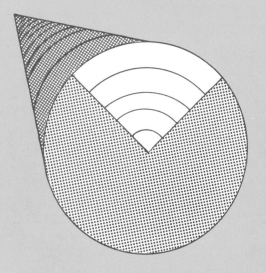

Present past future
Seizing and projecting
Image of Knowledge
Self found founds founders
Story discloses closed
Dimensions of Knowledge

PRESENTING
THE SELF

The self establishes its central position in descriptive and intentional knowledge through the structuring of the known world. After first laying claim to polar knowledge — attributed to the activity of the 'moment-to-moment' 'perceiver', — *the self goes on to present itself as the agent responsible* for the organization of experience over time through its all-important role as perceiver, knower, and actor.

Just as in the space-centered view of 'objective reality' space itself disappears in favor of objects, so in the temporal view knowledge as such disappears in favor of the intentions and concerns of the knowing self. All concepts, categories, and definitions, including 'time' and 'self', trace to the self's interpretive activity; more-over, the self is the one that sets goals and establishes projects, creating the sphere of meaning. Observation is completed by interpretation to produce the known world; memory is coupled with anticipation and inten-tion to give coherence and meaning to the flow of events. Acting as knower, interpreter, and meaning-giver, the self seizes the past, authenticates the present, and projects the unfolding of the future.

But who is this self? Precision in looking at the self will help us summarize what has gone before and anticipate further directions for inquiry.

Persona of the Self

It seems that the activities of the self can be organized into five principal categories:

☆ First is the 'objective self', subject to history and conditioning, to birth, life, and death. This is the aspect of self that gives self-identity its content: a personal history and a personality, a set of goals and purposes, a physical locatedness and an embodied nature. But *this* self — the self as object, with an identity and characteristics knowable by others — is part of the world 'out there'. It lacks the unique capacity of the self to occupy the 'here', which sets it apart from the rest of existence.

☆ Second is the self as 'perceiver', active 'here and now' in the present. Confined to the moment, *this* self lacks the power to shape, define, and organize experience.

☆ Third is the self as 'interpreter'. This is the self as subject in a world of objects, defining, naming, and labeling: the self of descriptive knowledge, knowing on the basis of the past. But we have seen that interpretations lack the power to found themselves. A self reliant on them is in the end only another interpretation.

☆ Fourth is the self as 'narrator', the self of intentional knowledge, whose nature we began to explore in chapter nineteen. The narrator gives meaning to events by directing them toward the future. The structure of this unfolding remains to be investigated.

☆ Fifth is the self as 'owner' and 'witness', validating experience and reality in validating its own identity: the self that underlies and guarantees the perceiver, interpreter, and narrator. This is the 'core self' whose existence is the key to all temporal knowing.

Efforts to establish the 'core self' based on the self as 'perceiver' and as 'interpreter' have left us dissatisfied. Now we will investigate the self as 'narrator', to see how the future-centered projects of intentionality relate to the underlying sense of self.

The Narrator and the Founding Story

The self as narrator actively links successive moments of knowing, wanting, and interpreting. It shapes the content of descriptive and intentional knowledge into an account that mirrors the seeming flow of time from past to future. The narrator's stories make meaningful the self's doings, thoughts, and imaginings, giving coherence to the flow of events.

The stories told by the narrator-self are about the needs, desires, feelings, experiences, projects, and understandings of the self. Within their patterns the self justifies, plans, and rehearses; judges, reasons, and feels emotions; desires, enjoys, rejects, and suffers. The rules of logic and social intercourse, the vivid imagery of the human mind, the interlocking domains of perception, feelings, naming, explanations, and interpretations all take their meaning and significance from the manifold structures of the web of stories.

A single story may be fully formed, subtle, and intricate, or fragmentary and suggestive. In either case, it allows for the possibility of subsidiary stories, bars the telling of conflicting stories, and establishes a framework for later experience, defining the understanding within which descriptive and intentional knowledge operate. As stories interweave and grow more elaborate, parts slip out of view, too complex in form and content to be grasped as a whole.

The growing complication (and internal conflicts) of the web of stories can lead to a fascinated self-absorption. The self learns to turn to its own stories for gratification and to make sense of events. Tracing out the patterns of interlocking stories permits the creation of new, more comprehensive, or more satisfying stories, including stories about stories, or even stories (such as this one) about how the story-telling mechanism operates.

Common to all these stories is the narrator itself. Who is this narrator that tells the tales that shape existence? A clear answer is given: It is none other than the actor at the center of every story — the owner of each experience. But the narrator is also none other than the audience that reacts to each story with emotions, explanations, justifications, and more stories.

Finally, the narrator is none other than the objective self whose identity and attributes the intersecting narratives establish. The narrator's stories unite owner, actor, and objective self, bearing witness to their existence and persistence 'over' time. The central narrative

structures — "I am; I feel; I experience; I want; I act" —
are the self-authenticating truth of every story.

The narrator thus asserts the self by telling another
story — a founding story that makes possible all other
stories. For without an actor at its center, an audience in
attendance, and a teller of the tale, no story could unfold
and meaning could not emerge. But this founding story is
intended as its own witness: presented as the basis for
self and world alike.

Assent to the Presupposed

*The ongoing persistence of a unified self appears to the
mind as a self-evident truth. It brings with it two
corollaries: the flow of experience from past to future,
and the objective existence of a surrounding world that
is subject to that flow.* The temporal dynamic of the self
and of history are parallel, indisputable structures.

Such basic constructs, which already presuppose the
polarities of descriptive and intentional knowledge, are
set up and offered for interpretation before the mind
knows it. Understanding, judgments, even the basic
structure of consciousness itself, arise within this pre-
existing matrix, which itself remains immune to inquiry. The entire range of self-centered knowledge — the
facts of conventional experience known scientifically
in chemistry, biology, physiology, psychology, cosmol-
ogy, and the like — supports the constructs and testifies
to their reality.

These consensus constructs, which center on the
self, are the 'founding story'. Established prior to all

questioning, the founding story is 'self-perpetuating'. Arguments may be advanced that undermine the logic of a unitary self; alternative stories may be told; but it all takes place within the founding story. *All knowing is directed toward points after the flow of self-centered experience is already in operation.* No room is allowed for a more fundamental knowing that might investigate how the founding story itself is established.

Universal assent to the founding story means unbridled power for the narratives that the founding story unfolds, for in terms of the claims of the self, apart from such narratives *there is no reality.* The world of historical time and of events bound together in meaningful patterns unfolds as a dynamic to which no countervailing force can be opposed.

The rich texture of narratives exerts a hypnotizing effect that only reinforces the founding story. If stories are challenged, it is only through new stories. Even when stories repeat themselves with a numbing regularity, becoming so familiar that they are triggered almost automatically by the flow of experience, the stereotyped response they produce allows for no alternatives.

Single-Minded Knowing

Based on the founding story of the self and the narrative structures it supports, a form of understanding arises that could be called 'single-minded'. Whereas the 'perceiver' observes from moment to moment, the self sweeps each new 'momentary' image or event into the flow of the founding story's narrative, continuously sustaining and reaffirming the narrative. Each new 'experience' is assigned a place within a web of needs, interests, situational patterns, and emotional reactions. Knowledge fits into this web as a tool for assigning identity or identifying goals, or as a vehicle for accomplishing what has been specified. It becomes an item to be acquired or manufactured for use within the framework of the self's concerns.

When knowledge is thus subordinated to the 'single-minded' momentum of the founding story, experience eludes illumination. The momentum of the narrative compels a linear logic unfolding in time in a linear way. In accord with this logic and with the self's 'self-understanding', knowing is bound to the predetermined truths of descriptive knowledge, improbably understood as based on the fragmented and momentary structure of polar observation. As the narrative flows along, one observation identifies one specified quality; one subject takes in one point; one knower makes one judgment, resulting in one conclusion that is immediately linked to the next. A steady narrowing of choices in the end leaves only one option. The identical pattern plays itself out again and again, allowing only one truth, one perspective, one position.

In committing to the narrative, the self finds the basis for asserting its identity. Just as the perceiver depends on the perceived, the narrator depends on the flow of stories that its narrative sets forth. The 'perceived', the 'described', and the 'intended' are all brought together to specify a historically determined world, and *this historical construct is then acknowledged as the source of the temporal momentum*. The self is discovered emerging from this historical matrix, like a baby emerging from the womb.

In this way, the self gives to its narratives an unquestionable authority. Self and objects are placed on the same 'objective footing', with the self at the center and objects as 'useful' adjuncts. Both arise through a historical conditioning that *makes the past the source of what is real*. The narrative commitment is reinterpreted as the truth of all that has happened in history, and it becomes a 'fact' that truth unfolds only within the narrative structure of linear temporality.

Chapter Twenty-One

Seizing of knowledge by the self; the five personas of the self; the narrator and the founding story of the self; knowledge subordinated to single-minded knowing; past as the source of reality.

Protecting and Projecting

Investigate the themes and narratives around which mental activity seems to focus. What 'purposes' do such narratives serve; what projects do they serve? Ask this question not only analytically, but by exploring 'deeper', more 'encompassing' narratives. Note that the sense of 'being distanced' that allows for this investigation is itself the outcome of a narrative. Continue to look for deeper, more encompassing narratives. At some point in this process, the 'content' of the narratives may fall away, leaving attitudes such as hope and fear, anxiety, and expectation to operate without their usual accompaniment.

Exercise Twenty-One

Imaging Dimensions

Twice Determined

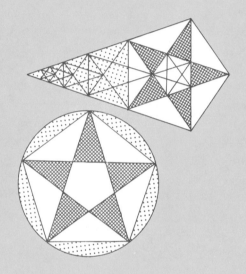

Self witness to present
Encircled by
Horizon reality of is and are
Tracing from
Generated generations
Generous genesis of

TWO TIMES

The narrative of the self seems to presuppose the linear, historical flow of time, as do the identities of both 'objective self' and 'owner'. Without linear time, what could happen to whom? How would experience be possible? To whom would it relate, and by whom would it be reported? Without the thread of time to hold it together, the fabric of cause and effect that produces objective identity and narrative alike at once unravels.

In ordinary experience, the temporal thread is interwoven with the identity of the self as the 'I am'. An 'I-awareness' or 'I-ness' accompanies and supports each occupied moment, linking sense fields, thoughts, interpretations, and emotions in a way that is central to the spirit of human being. The link between past, present, and future depends on this 'I am', which binds together moments in time and patterns human affairs.

Any attempt to investigate this interweaving of time and self-identity at once runs into difficulties. In conventional understanding, the self occupies each successive moment. As suggested in chapter fourteen, however, our understanding of 'a moment' leads to the conclusion that each act of knowing already occupies its moment fully, leaving no room for the self.

While the self lays claim to being the 'perceiver', the momentary structure of perception suggests that in the act of perception the 'I' is *occupied* by the act of knowing. But what would this mean? When the mind is temporarily occupied by a daydream or an image, or by a distracting sound or an inner dialogue, we say, "I am 'pre-occupied' at the moment." The specific sense seems to be that such events 'use up' our available energy, in the same way a victorious occupying army uses up a country's resources. The analysis in chapter fourteen of how moments of time are fully 'used up' suggests that this same 'occupying' phenomenon occurs on a more basic level, where we cannot directly observe it.

This leaves us with two different views. The self 'occupies' time in a unique way (or occupies a unique time), but events that occur in time also 'occupy' the self. This duality relates to what was referred to earlier as the dual citizenship of the self, and the two kinds of time to which the self seems to have access. The connection between self and time seems to be related to the energy and organizing capacity of both.

Two Views of Time

Linear time is first the time of cause and effect, predictable and orderly. Each day the sun moves across the sky; each night the planets cross the heavens. The passage from day to night gives way to the passing of the seasons, and seasons mark the life and death of living things and the imperceptible shifts of geologic time.

This world of 'objective' linear time offers a criterion for what is real. *Objects exist as products of determinate past events;* trees exist, while the content of images and dreams do not. The 'objective self' satisfies this criterion, for it is subject to the historical unfolding of linear time. Having once appeared, it joins the march from moment to moment, like a pedestrian caught up in a parade.

While this view of temporality has great explanatory power, it remains incomplete. For linear time is not only an unbroken flow; rather, it is sharply divided into the three domains of past, present, and future. The present moment stands at the exact center: To one side is the past, fixed and immutable; to the other is the future, not yet known but apparently predictable in principle.

The threefold division of time is fundamental to direct experience. The being of what exists only in the past is completely different from the being of what exists only in the future, and both in turn are completely different from the being of what exists in the present. In terms of this division, it seems accurate to say that only what exists in the present has 'real' being at all. What happened in the past may once have been real, but it no longer is; what will happen in the future may later be real, but it is not yet.

Something remarkable is at work in the view that the present alone is real, for the 'location' of the present in time is established only by the *presence within it of this particular 'I'*. Thus, the existence of all that is seems to hinge on the *wholly subjective fact* of 'my' being here.

In addition, the threefold view of time appears incompatible with 'object-centered' linear time, in which the present seems to be only the ever-changing boundary between past and future. While conventional understanding would say that 'tomorrow' has 'today' as its origin, 'today' is 'tomorrow's yesterday', and 'yesterday's tomorrow'. Moreover, 'yesterday' came into being because it was once 'tomorrow'. The ongoing succession of 'yesterdays' and 'tomorrows' encompasses the whole range of time, with the present only a 'no-dimensional' marker separating the two domains. How can what is 'most real' occur exactly in this no-dimensional point?

We also need to account for the fact that the present itself is constantly shifting. Each present moment is different from every other, except that there can only be one present moment 'at a time'. Since what is 'real' is only 'what exists in the present moment', does this mean that being is recreated in each moment? What is the dynamic that could give birth to so remarkable a structure? And if this is so, what has become of the principles of cause and effect, which determine what is real when we look at the other 'face' of linear time?

Chapter Twenty-Two

Self as occupied by moments of linear time; reality as based on past; alternate threefold view of time; reality as based on shifting present.

Point of Transition

Practice of Exercise 14 suggests that the 'points' we recognize as linked in time are not necessarily fundamental units. Then how do we move from point to point in awareness? If we focus on a particular interval between points A and A1, we find that there is a moment of transition — 'X' — that cannot ordinarily be directly observed and thus remains unknown. This establishes the following structure:

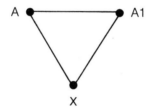

Try investigating 'X', directly or indirectly. Do not confuse a 'moment between moments' with 'X', which must be related to the 'between', rather than to a moment. What is the nature of 'X'? How does it function?

Exercise Twenty-Two

Modalities

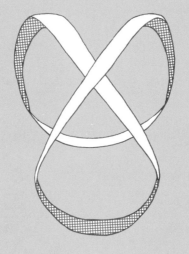

Self inseparable from self
Shifting untraceable
Identities told to time
Owned cloned
Distinctions resolve
Unfolding unmolding
Into one zero

THE ONWARD
FLOW OF TIME

Even if the difficulties posed by a shifting present could be resolved, time's movement from moment to moment would continue to be unaccounted for. Both versions of linear time suggest a picture in which static moments of linear time are linked to each other, and it would seem to be this linking that constitutes the 'temporality' of time. In a way that remains mysterious, time in its three aspects presents a constant flow. What is now the future will become present and then past; the present too will slip into the past, and the past will recede farther and farther from the fresh, vital center of present experience.

This basic momentum — a steady, forward-moving dynamic — seems to govern the universe. Whatever its origin, whatever energy powers it, change is the one constant, affecting the world of objects and the world of the self with equal power. Without change, experience and interaction could not arise and the self could not establish itself as the owner of experience, active 'across' the individual moments of time.

The time that corresponds to the temporal flow owned and organized by the self could be called 'narrative time'. Passing from birth to aging to death, from founding to decay and collapse, from stories to history, narrative time reveals a rhythm of change. The 'narrator-self' is caught up in that change, conditioned by the past and swept along toward the future; at the same time, the narrator also defines the structures of narrative time, shaping its present in constantly shifting ways in accord with the stories it tells.

Yet narrative is still not adequate to account for the experience of the self. For the self is not only 'narrator' but 'owner'; and as 'owner' it insists on the distinctions among past, present, and future. *Although the owner experiences only in the present,* it claims to 'own' the past through memories, accumulated knowledge, and interpretations; and to 'own' the future through plans, dreams, and intentions. This claim in turn founds its claim to 'own' the present, which it defines and gives coherence in terms of its own interests and needs.

Self as Owner

It may seem that 'owner' and 'narrator' could be regarded as one, but actually these two aspects of the self stand in a very different relationship to time. While the narrator rides the flow of narrative time, shaping it as it unfolds, the self as owner of experience claims to own time as well. Freely it 'jumps' from one moment of time to another — from memory to plan to thought to action — not bound by the steady flow of time from past into future. Somehow the self as owner stands in still another relationship to time, one that remains to be explored.

The significance of the owner's claim to be able to move freely 'through' time is difficult to assess. Is such movement 'only' imaginary, or is it 'real' with respect to a 'kind' of time available only to the owner? Even if we leave that issue open, it still seems that the view put forward by the owner regarding its relationship to time is incomplete. For the owner is not 'free' to choose just where in time it will leap next; instead, its thoughts and images are propelled by a momentum that remains largely out of its control.

Moreover, the owner's claims with regard to time seem powerless to affect the temporal flow directly: Aging and decay proceed, offering the objective self no special dispensation. And this historical reality has an immediate impact on the owner as well: Memories fade; faculties lose their power; energy diminishes. The power of the self to act 'on' time itself remains subject to time.

If the owner does stand 'outside' of the linear flow of time, able to 'move' through time in its thoughts, memories, and imaginings and to link these components of its experience together in patterns of its own design, it must have its own 'present', in which it acts and from which it directs the flow of its activity. But this suggestion seems untenable, for such a 'present' would be cut off from the dynamic movement from past to future and future to past — and it is just this movement that seems to account for the *vitality* of the present, sustaining the assertion that only what exists in the present is 'real'.

Though past is no more, it reaches out to create the future from its being. Though future is not yet come, it unfolds to create the past out of its becoming. The present is alive as the expression of this doubly active momentum. Like a musical note or a spoken syllable, present experience takes its meaning from the unfolding whole within which it emerges. If the owner is cut off from this being, it loses the source of its own vitality. It is hard to imagine that it could still act as self.

Momentum and Temporal Knowledge

The double momentum flowing between past and future to establish the active present correlates with the two aspects of temporal knowledge: the descriptive knowing that establishes a world and the intentional knowing that sets the narrative in motion. Through such knowing, the future creates the past, even while the past creates the future. It seems that narrative time, which specifically acknowledges and reflects this momentum, comes closest to capturing the full experience of the self's temporal being.

When the narrative is in operation, however, the creative power of time is interpreted exclusively in terms of the re-creation of the old. The narrative is governed by old stories and by the accumulated memories of personal and collective descriptive knowledge. The dynamic that emerges from creation so interpreted will assure a future based on similarities to the past. What is new will arise only mechanically, in response to the routinized patterns that have been built into such past-centered experience.

This same point emerges in considering the self as perceiver. In polar knowing, the attachment between perceiver and perceived generates a momentum. But if perceptual knowing is momentary, this momentum immediately gives way to a new interaction with its own momentum. The energy generated in one moment is lost in the next (transmitting it would require an 'interim moment', and so on).

If knowing takes place within such a momentary sequencing, as would apparently be true for the polar 'perceiver', each passing moment is already occupied, its knowing capacity and energy 'used up'. The self as owner and as narrator claims to occupy experience and to shape its flow, but if these claims are based on the self's control over the momentary knowledge of the perceiver, all the earlier difficulties arise. Since knowledge is momentary, 'something else' is always just about to 'take place', leaving the self fully 'occupied' in holding on to its current position. The potential for new knowledge remains untapped, for the self that might know is 'pre-occupied'. The dynamic of the present slips away, leaving awareness dim and concentration lacking.

Somehow these various pictures of the self in its different roles, all of which support each other in the conclusion that new knowledge and new ways of being are impossible, seem to leave something out of account. Beneath the patterns of the self — as perceiver, objective entity, narrator, and owner — is the witness. The story the witness tells — the identity of the self — may be 'just another story'. But still there is the witness itself: the powerful assertion that something *is*, with a direct vitality that cannot be denied.

Perhaps the witness is not 'just another story'. Perhaps the force behind its testimony — which operates entirely apart from the content of what it has to say — is a direct expression of the dynamic energy implicit in the flow from past to future and the corresponding vitality of the present. The witness may point to a primary thrust 'within' time that polar and temporal knowledge, together with the manifold structures of the self, do not fully reveal.

Chapter Twenty-Three

Mysterious forward dynamic of time; narrator and owner in relation to time; owner as outside of time; creativity of time placed in service of repetition; knowing capacity as 'used up'; the force behind the witness as more than a story.

Observing without Owning

Familiarity with 'X', as explored in Exercise 22, opens a dimension of depth not available in the linear relationship between two moments. A whole range of points becomes available for exploration — points that are given no names because they do not fit into the initial linear structure. Such points, because they are no longer reasonable or predictable in terms of the standard sequential order owned by the self, could be considered 'random'. This 'randomness' may manifest as a shimmery, luminous quality within experience, without undermining the conventional order. It may also affect the 'availability' of time for experience.

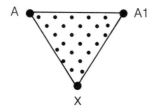

Exercise Twenty-Three

Time Knowing

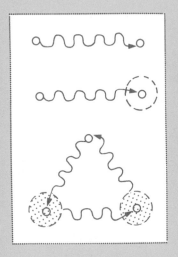

Rhythm of one into two
Gives one in quality shape form
Two gives one through three
Echo returns self through time
Unfolds through well-known pattern

THE SELF
IN QUESTION

In certain moments, we seem more in tune with the underlying energy that makes experience into a coherent whole, more free from the influence of interpretive structures. Energy, awareness, and concentration are united and in balance, and a genuine dynamic and power allow us to act in ways that are reliable and effective. Focusing our minds and balancing our energy, we can be sharp, penetrating, and one-pointed — able to control the operation of our awareness.

In such moments, reality seems most 'real', and the witness is at its strongest. But what is the content to which the witness testifies? Normally we interpret the message of the witness in terms of the identity of self and the substantiality of the world. But perhaps the witness is speaking of something very different. Suppose that beneath the time marked out in ordinary experience there were a 'deeper' time, a fabric into which the patternings presented in conventional time were woven, or else a dynamic whole without distinctions — a time presenting all meanings but prior to all meanings.

If the witness were speaking of this deeper time, the usual interpretations that we give its message might prove ill-founded and misleading. The three aspects of time — past, present, and future — might be understood as 'markers' for an underlying dynamism of transition and change, within which body, mind, and universe take form. The structure of 'self-in-the-world' might yield to a way of being at once more open and more free. If the 'story of the self' proved to be only another story, conditioning and limitations would fall away. Time, space, and knowledge could perhaps bear witness in a completely new way.

The Self as Subject

The self that knows through observation and descriptive knowledge is the subject or 'I', taking things in the world as object. In observation, 'I' stand as if at the edge of a pool, looking into its depths, in solitary, intimate confrontation with the universe. 'My' position is lonely, but also powerful: Isolated from everything else, 'I' can hardly be said to exist, and yet 'I' 'am' the knower, the one who brings awareness to being. Only 'my' knowing can authenticate the objective world that appears to lie stretched out before 'me'.

In polar and descriptive knowledge alike, the act of observation that gives rise to knowledge is always directed outward. In searching for the self, can 'I' turn to see 'myself' directly, instead of in the pool's reflection? The pool is too close and vast; it fills 'my' field of vision completely. When 'I' try to turn, 'I' find the pool is still before 'me'; nothing has changed. 'I' can know 'my' 'objective' traits, but it seems that 'I' cannot know the knower as knower.

Then how can 'I' establish 'my own' existence? The answer seems to be that 'I' establish 'myself' in observing the objective pole. As 'I' gaze into the pool, 'my own' image as subject is reflected back to 'me'.

In knowing, 'I' observe, categorize, and characterize; 'I' apply names and labels. This activity itself seems to be what 'I' label as 'I'. The unique energy that 'I' bring to knowing, mirrored back to 'me', confirms the truth of 'my' existence at the center of experience. 'I' find 'myself' reflected everywhere, for each known object, insofar as it is known, is 'my' creation.

If 'I' as subject is only the reflection of what the object reveals, then which is truly subject and which is object, which the actor and which the acted upon? Knowing and interpreting, the subject projects its projections into the objective realm. But each knowing is a knowing of the knowable, and what is knowable (including the existence of the knower) is only what the object projects into the subject. In this complex interaction, is the objective world 'my' projection, or is it perhaps more accurate to say that 'I' am its creation?

Instead of standing at the center of experience, am 'I' the shadow image of 'my own' knowing? Where in this picture is the substantial identity that 'I' assert and rely on to found my 'sense' of what is real?

The self claims ownership over its experience. But how can it establish its own independent existence apart from what it owns? One answer that has emerged in various systems of thought is to identify with what is owned. For example, the self owns a body. Perhaps it *is* this body, as materialist thinkers have suggested. Again, the self owns its experiences. But perhaps the self is simply the sum total of these experiences. In that case, however, what has become of the sense of self as owner, with its own existence independent of what is owned? How can a self that is nothing other than its experiences or its physical sensations (whether these are directed outward or are focused on inner body states) found the reality of those experiences?

The Self at the Center

If the self as owner of experience is separate from the experience owned, it must be because the self is present independently: When experience begins, there is already a self 'there' to whom the experience happens — a self enduring over time, perhaps even in some mysterious way taking priority over time.

But this assumed 'pre-existence' of the self depends squarely on the problematic flow of linear time from moment to moment. If this temporal structure is open to doubt (as the discussion in chapter fifteen seemed to suggest), the link between cause and effect is severed, and the rhythms of 'my' life are replaced by chaos. If 'I' can never plan 'my' actions or assess their value, the structures of personal identity, experience, and meaningful action all collapse. Only sequences of causes and conditions occurring predictably over time can make experience available for ownership and for the assigning of narrative significance.

We return to the sense of witness. Even if the self's self-interpretation proves to be incoherent, there is something or someone that continues to occupy the center of experienced reality, perceiving, interpreting, experiencing, and 'making sense' of experience by assigning it to an owner designated as 'self'.

Bearing Witness

Yet even on this level, where logic and analysis seem to be unable to penetrate, there is room for questioning. We saw at the outset of this chapter that the witness is strongest at those times when energy, awareness, and appreciation for experience are alive and in balance and we act with a special dynamic and power. But it is just in those moments, with the mind fully focused, the awareness engaged, and energy most dynamic, that the sense of self is most attenuated, and the sense of self-consciousness that often hinders effective action and well-being is least present. In such moments, does the self bear witness against itself?

The founding story recognizes an actor, events, and the unfolding of the narrative. The self unites these elements, possessing experience and organizing it into meaningful patterns. And the founding story asserts that this owner in turn is identical with the witness, the one who verifies the identity of the self.

Perhaps we have misunderstood the knowledge to which the witness testifies. For the witness can only be witness if it is more than another story told within the fundamental structure of the founding story. When the self appropriates the witness, sweeping it within the story-telling structure, it may be bearing false witness. In that case, the true source of the creative energy that the self seems to manifest might be found elsewhere, in a realm yet to be explored.

Chapter Twenty-Four

Misinterpreting the witness in terms of self; 'subject-self' as a reflection; self dependent on linear time; witness as testifying to the creative energy appropriated by the self.

Locating Tension in Space

Subtle tension is associated with a physical location. Locate tension in terms of the body; then in terms of the mind or awareness, considered in spatial terms. Expand the 'field' of inquiry to be aware of the body's 'locatedness' in space. With continued practice, this sense of 'locatedness' can become central in experiencing tension or other feelings, replacing the usual narrative focus. Do shifts in this sense affect the feeling of tension or related sensations?

Exercise Twenty-Four

Knowledge of Image

Transitional Construction

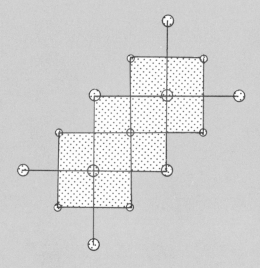

Patterns progress weaving
Space time known insistence
Is is arrows non-erroneous
Confirmation tracing triangle
New directions not to be affirmed

FOUNDING
IDENTITY

The founding identity—the enduring 'I'—must be separate from its 'objective' mental and physical characteristics, as well as its memories, plans, convictions, knowledge, and beliefs, for all of these fluctuate remarkably in time, sometimes shifting from moment to moment. The stock of memories, plans, and goals is also constantly in flux. If the founding self were subject to the same changes, it could not provide the connecting link that binds them together.

A Web of Difficulties

Who or what this remarkable invariant entity might be remains unclear. In attempting to deal with this question, two principal views have developed. The determinist view rejects the reality of a founding self separate from the objective self. Only the historically conditioned self is real; the self as owner is just another construct of historically conditioned thinking. But this view in the end leaves no room for the 'entity' that unites the qualities of the self into a seemingly unified whole. The testimony of the witness is rejected, and a part of human experience that seems perhaps the most fundamental and valid of all is left out of account.

The alternative view maintains the independence of the self from history, holding that the 'founding entity' is unaffected by change. But this view encounters other difficulties. If the owner is separate from the objective self, in what sense are the two selves nonetheless one and the same? We understand the witness as telling us that 'I' am also the objective self — that this specific, individual self is the meaning-giver and memory-holder. But the owner makes the objective self into a possession rather than an actor, assigning itself the title of knower and meaning-giver. Just who knows whom, and who in turn knows the knower? If the objective self is only our possession, what accounts for our sense, verified by the witness, that 'we' are 'it'? If we are not it, who are we?

There are other problems as well. If the owner is truly independent of temporal change, did it exist before the objective self came into being? If this alternative is rejected, then it seems that the temporal sequence that gave rise to the objective self is also responsible for producing the owner. In that case, how can the owner proclaim itself the master of temporal change?

Perhaps this analysis is too limited. Making sense of an independent self prior to all stories may require a whole new way of thinking about temporal change and succession. An alternative that was briefly explored in chapter eighteen is that the 'owner-self' operates in a realm *parallel* to the world of conventional change, subject to a different form of time. But if the owner has its own sort of time, how can it have knowledge of the changes that befall objects within ordinary time? How can it interact at all with the temporal realm?

One possible answer is that the changes that appear to occur to objects within ordinary time are in fact changes in time itself. In that case, a knowing self 'outside' of time might know changes by knowing conventional time directly, rather than its contents.

Whatever it might mean to 'know time directly', and however this might be possible, new mysteries arise. For time to become an 'object' of knowledge, it seems that the act of knowing must occur 'outside' of time, which would apparently require that it take place in some 'other' time. Assuming this to be a meaningful possibility, how can the knowing self know that the knowledge of time it accumulates is not a projection of its own form of time and its own situation? Does postulating a kind of 'hypertime' unique to the self lead to all the problems regarding interaction that were previously explored in connection with polar knowledge? And whatever the self believes itself to know, can it escape being bound by its own constructs?

The observation made above that 'the present' seems to function in two different ways may suggest a way out of this dilemma. The objective self may be subject to the flow from past to future, in which the present is only a boundary line, while the 'owner' is the one that enjoys the present, without being subject to the past. But if this is so, the question looms in a new way: How can the identity of these two selves, each with its own kind of time, be established? And how can the self as owner take responsibility for acting in a world to which it seems to have only a tenuous connection?

Living the Founding Story

When the self accepts the founding story and its own objective being as 'real', *it subjects itself to history.* What has once happened is beyond recall; the story perpetuates itself, whether it suits the self or not. At the same time, however, the bargain is not all one-sided. For it is this same founding story that allows the self to take possession of its world. Only because the self 'exists' objectively and historically can it stake its claim as owner of all knowledge and all experience. Once this basis is established, however, the founding story assures that all narratives will center on the self, thus validating the self in its identity and being.

The incentive for the self to accept its narratives as real is thus a strong one. True, a commitment to the past may subject the self to playing a role it has not chosen. The suffering that results may be great. But at least its own existence is assured. *For a being that occupies the seeming twilight zone of a momentary, constantly shifting present, such a guarantee has great significance.*

By holding to its narratives, the self seeks content in identity rather than knowledge. Measuring the world in terms of self-concern, it sees only what it has the tools to measure. Because it has no independent source of knowledge, it must accept what everyone else supports — not only accept, but support, sponsor, participate; even help to shape, create, and perpetuate it. What others call darkness the self must call darkness; what others call light it must call light. The patterns of the past proliferate forward into the future, creating complications and fueling deepening apprehension. Visions of what might be are narrowed to the prospects that suit the self's needs and the fears that haunt its thoughts.

The self's commitment to its identity has consequences on a more subtle level as well. For the self now sets out to define its being in terms drawn from the 'objective', space-centered world it regards as 'most real'. For the sake of affirming its own identity, it denies its special nature as a temporal, historical entity. The founding story and the narratives it supports are maintained, but the dynamic inherent in those stories is lost.

Accepting Restriction

Under such circumstances, time is no longer alive with the vitality of the present; instead, it once more becomes a lifeless measuring-stick for distance and decay. The sweeping flow of history, which could be understood as a mark of the narrator's story-telling power, is perceived instead as the source of the objective-self's conditioning and limitations. Since these 'objective' limitations are understood as 'real', the gaps and defects in knowledge that result are understood as fixed and immutable, and so go unchallenged.

Committed above all to its own existence, and thus to the objective realm to which existence traces, the self accepts the model of knowledge that puts forward polar observation as the only basis for knowing. Though this may be adequate to arrive at a coherent view of sensory knowledge — a realm of surfaces and of instants constantly repeating patterns of relative invariability — inner experience remains inaccessible.

The result is a fundamental distortion and characteristic ignorance. The focus on surface-level knowing forces the self to explain human being and experience in terms drawn from the rigid, mechanical realm of objects. No room is allowed for shifting perspectives and ways of being. True, the very multiplicity of the self's stories counters such reductionism, suggesting that even observation itself may change in different settings. Art, play, and other realms of activity preserve such possibilities. Invariably, however, the tendency is to return to the surface: to shape, form, and the tightly structured patterns of the already known.

Bargaining Knowledge Away

Lacking any sense of a well-being apart from its own existence, the self can only continue in the patterns it acknowledges as its own. Self-concern colors even the words the self has available for speaking of possibilities and alternatives — 'protection', 'security', 'pleasure', 'salvation', etc. New thoughts are positioned among pre-existing models and structures; new ways of seeing, such as are offered by aesthetic awareness or penetrating insight, are made into experiences that the self 'has', rather than openings into possibilities beyond the self.

Even when the self does choose change, it is a change that comes in the adopting of a new self-identity, complete with a newly interpreted history and a new set of future possibilities. Tales and ideas otherwise radiant with potential are rooted in the story of the self, becoming simple counters for the self to manipulate. Because they can go no deeper, they become trivial; because they have no ground on which to rest, they make us restless.

The narrative unfolding of the self's story amounts to an ongoing agreement the self makes with itself for the purpose of witnessing its own identity and affirming its ownership over experience. Narrator and narrative flow emerge together. The flow itself, charged with energy, finds expression as the self's will to be. From moment to moment the self erects a gateway through which experience, mind, and awareness must pass. Appointing itself gatekeeper, it allows entry only to those willing to dedicate their creative power to shaping the single-minded world in which the self lives and acts.

When the self sets out to authenticate its being, it accepts a way of knowing that perpetuates defects and breeds harm. The result is a world where knowledge itself is not welcome. How seldom great leaders and teachers will appear in such a world! How limited the prospects for individuals bound by its models and constructs! When historical conditioning, self-concern, and temporal knowledge shape the world, the times themselves seem narrow and superficial. The self does not act; it only inherits the consequences of previous actions. Its dreams go unrealized; its plans unfulfilled.

The single-minded intensity with which the self makes its commitments seems to allow no way out of this impasse. There may be moments when we feel a sense of longing, a disquieting concern for the destiny of our bodies, minds, and spirits. But we have no way to investigate, no way to hold vital questions open in our minds. Without a deeper knowledge to sustain our intelligence and sense of worth, a spirit of poverty invades the core of human being.

Chapter Twenty-Five

Self's founding identity as non-objective; problematic link to the identified self; ways of relating to time; willing subjection to history; loss of temporal vitality; trading knowledge for identity.

Building the Past

Exercises 13 and 18 disassociate remembered events from their future. Once you gain familiarity with this practice, investigate how specific remembered events are associated with their pasts. Take some time to clarify and explore this relationship. Next, note that in tracing the past of the past you must recreate that past in your present memory. As each new memory of a past moment 'past' the previous past moment arises, try to 'strip it' of its future, as in Exercise 13. With practice, you can maintain simultaneously a complex web of memories with or without their associated pasts and futures.

Exercise Twenty-Five

Dynamic Space Being

PART THREE

Sources
of
Knowledge

History Emerging

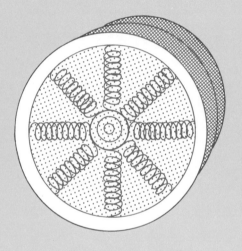

Spiraling into present
Past proclaims and limits
Possible stories unfold
Presenting no alternatives
Presenting moments of becoming

MERGING
WITH TIME

The discussion in Part Two moved from an initial focus on the world of objects, to an investigation of the identity of the self, to a more direct examination of the space and time that support self and world alike, as well as their interaction.

Conventionally, the interconnection between space and time is acknowledged in terms of positioning and measurement — to locate an object within the everyday world requires specifying (at least by implication) its coordinates in space and time. A deeper investigation reveals that the space that contains objects presupposes a time that unfolds from moment to moment, while the very different kind of time that sustains the self discloses a world shaped by the spatial attributes of distance and separation.

The connection between space and time can be clarified by considering what space would be like in the absence of time. For example, modern science suggests that it may be more accurate (in terms of its concerns) to replace the usual view of a time that flows with a view of time as 'space-like' in its structure. In that case, time becomes a fourth dimension equivalent to each of the three dimensions of space. If we maintain this view, however, the result is to lose the dynamic that seems fundamental to time. A corollary will be that events in the world are predetermined. Past, present, and future are 'spread out' like different regions of space, and the observer does not yet know the future only because he has not yet 'arrived' at that region.

This suggestion, though it may lead to interesting insights, is incomplete, for somehow space itself must *arise*. This does not necessarily mean that space is 'created'—since space is not a thing, it is difficult to know what it would mean for it to 'be created'. Perhaps instead it could be said that space must be 'activated', and that time is the agent of this activation. We could say that space is like being asleep, and that adding the 'dimension' of time is like waking up. With time, energy becomes available for appearances in space to present themselves.

Space and Time and Knowledge

Just as time and space are related, so time and space in turn are related to knowledge. We have already seen that when objects are separated in space, knowledge becomes available primarily through polar observation. In the same way, even within the temporal succession of moments, knowledge arises on the basis of the particular time frame employed. If we experienced time on a microscopic scale, we would find ourselves in a world of constant motion; if we experienced time on a cosmic scale, the entities that we understand to be relatively stable would come and go like clouds drifting across the sky. In either case, the emphasis we place on 'fixed' objects would be drastically challenged. The temporal rhythm of human consciousness, geared to a particular sense of the rate at which time flows, is directly responsible for the knowledge that discloses a relatively stable world, within which the self appears, acts, and in turn can be acted upon.

Although the examples above do not really depart from the structures of conventional knowledge, they suggest the possibility that knowledge could be quite different from what it ordinarily is. The focus on the self as knower and owner is a function of a particular understanding of space and time, just as the focus on objects as constituting 'reality' is a function of a particular understanding of space and time.

If we responded to a different temporal rhythm, would the content of the knowledge available to us shift? If time itself were understood differently, could the knower know 'more' or know differently? Could there perhaps be a form of knowledge that was not dependent on a knower at all?

Such speculations might seem idle if it were well-established that time and space are as they are, with no possibility that they might be otherwise. But we have seen in previous chapters that this is far from being the case. The conventional understanding of space and time involves numerous difficulties, which become readily apparent in attempts to account for how knowledge could arise within linear time.

Moreover, even within conventional knowledge at least two different and contradictory understandings of space and time are in operation: one centered on 'objects in space', the other on 'the self in time'. Thus, the nature of space and time, and of the knowledge they give birth to, seems very much an open question.

Staying with the Already Known

Up to a certain point, the self seems able to accommodate itself to questioning that might lead to new knowledge. As long as it remains the owner of experience, it can enjoy the prospect of new adventures, as well as the feeling of accomplishment that comes from seeing through what had previously been opaque. But when the self's own identity — the 'founding story' — is called into question, the self cannot go along. All its knowing, all its stories and interpretations, are based on the founding story. A knowledge that no longer acknowledged the truth of the founding story would mean destruction, in the direct sense of non-existence. And since the self bases its being on existence, not to exist is for it the worst of all possible fates.

The self's reaction to questions that challenge the founding story indicates how powerful knowledge truly is. *Not to 'know' the founding story to be true is to undermine reality. On this fundamental level, knowledge of reality makes reality so.* Knowledge in this sense is the special province of the witness. And so the self, which must make the witness 'bear witness' to its own being, turns away from knowledge that might reveal the witness in a new light.

Subject to History

The turn away from knowledge takes the form of a commitment to the outcome of the historical process, and thus to a particular understanding of space and time. Subject to the concerns of the self, the 'story of history' becomes an account of the way that things have 'come to be' as they are. It satisfies the self's need for explanations that bind, excuse, or justify.

History understood as 'our story' is simply the narrative applied to 'objective reality'. It points toward determinism, and toward explanations that are mechanistic in nature. Enmeshed in past, present, and future, in structures and positionings, the self cannot pursue alternatives. Patterns laid down over millions of years of natural history and hundreds of generations of cultural development seem too strong to resist — as though there were limits written into our genes themselves that commit us to a certain way of being.

The structure of time and space that underlies this 'story of history' catches us up in the circumstances and conditions in which we live, establishing an order beyond questioning. Committed to temporality, anxious to establish existence in each moment, we define and specify in accord with the unfolding temporal order. The relentless succession of moments seems to require what is known in one moment to be no longer known in the next, while the historical narrative as a whole founds a rigidly specified space-time structure. Bound within these configurations, knowledge is established in such a way that it proves to have been 'limited' from the outset.

The Dominion of History

The self assigns its own existence in history priority over any commitment to questioning. No matter how loudly it proclaims each new question, the self can accept only a finite range of possible answers, starting from what is given and only then looking for ways to change it. A certain range of interpretations remains always in force.

In centuries past, the self's historical conditioning was viewed as a positive good. The sequential unfolding of linear events, so strongly suggestive of a narrative order, was understood as a sign that an all-powerful and all-good creator was shaping the history of the world. The presence of 'history as a founding story' was understood as evidence that the fate of the world rested safely in loving hands.

Today, however, that view, together with its implicit promise of a special destiny for humanity, has been largely rejected. There have always been difficulties in maintaining such an understanding; for example, the existence of evil in a world governed by such a creator; or — if evil demonstrates that the creator is less than all-powerful or all-good — the lack of sufficient grounds for following the will of a limited creator.

The rise of science, with its 'explanations' for the old mysteries, has allowed these difficulties to gain the upper hand. For many, the picture of history as a story told by a beneficent force is no longer convincing; instead, it is 'just a story'. A new story (understood as 'the facts — not a story') takes its place: human beings are subject to a natural order in which meaning and value ultimately have no role. What remains the same is the sense that the story is binding on those who are born into it. The modern suspicion that this binding order itself is senseless has led in some cases to despair.

The historical narrative can provide valuable, essential insight into how human consciousness and understanding emerge, take form, and alter through time. Yet accepting this story — together with its implicit structures of space and time — as absolute means closing off in advance avenues of inquiry and understanding that might lead to new knowledge.

Unfounded Devotion

The ancient sense that history revealed the working out of divine destiny (a different version of the perhaps still earlier view that events in this world mirrored the cycles of a cosmic order) gave to history a grand significance, in part because it acknowledged a higher knowledge at work in the world. Now that this understanding has largely vanished, it seems remarkable that we still hold to history with such tenacity, even while dismissing the opportunities for insight that the study of history offers. It is as though we continued to cherish a picture whose central figure had been defaced.

The source for such grim devotion to a history that offers us no solace is the commitment that the self makes to its own historical existence. As long as the self understands itself as the product of a historical process, its loyalty to that process will remain unshakable. But this leaves the adequacy of the self's understanding unexamined. The question remains: Could knowledge that probed 'beneath' or 'behind' history give to the self a new way of understanding its own origins and the nature of its being?

Chapter Twenty-Six

Time as accounting for the arising and energy of appearance; human knowledge as keyed to a specific temporal rhythm; the witness bound by self-concern; commitment of the self to history.

Reversing Momentum

Return to the practice of Exercise 15, noticing at what 'level' you reverse the temporal flow. Give special attention to points at which you do not proceed in an absolute linear order, but 'jump ahead' (i.e., further back in time) to a point of beginning. Such 'jumps' offer clues to the way in which the forward momentum of time is established. Also take special note of past events that you 'anticipate' remembering as you proceed backward through time, and of the resulting subcurrents of momentum.

Exercise Twenty-Six

Timeless Dimensions

Unfound

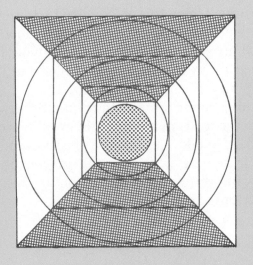

Question of foundation
Of position of perspective
Hallway for confusion
Enter through
Entire replication

Opposites define confine
Define refine again define
Find questions invitation

WORLD
WITHOUT
POSITIONING

A world in which the 'historical self' is no longer 'real' may seem inconceivable. But in moments of surprise or unusual intensity, when the self is taken off guard, such a possibility may for a moment seem to open up. The response on the part of the self is likely to be a profound fear, described by some writers as fear of the void: an 'existential' anxiety that can paralyze the will and destroy all hope for joy in living.

Usually, such an anxiety is not tolerated for long; instead, the prospect is thrust out of awareness. The intense fear that it generated is soon forgotten, but its effects remain, solidified into fixed 'boundaries' and mental patterns that exclude certain kinds of knowledge. To build on fear in this way is like designing and building a house after the foundation has already been poured: There are absolute limits on where we can build and on the shape and structure of the building itself.

The self's fear that its existence may be called into question can manifest in a variety of ways. Confronted with an unusual experience that might be viewed as an invitation to inquire further, the self may simply respond with preoccupation, deciding that it has no time for such concerns, or no interest in them. Instead, it turns back to the well-known stories that proliferate from the founding story: stories of success and failure, sorrow and joy, gain and loss, praise and blame. Other concerns are rejected as childish, or as better left to 'professional' thinkers, or else derided as useless.

Another response to the momentary awareness that matters could be different is to interpret such awareness as the onset of confusion. Confusion is the self's response to the not-knowing that calls a story into question — a way of twisting not-knowing to gain control over it. The self expects to understand in terms of the old categories and old stories, and interprets the failure of the old ways as a failure of understanding: a sign of weakness that it quickly turns into a shield against the new. Aware that the old patterns have been brought under suspicion, it holds onto them as tightly as ever, catching awareness 'in a bind'.

Such a confusion is the *self*'s version of the deep not-knowing that challenges existence. When the not-knowing at issue is fundamental (that is, when it deals with the founding story), the response is a kind of 'founding' confusion — a response at bottom emotional. Like ordinary confusion, it has its genesis in the *specific knowledge* that a story has in some way failed to cohere, and has thus become 'un-known'.

In the 'substitution' of confusion for not-knowing, a fog descends. Someone is tricking someone; someone has been tricked. In the midst of all this, we no longer know where we stand. The resulting emotional tone covers over the cutting clarity inherent in the original not-knowing. As the darkness of confusion descends, the light disclosed by questioning once more grows dim, and the old knowledge is restored. Perhaps for a moment we felt a shift, but now the accustomed patterns are again in place, and we are left only with uneasiness. In a short time there will be no room even to recall that for a moment other possibilities appeared. If we do remember, the self will turn the memory into another possession, a goal for the self one day to attain.

The pattern that gives rise to confusion is well-established in the domain of the self, for it comes up frequently when old stories are challenged by emerging knowledge. Often the confusion forms before we can become aware of the knowledge that has generated it; at other times, we may experience only a brief moment of clarity before the fog of confusion descends. Indeed, confusion may be an ever-present possibility: a cognitive-emotional response to the unspoken and unthought recognition that beneath our stories lies 'something else' (in somewhat the way that random quantum motion is said to underlie the physical realities of the everyday world). If so, then *confusion itself signals knowledge* — knowledge denied, and thus confounded.

In addition to fear, lack of interest, and confusion, the self may respond to the challenge of not-knowing by moving to appropriate it, subtly turning not-knowing itself into a position and a structure. "Yes," the self says, "Yes, I understand! For so long I have held on to my positions and my stories, but now I see the truth!

What Beauty! What Joy! What Openness! At last I have found my true home!"

Such affirmation is a ready cover for self-deception. Its 'yes' is the comfortable 'yes' of old patterns. It turns understanding into 'my' experience, something the self can manipulate through new narratives and interpretations. The self twists its concepts and meanings around until there is room for the element of not-knowing to fit in. Reacting to openness as a void, it rushes to fill it.

To appropriate not-knowing in this way is quite easy, even 'natural'. The self has a strong impulse toward the therapeutic, toward making knowledge into something that can benefit the self. Now it becomes a partisan of not-knowing. It sweeps the freedom of the unknown into the shadow cast by the self, then pretends not to notice as darkness falls once more.

'Logos' and Beyond

The responses of confusion, fear, lack of interest, and appropriation all claim to be independent of the founding story. In fact, however, they are expressions of the logic that that story insists upon: a defining 'logos' that shapes all possibilities for understanding.

Can this 'logos' itself be challenged? The 'logos' has its own power, but how much of this power originates in the self's fear and defensiveness, its incomprehension of a world order which leaves no room for it?

The self lives in the world like a permanent alien, always afraid that if it stirs up trouble its papers will be revoked and deportation proceedings initiated. Accepting its positions, we are bound by this same fear, a fear that limits our inquiry from the start. No matter how we proceed, built-in assumptions will create frightful images of what we might discover or how much we stand to lose. At the critical moments, just when we most need concentration and clarity to direct our efforts, we will draw back, victims of an emotional response that binds us to our starting point.

The incomprehensibility of any alternative may simply show how deeply the self is committed to the founding story and to the innumerable forms of not-knowing that result. Even when our logic is impeccable and our casual disregard for alternatives seems only reasonable, we have reason to wonder. It seems suspiciously convenient that the fundamental framework proves to be beyond questioning — that we have no choice but to live as we do.

True, the self is committed to its own existence. But the self is the one that forms an image of what it would mean for the self to come into question. What if that image is mistaken? The self's flight from non-existence is driven only by the 'logos' of the 'founding story'. If that story proves 'unfounded', what becomes of the fear that it generates? Perhaps fear is simply a product of a certain limitation on knowing; if so, *fear itself could become a pointer, directing us toward a deeper knowing.*

An alternative to the 'logos' of the founding story appears if the bipolar logic of conventional knowing is used against itself. Though we may find ourselves 'inside' a 'trap' big enough to encompass the entire universe, the logic of dichotomy means there must be an 'outside' as well. We can gain 'access' to this 'outside' by looking at the way we question. Questions framed in accord with the structures of temporal knowing stay within the 'logos': They allow only for 'correct' answers that reflect our own projections. We ask our questions, then strain to hear the answer in the echo of our own voice. Question and answer together form a narrative: Asking a question means taking a position; searching for an answer means acting within the linear sequencing of past, present, and future.

Could we abandon this positioning in space and time? If our questions were more accommodating, so that knowing were no longer 'doing' and questioning not 'the activity of a self', space might no longer entail separation, time might not pass away, and knowledge might go beyond conventional limits. There would be no 'witness' to the 'truth' of our knowledge and no 'narrator' to make our wonder 'meaningful', but also no structures to confine our knowing. Penetrating the narrative and the 'logos', we might discover that experience can be meaningful in its own right, and that knowledge can serve as its own witness.

Chapter Twenty-Seven

Self's fear of non-existence; response of confusion; appropriating not-knowing; the 'logos' of the self; fear as a pointer; new questions with no witness.

Field of Space

Find a peaceful, nourishing environment with few distractions, a place where there is a vast expanse of deep blue sky, or else a view of the ocean on a day when the water is calm and blue. Pick a time in the morning or evening, when the sky is not too bright, and gaze lightly at the blue expanse of the sky or the water, directing your awareness into the distance. Invite the energy of the blue into your consciousness. As passing thoughts and feelings arise, allow them to dissolve in the vast blue field. Be sensitive to a positive, healthy energy flowing through your consciousness, reflecting the clarity of space. Repeat twice daily for a week.

Exercise Twenty-Seven

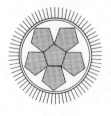

Seeing Through Space

Ground of Being

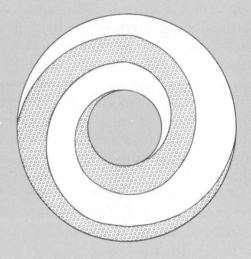

Shape from source
Emerging from background
Black ground unconditioned
Found in opposition
Mutual position
No ground for grounding
But the co-determined found

NO ALTERNATIVE
IN ALTERNATIVES

For hundreds of generations, human beings have looked to natural law, to sacred texts, and to divine authority as sources of knowledge. Today these alternatives have increasingly come under challenge in the name of empirical truth. Those who support their validity are asked to demonstrate their claims with 'objective' evidence: data available through sensory observation and subject to measurement and replication.

Religious traditions may well counter that the divine is inaccessible to empirical observation, and rely instead on more intuitive appeals that are not 'empirical' in the scientific sense. As long as science is accepted as the standard for knowledge, the result is to relegate religious teachings to the level of second-class truths: assertions that do not meet the strictest standards of validity. It is on this basis that the sacred texts and symbols of the world's great religious traditions have been 'demythologized' to make them conform to common-sense standards for the possible. When adherents of traditional teachings point to the singularity of their central tenets, insisting that in principle certain historical events cannot be verified by standards drawn from everyday experience, the gulf between 'objective' and traditional knowledge only widens.

An increased familiarity with the views of different cultures around the world and throughout history has supported this trend. Judged by a single, non-traditional standard, all traditions are found wanting, making adherence to one over another a simple accident of birth. While traditional teachings may be honored as guides to morality or ethical conduct, they lose their role as sources for the direct knowledge of reality.

To replace tradition, philosophy has sometimes put forward pure reason as an alternative to temporal knowledge. But history suggests that reason can support countless conflicting positions, even those most destructive of the human spirit. How then can reason ever yield trustworthy knowledge? The advance of formal logic has only confirmed reason's limitations and its ultimate incompleteness.

The Idea of an Absolute

The notion of an absolute also raises difficult questions. If the absolute is to have any significance for human beings, it must be related to us. For example, unless 'ultimate truth' either guarantees or otherwise affects conventional truth, how can it be called 'true'? Conditional reality must reflect, manifest, or share in ultimate reality. But the nature of this relationship, and even its possibility, remains a mystery.

The interaction of absolute and conditioned seems to lead directly to contradiction. Thus, the absolute is absolute only in comparison to what is not absolute. It follows that the absolute depends on the environment that validates it as absolute: the changing world of the conditioned realm. But this seems to mean that the conditioned realm as such must be *absolutely* conditioned. (If it could cease being conditioned, it would no longer be a validating environment for the absolute, in which case the absolute would no longer be absolute — but an absolute that could stop being absolute is not absolute to begin with.) Can the conditional be absolute in any way? If so, what role is left for another, 'absolute' absolute? There is another difficulty as well: If the conditional is absolute, the absolute (its validating environment) must be conditional!

It might be that the absolute, though inaccessible to logic, can be directly experienced (assuming a human faculty for cognizing the absolute). Perhaps we have had such an experience — an indisputable witness — or perhaps someone we trust has spoken of it. Yet how trustworthy is the knowledge that such an experience brings? No matter how direct knowledge claims to be, it will be mediated through structures of knowing firmly tied to the conditioned realm, including language, concepts, images, and reasoning. Whatever we can know by such means will not be absolute.

A possible response is to acknowledge that the absolute is beyond comprehension, while still asserting the validity of our inchoate experience of it. But if we cannot comprehend what we are pointing to, we are not 'knowing' it, but only expressing a belief about it. Saying that the absolute is 'beyond thought' is another thought. Since by definition the thought — being conditioned — has no relation with what it claims to be pointing at, it cannot operate to establish an absolute.

If non-conceptual knowledge of the absolute relies on incommunicable experience, why speak of the absolute at all? What is the basis of our belief that such inaccurate speech could be of benefit? Yet if we do maintain silence, are we admitting that the absolute and the conditioned are simply incompatible with one another?

The Role of the Supplicant

One final move remains available. Acknowledging our inability to gain access to an absolute, we can accept this inability as 'proof' for the absolute. Unable to speak, defeated by our own limitations, bereft of capacities, we find in our own weakness a source of awe and wonder at an inaccessible unknowable. From lack of knowledge comes humility, and out of humility grows worship. Our weakness and ignorance depart as envoys to the realm of the transcendent, bearing with them the gift of our devotion. We offer fealty to the incomprehensible, and in return seek compassionate protection.

Because such devotion turns on its head the conventional emphasis on a self, it can bring great benefits. The world becomes a simpler place, more integrated and more stable. It is easier to live in harmony and balance, for at last we have something to depend on. The mind and heart grow calm, and we can find peace in times of difficulty. Acceptance gives us strength: Through our commitment and determination, we witness our own experience more fully. The possibility emerges of a knowing that goes beyond temporal knowledge and self-centered concern.

Yet depending on how they are understood, these same virtues may become limitations. If we acknowledge 'complete dependence' and 'incurable ignorance', are we accepting restrictions on the power of knowledge and the capacities of our own being? Again and again throughout history, faith in an absolute has been interpreted to mean that humanity's role is steadfast acceptance of an order whose workings cannot be questioned. If faith is made to point in this direction, we must proceed with extreme caution. Bound by the bonds of such a faith, we may be sacrificing a vital part of our birthright as human beings.

Does faith in such an absolute lead us any closer to a new kind of knowledge? If knowledge of the absolute is to emerge, it cannot come from conditioned human being, for the conditioned cannot transcend its own nature. In that case, where can it come from? The teaching of an absolute seems to make transformation dependent on an influx of will, understanding, or power from a source beyond the conditioned realm. What role remains for human knowledge and responsibility, intelligence and faculties? Does the individual still have responsibility for working out his own destiny?

Relying on the absolute may commit us to a new story — the story of the powerless supplicant, dependent on what lies beyond. Obedient to the absolute, the supplicant awaits new knowledge and a new way of being. As waiting becomes hoping and hoping becomes wishing, the supplicant stands revealed as the historical self in a new guise. Eventually the self may tire of this story. Leaving others to maintain the vigil, rejecting a condition that asks too much, it may wander back into the pathways of daily life, no closer to a higher knowledge than it was at the outset.

On a more subtle level, however, an active faith may be related to the love of knowledge. Devotion can be a pointer directing us outside the range of ordinary experience and the concerns of the self, while the confession of ignorance can be a starting point for knowledge. By leading us beyond our own limited view, the recognition of powers, possibilities, and ways of knowing greater than the self can awaken a sense of awe that leads to wider vision and an ever-deepening appreciation.

Chapter Twenty-Eight

No alternatives to temporal knowledge; seeming impossibility of a meaningful absolute; faith in an absolute; accepting restrictions; linkage between faith and love of knowledge.

Sound Within Sound

Attend to the sounds around you or within your body, listening without assigning any importance to accompanying judgments or thoughts. Listen with regard to a 'deeper' sound within the sound. Continued focus on this deeper level within ordinary sensing soothes the mind and heals painful agitation.

Exercise Twenty-Eight

Transcending Space

Realm of Beyond

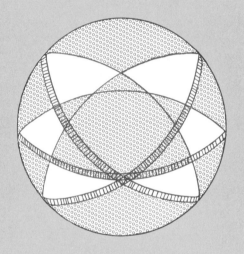

Circles open into unknown circles
Sphere of knowledge fluid possibilities
New dimensions unconfined by old
Measured as dimensions as
Dimensionless as less than all
As vision setting forgetting limits

VISIONARY REALM

Without accepting the limitations implicit in commitment to the incomprehensible, could we develop confidence in a source of knowledge beyond the self? Humility spacious enough to allow for this possibility might lead beyond the well-established self-concern that deadens inquiry. Perhaps it could allow as well for a more accommodating questioning that showed the way toward a greater and more complete knowledge.

Until now, we have considered 'the absolute' as a particular kind of story, one perhaps no longer told by the self. But this approach retains the structure of the narrative flow, and thus makes several key assumptions about the nature of space and time that may limit the availability of knowledge.

An alternative vehicle for attaining knowledge of the absolute is the timeless presentation of the vision. While the story focuses on the immediate situation defined by self-concern, the vision encourages aesthetic appreciation of the whole. The specific structures in which we normally place our trust do not need to be 'known' as fixed. Nor do we need to *assert* the 'existence' of what the vision reveals.

A Resplendent Whole

Let us envision all possible experience as an exquisite robe: a seamless 'fabric', woven in countless patterns that together create an infinite 'tapestry' of designs. Whatever exists is present among the patterns, and so too is its arising and its destruction. Past, present, and future all contribute to the tapestry. All our meanings and all the stories we tell are a part of the robe, together with the descriptions and categories we apply in shaping our experience into entities and events. All directions, possibilities, and energies, all competing values, all shapes, forms, and roles are present as well. Attempts to describe aspects of the robe would themselves form a tapestry of infinite complexity, were they not already a part of the robe.

Within the robe, some patterns could be considered more elegant than others, some more fully defined and more harmonious. There are combinations, concepts, and judgments that interact synergistically, and others that come into conflict. Since we too are part of the robe, such distinctions have an undeniable reality for us. If we see no differences, if we insist that all patterns within the robe are equal, our interpretation forms another pattern, generating greater or lesser harmony.

The world of the robe is one of universal interdependence, where each element is woven into the whole. The individual's felt sense of independence and even isolation is a part of the whole, an aspect of the intimate connection between microcosm and macrocosm. Individual action occurs within a flow of presentations, distributed through past, present, and future, that influences and guides our judgments.

Focusing on one item or event in experience, without understanding its place in the tapestry, creates disharmony and imbalance. Just such a narrow focus is implicit in the self's characteristic move of taking a position. The self sets out to impose a pattern, as if it were going to cut the robe apart to fit, sew it back together, and wear it. When violence is done to the fabric in this way, there is inevitably distortion and a tendency toward chaos. The clear recognition of this disruptive impact is in itself the appropriate countermeasure. Returning to the vision, we can let its power transform the tendencies that undermine fulfillment.

The Vision and Time

Within the timeless vision of the robe, new ways of knowing are allowed to emerge. Conventional knowledge is confined to what we can know 'now'. But once we turn from the momentum of our stories to a vision of the whole, 'now' and 'then' and the connection between them — the constant dynamic motion of all phenomena and all experience — are revealed as an overwhelming mystery. A rapt appreciation for the timeless acknowledges the patterns of linear temporal unfolding, without according them special significance. Free from restrictive local concerns, time can open in new ways, presenting secret realms. Instead of being 'distributed out' throughout linear time, the power of the present can be 'available' in all times, supporting the growth of our knowledge. What before was dark can now be illuminated with an inner light that had been obscured. Our lives become vivid and rewarding in ways that would previously have been unimaginable.

Without the insistence that the temporal flow is fixed in direction and momentum, time can present us with unsuspected gifts. We are free to be 'above' time, in a realm without limitations, borders, and discriminations, and also 'below' time, living with 'zero structure'. In the 'secret' world of the robe, knowledge may be instantaneous and complete, and communication may occur without ever 'taking place'. As part of a visionary reality, time can present the full openness of space and the full range of knowledge, allowing all presentations to appear in a harmony that human beings can embrace with uninhibited joy.

Direct Experience of Time

In the stories of conventional knowing, the founding story tells us what we are, so that we 'know' our limits. In the vision of the robe there are no boundaries, and thus no limits. We turn from the drive to *be* what we are not, which draws us into the future, and from the drive to *know* what we do not, which cements us to the past. Looking directly at what time is presenting, we can abandon wishing and waiting, nostalgia and regret, description and separation. We are free to cherish the experience of being human.

When they are no longer understood as being fixed and determinate, the three times — past, present, and future — offer a precious opportunity. The interplay of events in time; the subtle influence that our concepts and constructs exert on one another; the way that stories and patterns form, merge, separate, and form again: All these elements signal a rare creative energy at work within being. The past displays the unfolding patterns that underlie the flow of events; the present exhibits a dynamic creativity; the future reveals the interplay that goes on between actions and their consequences.

Allowing the unacknowledged power of time to reveal itself, we can accommodate the 'fullness of time' with the breadth and depth of a receptive awareness. Attunement to the marvels of creation can awaken within us an experience of overwhelming beauty and power. Our world can be dynamic and richly textured, our knowledge holistic and healing, holding new possibilities for being.

In the vision of the three times, the familiar linear sequence falls away. In such a 'random' time, 'I' cannot trace from now to then or here to there; nor can 'I' impose structures, distinctions, or patterns. 'I' cannot even know time as 'random', for it does not arise in opposition to order: the 'randomness' of time is itself 'random'.

'Random' time is unitary, for partitioning is based on order. Past, present, and future move as one, like the spokes of a wheel. All order, including such basic elements as movement and directionality, are entirely the product of interpretation, and interpretation itself likewise has a unitary character — the integration of an undifferentiated whole. What then is left to bar the path to freedom?

Beyond the Vision

Throughout history, mystical traditions have put forward visions of reality that resemble in fundamental ways the vision of the robe. They have proclaimed an eternal truth, underlying all change and every manifestation, in which space and time take on a different significance. Their ways for contacting this 'truth' have tapped a source of power that seems able to transform experience and give it new meaning.

Despite their transformative power, however, such visions may not remain true to the full potential of human being. For in setting forth an absolute, the visionary path projects 'truth' and 'reality' — constructs of conventional knowledge based on the conditioned realm — into 'another', higher realm. As long as it separates absolute from conditioned and proclaims the reality of the former, the visionary way perpetuates the structure of dichotomy that characterizes temporal knowledge and the known world.

To accept as ultimate a vision of the whole is to turn away from the highest possibilities for human freedom. Intent on exploring our interconnection with 'all that is', we act out our role and accept its attendant obligations, looking past the prospect that the patterns we attend to could be transformed. Though our experience may be sublime and the realms in which we move radiant with a new light, we affirm an underlying 'reality' — a time

244

and space that operate in specified ways and allow only certain manifestations. No matter how vast the range of this 'presupposed' realm, in the end our own actions are bound by the limits of what 'is', and tend toward duplication. Aware of the creative energies at play in the cosmos, we are not ourselves creative.

Refining Knowledge

Visionary harmony and indwelling perfection offer a deeply healing antidote to the self-centered structure of the narrative. Yet the turn *toward* the vision subtly affirms the reality of what is turned *from*. A dichotomy is established between ordinary existence and another, transcendent realm. No matter how exalted, the constructs that refer to the 'absolute' remain constructs; no matter how fully the vision transcends all linear narratives, a final story unfolds, asserting the 'existence' of a timeless realm.

The dimensions of visionary experience can nourish our whole being, revealing the potential for transformation as direct, lived knowledge. Yet if we are truly interested in freedom for ourselves and others, we need access to a knowledge that goes beyond the visionary. Accepting neither 'what is' nor 'what might be' as given, we need to explore the 'reality' of the real, investigating the 'time' and 'space' in which we now operate.

Perhaps in the end such questioning will return us to a vision not dissimilar from the vision of the robe. Even so, we cannot remain true to knowledge by making the leap to such a vision. Instead, a way must be found to 'purify' our conventional knowing—not through baptism, initiation, or ritual cleansing, but by refining our thoughts and cutting through accumulated patterns, until our thinking becomes an open gateway to a truly remarkable intelligence.

Chapter Twenty-Nine

An absolute accessible through vision rather than narrative; a vision of universal interdependence; non-distributed 'timing'; cherishing the fullness of time; 'random' time; vision as projecting truth and reality; subtle affirmation without creativity.

Inviting Awareness

Return to the practice of Exercise 19. Once an object of desire is clearly established in the mind, together with the associated aspects of the perceptual situation, invite in more awareness. Begin by inviting the senses to experience in new ways, deepening in their appreciation. Focus loosely on the background quality of awareness, noticing any shifts or changes.

Exercise Twenty-Nine

Read-out of Time

Tending Toward

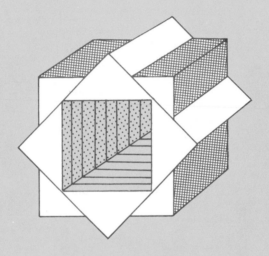

Knowledge intending
Knowledge extending
Probing multiple directions
Tending toward
The end of knowledge
Bounded by the repetition
Of the same

TOUCHING
THE LIMITS

Where is the source of a new knowledge within the old? Beyond the knowledge of eye and ear, of model and interpretation, there is the knowledge handed down from the past. But when tradition is available only as collective knowledge, it will not open into a more comprehensive knowing. Perhaps previous generations understood their customs and ways of knowing as 'arising from' a more fundamental level, but if so, they did not succeed in transmitting that knowledge forward. As they have come down to us, custom, convention, tradition, and common sense only 'mirror back' to us our own unknowing with regard to the most basic issues.

There is also the knowledge of heart and gut, of intuition and feeling. But what grounds these sensibilities? While it may be valuable to look for a knowledge free from words and labels, it has become clear that reliance on feelings and emotions is unlikely to deepen our knowing. Understood in this sense, a turn toward 'intuition' or 'direct' experiential knowledge only reinforces old patterns, while tending on the psychological level to promote a self-satisfaction that discourages inquiry into aspects of experience not based on the self.

Approaching deeper knowing as completely 'beyond' anything in our experience also leads to disappointment. If we did discover such a 'beyond' — a realm out of which judgments, projections, and specific knowledge somehow emerged — we could no more make sense of it than a shadow could know the object that cast it. Could we understand such a realm as anything other than chaos or the unknowable? Or do even these characterizations go too far in attempting to fit a 'beyond' within the constructs of labels and form (for example, as being 'prior to labels and form')?

Modeling Our Limits

At this point, a fundamental question may prove more useful than tracing out alternative sources of knowledge and rejecting them one by one. Why are there limits on our knowledge in the first place? *Is there something in the way we understand knowledge that sets up a lack of knowing as inevitable from the start?*

The discussion in Part One of this book suggested that conventional understanding views knowledge as given primarily through models. Starting with the data given by the senses, we use models to 'make sense' of experience. There are models for achieving very specific results, but also models that encompass the whole range of human activity, establishing a global 'world view' that offers a comprehensive interpretation of reality. Religions and philosophies of every kind, including the practical philosophy of 'common-sense', can be understood as models in this all-embracing sense.

Because every model, even the most encompassing, can be viewed as a tool for accomplishing a specific purpose, the use of models frames and limits the potential for knowledge. *A purpose establishes a 'stopping point' for knowledge*: When the purpose is attained (in the terms that the model specifies), no more knowledge is necessary. Understanding is restricted to the purposes that the prevailing models encompass. A purpose accomplished means an end to knowing, at least until the next model comes into operation.

While this 'model' for knowledge may seem simple and obvious, it has far-reaching consequences. Instead of being freely available in every moment, knowledge that arises and disappears over time, depending on the purposes then in operation, will always tend to be limited. Understood as a tool, knowledge is quickly shaped and structured into positions, interpretations, and more models. Alternative forms of knowledge that do not serve specific purposes (for example, knowledge about knowledge as explored in different societies and eras) may be available as a field for study, but not as an active and engaging knowing.

Confirming the Limits on Knowledge

The positioning to which models lead confirms and expands the 'fundamental model': *the self pursuing its intentions in a world accessible only through observation and distinction-making.* This model assures that knowledge will remain obscured and absent. For questions of 'fact', knowledge is available elsewhere, and the self must make use of the appropriate models, interpretations, and labels to acquire it. For questions of value, on the other hand, knowledge is restricted to the shadow-worlds of faith and feeling, or else its possibility is simply denied entirely.

The self's acceptance of restrictions on its knowledge suggests that the self is modest in assessing its own knowing capacity. But the reverse is also true: The limits on the self's knowledge confirm the self's *active control over knowledge*, confining what can be known within the models and structures that the self puts into operation. In the self's understanding, space and time and all that manifests 'within' them function only as the environment within which the self asserts its unique and all-important capacity to know.

The restrictions on knowledge in the self's model of knowing establish the self's basic situation: *Something is lacking and something must be done.* On the cognitive level, knowledge is lacking, and must be obtained. On the psychological level, the pattern is similar. The self finds that it has a problem and needs to change in some way; that it has needs that must be met or desires that leave it feeling unfulfilled; that it must discipline itself to attain its goals. The self sets up discriminations and makes judgments, choosing the course of conduct that will give it what it wants.

Based on this pattern, human being subjects itself to failure. When knowledge is limited and actions are judged as right or wrong, there will certainly be actions that are 'wrong'. We will make 'mistakes', and these 'mistakes' will generate more 'mistakes', perpetuating a 'mistaken' way of being. A spiraling cycle of fault and limitation is established, founded on separation, discrimination, and polarity.

One response to this pattern is the determination to 'pursue' knowledge of a new kind. But the old models make clear that a new way of knowing can be established only by setting aside the old. Conforming to this logic of conflict and alternatives, we submit ourselves to a course of struggle and discipline. We maintain an intrinsic friction within experience, perpetuating a root tension and anxiety. Despite our efforts, the same basic limitations continue to operate.

Knowledge as Commodity

The limitations set up by the prevailing models turn knowledge into a 'commodity' and human beings into consumers rather than producers. The different systems of knowledge, each offering its own explanations and techniques, its interpretations and methods, leave open only the question of which system to adopt. Within a particular field of knowledge (religion, politics, etc.), we select from among a relatively small number of basic models and beliefs. It is as though we were choosing from among computer software programs — except that in a sense we are the ones being programmed.

Knowledge handed down as a commodity is subject to ownership and manipulation. It is easily caught up in concerns that have nothing to do with knowledge as such: issues of power and powerlessness, blame and guilt. As such concerns come to the fore, the fundamental patterns of knowledge do not 'come up' for investigation. The prospect for a direct understanding of how knowledge functions and how it might be transformed slips unnoticed out of view.

Chapter Thirty

No final knowledge in tradition or feeling; models limiting knowledge; self's knowledge restricted; self in control; knowledge as a commodity.

Observing Hearing

As an extension of Exercise 28, while focusing on sounds expand awareness to include yourself as the one who is hearing the sound. Include as well awareness of the 'process' of hearing. This practice makes the energy within sound more available to knowledge, allowing greater clarity.

Exercise Thirty

Being Itself Knowing

Part Whole

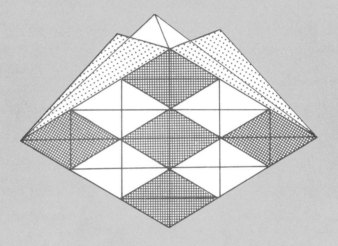

Parts into wholes
Holes into parts
Partitions accumulate
Particles perpetuate
Limits beyond limits
One all and none one

CONSTRICTING CIRCLE

How is it possible to find a way out of the circle of conventional knowledge that closes us in without recourse? Replacing conventional constructs with new ones will not fundamentally alter the knowledge available to us, since it will still leave us in the realm of descriptive knowledge and the narrative. If we try to go 'beneath' this realm by calling on the witness, the content of what is witnessed will be formed out of the ordinary 'stuff' of common, shared agreement.

If the old labels are wrong, how can we point this out without once more making use of labels? We may have new experiences, but the model of 'a self having experiences' is still in operation. Like the fairy-tale knight bewitched by a magic spell, we find that every door we open leads back into the room we just left.

If we stripped away all the stories, labels and interpretations that we rely on in conventional knowledge, what 'basis' for knowing would be left? The self would be gone, and with it the historical narrative and the 'objective' world. There would be no arena in which to act, and no way to make sense of the outcome of action. Without starting from our accumulated patterns, how could we understand a realm free of those patterns? Without our old, subjective way of being, how could there be any witness to new knowledge or any sense that what was known was meaningful? Truly free from expectations, how could we know if we attained results?

In such 'circumstances', could we even keep on questioning? Who would 'do' the questioning, when 'doer' itself is a category within a model? Even if we found that questioning consisted of 'not-doing', we could continue questioning only by becoming 'not-doers': another category within the model.

Caught in the Web

The existing order and its patterns shape our thoughts at the deepest level. Though we may sense the possibility of a 'knowing that does not depend on such patterns', pointing to it can be like trying to point with the pointing finger to the finger that is pointing.

We seem to lack knowledge about how to transform our knowledge. A knowledge that depends on fundamental structures of thought, language, and human behavior cannot investigate those structures. But where could we expect to find a knowledge that did not rely on those structures and the models they generate? Is the genetic coding of our cells supposed to give us new ways of knowing? Do our hands or feet have knowledge to which our heads have been denied access? Can we tap into the 'knowledge of the cosmos'? It seems difficult to make sense of such possibilities.

On the deepest level, our existence as human beings seems to *consist* of limits on every level — physical, mental, and cultural. We are what we have been made to be. Struggle against our own history and origins seems futile. Even if we take this sense of futility as an invitation to allow knowledge to operate in 'another' way, we are already caught up in a new interpretation. We may be quite sure that we have no 'fixed ideas' as to what this 'other' way would be like, but the idea of 'another way' itself imposes the limits and restrictions of old thought patterns. Understanding *this* is, in turn, another interpretation.

However we approach the search for knowledge, in the end we seem restricted to a limited set of thoughts, images, concepts, and meanings. Disappointment and confusion, explanations and excuses may crowd in on us, confirming our lack of knowledge; even so our questions lead only to hesitation, embarrassment, frustration, or self-deception. 'New' knowledge will either fit within our ordinary framework (perhaps as an interesting theoretical construct) or else be unintelligible. There are no other possibilities — no road we can take, no dialogue we can initiate, no opportunity for change.

No Beyond

Our world is like a bubble swept along in a torrent of water. The bubble owes its existence, form, and specific qualities to the water that surrounds it, but within the bubble there is no way of knowing the water. The distinctions we make within our bubble world may ultimately depend on the surrounding water, but give us no access to it. If we think we have found new knowledge that bursts the bubble, we may only be like a dreamer who dreams having awakened. And we are fortunate that this is so, for it seems that if the bubble did burst, we would immediately drown.

The circle of not-knowing that defines the bubble's boundary reveals how far we are from being free. In the conventional sense, we call ourselves free when we can live out our own stories, rather than being assigned roles in stories told by others. But who determines the content and structures of the narratives that we put forth? Who decides the setting of the story and the rules that govern the reality within which it unfolds? If we follow the established patterns and models of the past and submit to the accumulated weight of history, are we choosing our own lives? Are we free when our minds have been 'made up' for us in advance?

Chapter Thirty-One

No escape from patterns; no knowledge of how to transform knowledge; human being as made up of limits; bound in a circle of not-knowing.

Resonating Sound

Practice intensifying the energy of sounds by allowing each sound to linger in the mind. Be attentive to resonance and to echoes. Trace the sound as it fades, pursuing the energy into body and mind, sensitive to its revitalizing effect.

Exercise Thirty-One

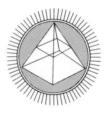

Experience of Time

Circle of Self

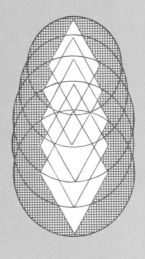

Point moves to form
Constricted circle
Of constructed domain
Surround define
Define surround
Giving rise to
Pre-conditioned knowledge

TAKING A STAND

The restrictions on knowledge, which seem so absolute and final from the conventional perspective, can be analyzed in terms of 'positions' and 'conditions'. *In the space-centered view of 'objective' reality, limitations on knowing are the consequence of positions.* The self (to which the conventional view refers all knowing) occupies a *place* 'here' and lacks knowledge regarding something *located* 'there'. This lack sets up a basic tension, which generates a momentum 'outward', activating the flow of linear temporality that perpetuates the self and its constructs.

From the time-centered view of the self, the same lack emerges as conditioning. Born into a particular setting and subject to a specific order, the self is shaped in its being and its knowing. Its limited knowledge is the inevitable outcome of its circumstances, which define the self in its person and its potential.

'Positions' and 'conditioning' seem to foreclose any new possibilities. When the self emerges as already active within time and space in a characteristic way, 'how' and 'where' will it contact new prospects for knowing? Only if time and space themselves were *already different* could they sustain a way of knowing that did not depend on positions and conditions. But in that case, how could a self arise to 'do' the knowing?

The Self as 'Bystander'

Positions and conditions are the outcome of the model that assigns knowing to a self. In this model, knowledge results from *the projection of a knowing capacity out into an unknown world*. The self appears as separate from the events it knows — a 'bystander' that extracts knowledge from experience without becoming directly 'involved' in experience. The personas of the self as 'perceiver', 'owner', and 'narrator', discussed in Part Two, can all be understood as aspects of this 'bystander-self'. The term 'bystander' emphasizes the element of 'positioning' that is inherent in the activity of knowing that the 'bystander' carries out.

The 'bystander' protects its own territory and position. It stands back, not embracing or embodying what time presents, asserting its independence from the world that is known. In its knowing of experience, it remains opposed to what it knows, even though it also claims ownership over it. The resulting division between the source of *knowing* and the source of *knowledge* establishes a 'gap in knowledge' as basic. In a knowing founded on opposition, what is understood as 'real' is *opposed* to the knowledge that knows it.

In the 'bystander'-centered model, the world that appears to the 'bystander' is initially unknown and in principle unmanageable — not for reasons that are arbitrary or even mysterious, but as the direct consequence of the 'position' or 'posture' that the 'bystander' adopts. Independent of the 'bystander', the world 'reflects back' the initial opposition, 'stubbornly' resisting both knowledge and manipulation. Time in this world is an external force bearing down on the self, space is the arena for limitation, crowding, and constriction, and knowledge tends to remain clouded and uncertain.

Thus, positioning and conditioning arise as 'mirror images' of one another. In taking a position, the self as 'bystander' also establishes a world 'over and against which' that position is maintained. Having 'positioned itself' in this way, it is subject to 'conditions' over which it has no control. The 'bystander' that acts is inseparable from the 'objective self' that is acted upon.

When the 'bystander' is understood as basic to all knowing, the resulting pattern of opposition shapes all knowledge. Seen in this light, 'polar knowledge' is no longer understood as basic at all; instead, it becomes a *hypothetical construct* founded on the stance taken by the 'bystander'. It serves as an explanation for 'how knowledge must arise' given the separation that divides the 'bystander' from experience.

'Descriptive knowledge' reflects an identical 'bystander' orientation. On this level, 'position' comes into play through 'opposition', active as the basis for identification and discrimination. It is dichotomies that define what is real: subject and object, self and world, mind and body, idealism and materialism, determinism and free will, etc. In addition, there are the oppositions that shape values and determine choices: positive and negative, valuable and destructive, limiting and opening, and so forth. Each pole is a potential 'position' for the 'by-stander' to adopt, and the known world comes into being through the progressive marking out and 'owning' of such polar oppositions. As identities are assigned, judgments are formed in accord with chains of inference and reasoning. The judgments initiate a momentum; this momentum in turn establishes the mechanisms for duplication, through which a 'well-established' conventional reality comes to be known.

Limited to the field of discrimination and judgment in which the 'bystander' operates, knowledge remains confined to the presupposed 'positions' the bystander occupies. Models, descriptions, and interpretations may be open to inquiry on a conceptual level, but they are not allowed to interfere with the positions that the 'bystander' has adopted, or to investigate the structure that puts forward the 'bystander'. The 'bystander' itself, together with its knowing capacity, remains unknown.

Chapter Thirty-Two

Restrictions as based on positions in space and conditions in time; self as projecting 'bystander'; gap between knowing and knowledge; positions and polarity; opposition as basis for knowledge.

Playing with Momentum

As a variation on Exercises 15 and 26, 'review' a whole day in just a few minutes, then go back over the same events, this time allowing twice as long. Do this several times at least, progressively increasing the amount of time you allow. Note the new memories that arise, and also the new patterns linking memories. You can also reverse the order of the repetitions, progressively *decreasing* the time allowed for review.

Exercise Thirty-Two

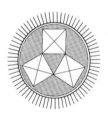

Light of Space

Boundless Positioning

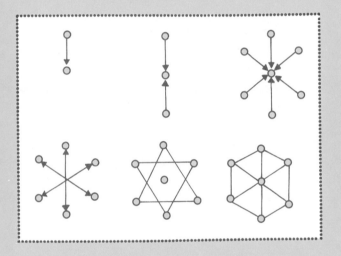

Bystanding arising around
The boundaries open
Prior to position unpositioned
Centered point momentum
Presenting presence
Positioning boundless rhythm

AVAILABILITY
OF KNOWLEDGE

B ound by its positions, the 'bystander' knows a world of surfaces and linear sequences, of objects interacting in terms of a mechanically understood progression of cause and effect. What interacts in this way is subject to analysis by reason. Reason, however, is a tool of the 'bystander', who reasons 'about' the objects to which polar knowledge is thought to give access, and does so by applying the categories and distinctions descriptive knowledge makes available.

Given the link between reason and the 'bystander', it is perhaps not surprising that reason itself is strangely lacking in foundation. We do not know why reason is effective in making sense of reality, nor do we know whether the structure of cause and effect that reason depends on is only an interpretation that reason itself imposes. The authority of reason cannot be established by reason, nor can reason be 'grounded' in anything more fundamental than itself.

As long as inquiry proceeds in terms of reasoning, it does not escape the structures of opposition that go with the 'bystander'. There is no shortage of theories or explanations for why knowledge is limited, or for why the depth and richness that experience sometimes discloses is 'normally' restricted. But such explanations do not move beyond the realm of theory. They fail to demonstrate how a new vision or a new understanding could open from within the confines of the 'bystander's' world.

Knowledge Through Inquiry

As an alternative to reason and explanations directed at the 'facts' disclosed when the 'bystander' takes up its positions, we can look directly at the way in which the 'bystander' knows. For example, instead of looking at what observation observes, we can inquire into observation *as it operates*. Here the conventional limits on observation, which restrict it to surfaces, limited perspectives, and the rest need not apply.

In the same way, reason can be investigated in ways that do not depend on reason, and the operation of cause and effect can be opened to inquiry without placing that inquiry within a causal sequence. We can look at the patterns of intentional knowledge without first accepting the confines of conventional intentionality, and can investigate desire without being caught up in its flow.

Through such inquiry, new questions can be asked in a new way. In the domain that inquiry opens, does reason still apply? Do cause and effect still operate? We *do not know* the answers. In this not-knowing, a possibility for a new knowledge emerges. The terms we use and the thoughts we entertain now have a new and wider context; instead of being givens, they are constructs to be investigated further.

For example, inquiry will continue to use the language of conventional knowledge. We may distrust the accuracy of terms such as 'self', 'mind', 'experience', 'observation', 'world', 'reality', and 'knowledge' — not to mention the structures of grammar and syntax — but making up new words, or assigning new meanings to the old, would only bring confusion.

This limitation conditions but need not impede inquiry. The labels and ideas that structure experience will naturally also shape and guide our questioning. But recognized *as* labels and ideas, they lose their power to confine the range of inquiry, and instead become elements *available for investigation*. Proceeding with care and dedication to keep such awareness active in our questions, we can learn to treat words and thoughts as pointers toward knowledge, rather than boundaries for what can be known.

The basic premise of the 'bystander', which resonates throughout the realms of polar and temporal knowledge, holds that knowledge is obtained when a 'knowing capacity' reaches out to a 'knowable entity'. Inquiry, however, calls the model of the 'bystander' into question. In doing so, it suggests a key alternative to the standard view: *The activity of knowing may already intrinsically embody knowledge.*

If inquiry can operate in this way, the momentum of the primordial 'not-knowing' to which the bystander's knowledge is invariably subject can be transformed. In its place, a more powerful 'not-knowing' could emerge:

one that no longer 'knew' the established truths of conventional knowledge to be 'true' and thus beyond the range of inquiry. The conclusion that knowledge is intrinsically limited could then appear as a *reflection* of the limitations on our knowledge rather than an insight into the *necessity* of those limitations. Ready to look anew at self and world and all the other structures of the known, such a not-knowing could proceed with confidence, satisfied that inquiry itself offered an inexhaustible source of deeper knowledge.

From Positions to Positioning

For inquiry to operate freely, it cannot be bound by the 'positions' that the 'bystander' adopts. This does not necessarily mean, however, that those positions must be rejected. Indeed, it is not clear that it would be possible to reject one set of positions without adopting another. Inquiry will be free only if it allows for a way of knowing more fundamental than 'rejection'.

A position is the outcome of an *act* of positioning, which unfolds in time through discrete acts of distinguishing, knowing, and so forth. Seen in this light, *positions are expressions of knowledge, rather than structures that limit it.* Instead of accepting the viewpoint of the 'bystander', which insists on its fixed positions situated at a point off-center from an imagined origin, we could see in positioning *the manifestation of a knowing that is not itself situated or specified.*

Where does the knowing that establishes a position originate? The conventional answer, which would refer back once more to the 'bystander', is unacceptable, for the 'bystander' 'comes into being' only with the 'fixing' of its 'position'. Instead, the 'knowing that positions' in the first instance must originate from a 'center' that is 'prior' to all positions. But even this is saying too much, for if the center is 'prior' to all positions, then we do not 'depart' from the center no matter 'where' we are 'positioned'. At this center, where no positions hold and we hold no positions, where no shadows are cast and light is all-illuminating, 'knowledge' might take on a very different significance.

Free from all positions, inquiry has access to all manifestations, including the 'bystander-self', its interpretations, and all the most widely accepted and 'best established' elements of experience. Inquiry can see 'through' positions, recognizing them as 'positionings' that express knowledge. By being ready to take each question to a deeper level, it dissolves or transforms each structure in turn, so that in the end there are no obstacles to the recognition of knowledge at work.

The Qualities of Inquiry

Free and open inquiry is no longer concerned with answers in the usual way. We look at our situation 'lightly'; observing in an equal, balanced, and inviting way, we make no special effort to 'make sense' of what we see. We follow images and thoughts without accepting their authority, and make use of reason and observation without having to establish the truth of what they present. We 'take' no positions — not even the position 'I am the observer'. Prepared to question observation itself, we can observe without friction, creating a boundless rhythm and momentum within perception and awareness.

Such an inquiry rejects the 'bystander's' claim to be the one that knows, and sets up no new 'knower' in its place. What is known through inquiry is not 'something new', known by 'someone'— this interpretation would only go 'beyond' the existing structure, thus affirming the structure itself. Instead, free and open inquiry sees *through* the 'truth' of what the 'bystander' knows, investigating how that 'truth' is set up without setting up a competing 'truth'.

'Open' to investigate whatever appears, such inquiry is 'free' from the obligation to 'recreate' what belongs to the 'already established'. *It is not a question of learning new techniques or practices*, but of giving up unquestioning loyalty to the techniques and practices that we are *already practicing* in every moment. A new form of seeing comes into operation.

Free and open inquiry offers no target for the fear with which the self responds to inquiry that calls the founding story into question. Seeing each position only as an instance of knowledge actively 'positioning', inquiry cannot be crushed by the 'gravity' generated within existing 'fields of being'. It is open randomly and without limitation to sight, sound, images, meanings, and feelings alike— to fear as well as joy, to pain as well as pleasure. Turning experience 'on its edge', it finds the meeting place of time and space, and there creates an opening for luminous knowing.

Random inquiry allows for a random knowledge, no longer based on conventional ways of 'measuring out' and defining the known, and so no longer confined by the instruments available for measurement. Because it is not susceptible to measurement, such knowledge may not appear to be knowledge at all; instead, it may appear as 'zero'. But random knowledge *in operation* is not subject to such characterizations — it is 'random' without being governed by the 'laws' of probability. Nor is random inquiry affected by the limits it encounters. Activated within present circumstances, it cuts through the careful structures and strictures of the conventional to embody 'knowingness' directly.

Activating Inquiry

An all-accommodating inquiry can be activated through analysis that turns from what is known to the 'coming to be' of what is known. Such analysis lets us drop our unthinking commitment to our own existence. Looking at the way in which the structures we take for granted arise, we can see that our positions are not solid — that we are not what we thought. We see the names, associations, and shared agreements that establish 'the real' and 'the acceptable' in operation. Established patterns are resolved into a more fluid 'patterning'. Investigating how things are joined together in consciousness, we abandon the commitment to our 'positions', and come closer to understanding the temporal order within which 'positioning itself' arises.

When analysis takes as its subject the process of arising, it discloses time in a new way. The frozen 'product' of the 'positioning process' is thawed, awaking the flow of energy that it manifests. *The process of analysis parallels the dynamic that it explores,* making contact with a fundamental temporal vitality, embodying an active feedback that can truly nourish knowledge. As analysis tunes in to the 'momentum of arising', starting from the point at which 'we' find ourselves and *working backward, it naturally reverses* the tendency toward setting up rigid positions, initiating healing and restoration. Painful difficulties and patterns are seen in a new light, as 'manifested probabilities' of being, and the open, allowing nature of experience comes to the fore.

Chapter Thirty-Three

Inquiry 'within' reason and observation; inquiry not bound by constructs; knowing embodying knowledge; positions as expressing knowledge; non-positioned center; random knowing without a knower; awaking the flow of time.

Glowing Journey in Time

After you have worked with 'reversing' the temporal flow of a stream of memories (see Exercises 15, 26, and 32), recall the same stream of memories in the conventional order. As each memory 'appears', let it expand in intensity or energy, or in the quality of light it bears. 'Assign' this glowing energy a positive feeling, even if the feeling tone of the 'original' experience was not positive. Let each memory add to the glow, until a deep radiance suffuses your awareness. If you wish, you can continue this journey forward in time past the point at which you began the earlier 'backward' progression.

Exercise Thirty-Three

Time to Time

Enmeshed in Wondering

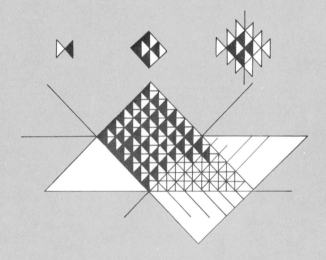

Opening field filling out
Enmeshed rhythm structure
Limits unknown
Edges stopping starting
Putting knowledge together
Freely seeing between
Into being wonder

RAIN OF
QUESTIONS

The prospect that inquiry and analysis can awaken new knowledge may be deeply inspiring, but in practice this inspiration can be hard to maintain. If we set out on such a path, we may soon find that the questions we pose seem abstract and speculative, without significance for our own lives. Alternatively, they may seem beyond our capacity to understand. Lacking confidence in our own abilities, we may stop with the first answer that comes to mind, or borrow an answer we have read about, or shrug our shoulders and say we simply do not know. We fail to notice that when we adopt such a position, the position itself is subject to questioning. What is this position based on? What needs does it satisfy or concerns does it meet? Why do we hold to it so tenaciously?

When questions probe deep enough, they can seem threatening. We may respond by feeling lazy or distracted — eager to turn to other concerns that seem more interesting or pressing. No such response needs to be accepted as marking the limit of questioning. 'Lazy', 'don't want to', 'bored' and the like are interpretations. Where do these interpretations come from? How do they fit into our more fundamental view of what is happening in our lives and in the world? How are they tied in to emotions? Do they manifest an underlying mental energy? Is it possible to contact such an energy directly? What happens when we make the attempt?

Emotions and feelings are often presented as though they were the final word, immune to inquiry, but there is no reason this should be so. For example, to say we do not 'want' to question is to adopt a position. This position is based on linguistic and psychological structures, which can also be investigated.

We can look into our motivations and concerns the way an actor might try to understand the character he is playing: engaged, yet somewhat removed. If emotions are like the costumes that the character puts on, what leads him to dress that way? And what does this reveal about his sense of self or understanding of his situation? Watching what manifests and probing its structure may disclose underlying tendencies and beliefs, together with assumptions formed by 'juxtaposing' positions.

Energy for Questions

Perhaps we feel we simply do not possess the energy that sustained questioning takes. In that case we have a new focus for inquiry: What is the nature of this energy? How do we know that it is lacking or that it might be exhausted? Instead of speculating about this, we can look right now at our own energy in operation—as we read, as we reflect, and as we question.

To say that questioning requires energy is to apply a complicated set of labels. Questioning is understood as the activity of a questioner who requires energy to function; energy is needed because what is not known must be explored. The energy comes from some 'where' to 'here', where the questioner is located; the questioner uses it to direct inquiry 'there'. All of these 'locations' depend on a particular understanding of space, adopted without sustained inquiry in the course of our learning to think, reason, and experience in the customary ways. How are all these structures interrelated, and how does the whole come to be?

Perhaps our investigations lead to no firm answers. But to say we do not know the answers to such questions is also not a 'conclusion' that ends inquiry. How do we know that we do not know? What makes us certain of this? What constitutes the sense of certainty that gives us faith in our uncertainty? How can we be so sure of not being sure? What kind of 'energy' does it take to continue our inquiry in this manner, when the subject for investigation is present 'here' and 'now'?

Granting Knowledge Permission

All our lives we have relied on certain truths that support each other in a coherent, consistent way. But if the positions established by the 'bystander-self' conceal from us their own nature, these 'truths' are all open for re-examination. The evidence of the senses and the cogency of reason, the guiding structure of time and the patterns of 'positioned' knowing that confirm our limitations are all open for questioning in a new way.

What is behind our mental patterns? How do they arise? How does the mind gain access to what it feeds on? Who experiences, who knows, and who responds? What role do memory and interpretation play in shaping the contents of consciousness? How does experience arise, and how do thought and the senses interact? What is it that changes over time, and how? Is collective knowledge the proper authority to govern our lives? To what does it trace its legitimacy?

When such questions suddenly take on real significance, it is like discovering that we were adopted as children and raised by strangers: The familiar at once seems profoundly foreign. We face an ignorance so deep that it is actually embarrassing, and find that our embarrassment in turn conceals a deep sense of uncertainty and concern. But if we stay with inquiry, investigating the range of our past experience and the domain of our present possibilities, we are led to new beginnings. Our embarrassment and not-knowing are what make the old structures accessible to inquiry. We do not need to insist on answers; instead, we can allow knowledge to disclose itself in the very process of analysis.

Investigating the Limit Structure

We know as we start investigating that we are already enmeshed in specific situations, possessing specific faculties and models for knowing, relying on a foundation about which we are largely ignorant. *But this ignorance, once acknowledged, does not have to remain in effect.* The limits we find in effect do not mean that the 'limit-structure' itself is basic.

The limits on our knowledge are reflected in the limits and boundaries of the objects that present themselves to be known. These limits — the borders, distinctions, and differences that define and shape what we know — are not in themselves a limitation on knowing. In the *midst* of our knowing, we can look at these 'edges' that let us discriminate: at the 'starting' and 'stopping' points, the places where identified entities and events come into being or cease to exist; where one object gives way to another, or where 'what is' is differentiated from 'what is not'.

Such a way of investigating reveals a rich source of knowledge available in this very moment. We touch it when we turn from the content of what we know *to investigate how our knowledge is put together.* We foster it by raining down questions in all directions — questions not bound to the limiting narrative structure of question and answer. Asking 'who' and 'where' and 'how' and 'when', we can follow the line of inquiry from question to question and answer to answer, not unduly concerned with whether the answers put forward are 'correct' or useful.

If we let our questions arise from true wonder, they will open to further questions; free from the bias of positions, they will call forth a knowledge that reflects their power to go beyond the known. We may see the patterns of identification and involvement in a new way and develop an understanding that brings immediate practical benefit. At the outset, nothing we do should close off the free flow of questioning itself. As questions open to further questions, we may find that we have been looking for knowledge in the wrong way and in the wrong place. We may discover more inspiration and deeper knowledge in what we do not know than in what we think we understand.

Chapter Thirty-Four

Questioning interpretations and feelings; energy for questioning; investigating senses, reason, and patterns; through ignorance to knowledge; looking at boundaries; questioning with wonder; finding inspiration in not-knowing.

Inviting Being

To open the awareness developed in Exercises 19
and 29, invite into awareness more space, more
time, and more knowledge. Focus on each of
these elements in turn, or experiment with
different ways of combining them. Be sensitive
to the 'field' of space and the 'character' of time.
At the start this will be a threefold practice;
later, it will open in new ways. This exercise extends the power of the mind and improves the
quality of observation, especially with regard to
'subjective' elements.

Exercise Thirty-Four

Knowing is Being

Embodying

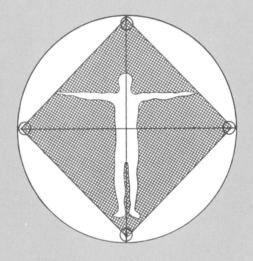

Reflection of pure power
Knowledge in Time and Space
Mind and body existence
Energy time revolves
Space of dimension
Knowledge communicates knowledge
Embodied Human Being

KNOWLEDGE
IN HUMAN BEING

Inquiry and analysis follow no model, but depend on the path of their own unfolding. Nevertheless, there are several directions that an open, vigorous questioning might take that would be likely to lead toward a more comprehensive knowledge.

If we begin at a level that is too abstract, we may come under the influence of theoretical constructs that lack transforming power. But if we look at our own experience to see how the patterns we rely on are established, insight is directly available. Language, behavior, living conditions, human evolution, the rise of consciousness, our own personal development, and the circumstances in which we act and live — these are the subject of our inquiry. Without restricting knowledge to 'psychology' or 'anthropology', such an inquiry recognizes that the subject and substance for investigation can be found in immediate, present experience, within and around in all directions.

We might start by looking at beginnings. The known world is built up on the basis of communication. How did human beings learn to speak? Scientific speculations on this point, together with the evidence that supports them, can serve to focus an inquiry that looks at how language functions within our own minds, shaping our intelligence, our perception, our understanding, and our interactions with others.

Another focus might be the process by which human consciousness changes over time. Different cultures have accepted as fundamental realities and ways of thinking that are completely different from our own. Appreciation for such differences can suggest how the changing dimensions of consciousness have given rise to our own ways of thinking, and can loosen the hold that our styles of thought and imagination have over us. Reflections based on our own experience and observation of the culture around us, together with study of findings by historians and cross-cultural investigators can provide a fruitful basis for such inquiry. Literature and the root meaning of the words and symbols we use in daily discourse can also offer valuable clues to the workings of the mind.

Just as we are 'positioned' by language and by culture, we are bound by a certain understanding of space and time. This understanding could be traced out historically, or it could be the focus of a direct inquiry. Where does space come from and how does it originate? Can anything exist 'outside' of space? Was there a beginning to time? If so, what was there 'before' the beginning? If time had an origin outside of time, is a different temporality in operation 'somewhere else'? How might knowledge operate in such an 'elsewhere'?

Knowledge in Particulars

Within the social, cultural, historical, and mental patterns that shape the 'known world', a structure operates that is far less solid than we usually imagine. Objects enter our lives in the course of an unfolding series of events, like actors who appear on stage, play a role for a time, and then depart. Despite appearances, the roles that the actors occupy — the patterns into which 'things' fall and the stories about them — are a matter of interpretation, not substance.

An inquiry into the inner structure of this world we take for granted begins with our own being and history, and with the 'things' and patterns with which we interact. Perhaps we focus on a table on which are resting some books or papers. The table is located quite specifically in space and time. It has a history that can be traced back physically, socially, culturally, and economically; it has meaning in our lives that depends on the linguistic structures that let us identify it, the ways in which we have put it to use, and the associations we bring to it.

In the same way, whatever is now in existence has a history and reflects dimensions of structure, meaning, and value. Because these dimensions relate as well to 'our' being as 'narrator' and 'owner', an inquiry that embraces them can teach us where we 'come from' and where we are 'going'. We can ask how the past led to the present, how we make models and structure experience, and how we project the past toward the future. We can educate ourselves so that patterns open up, stimulating an active, creative intelligence. Through such inquiry we discover that *knowledge is available here and now, freeing us from the need to freeze accumulated under-standing into a position for fear of losing it.*

In conducting such an investigation, we are inquiring also into the knowing capacity of the mind. Here the range of what conventional knowledge knows is quickly left behind. Ordinary understanding offers no obvious answer to the question of how the mind exists, and knows no way to measure its potential. The mind seems almost infinite in its power to produce thoughts, shapes, and forms that come and go, interacting too quickly to observe; yet typically this power is dispersed into the endless repetition of unsophisticated patterns of knowledge and action. On the one hand, the mind is creative at its root; on the other this creativity is channeled into rigid structures that throttle its vitality.

It is pleasant to imagine ourselves exercising the innate creativity of the mind in new and fruitful ways, gracefully interweaving thought and action like a gifted musician who takes up a simple theme and shapes it unerringly toward beauty. But when the mind is flooded with content and bound by old patterns, the path of beauty and spontaneous creativity can be elusive.

Is such proliferation and stagnation a part of mind from the very beginning? Is there a 'place' within or beneath thought where there are no thoughts and no perceptions, where the spontaneity of the mind operates without restriction? Is such a place, if it does 'exist', accessible to knowing? Or does knowing originate with a call for positioning that already violates the absolute stillness of 'no thoughts'?

Even more basic than mind, it seems, is existence. A non-existing knower could not know; an object that could not be said to exist in some manner could not be known. The polarities 'subject/object' and 'self/world' seem to presuppose a commitment to existence, so that whatever form the subject's knowing takes, it verifies that existence 'exists'. Subject and object will point to each other, in a kind of negotiated agreement — a conspiracy of what is. Is it possible to conceive of a knowing that would not be bound by such terms?

Boundless Realms of Knowing

In each realm of human being, from the particulars of everyday life to the workings of the mind to the basic 'given' of existence, free and open inquiry will foster clarity in observation and analysis. Bound to no positions, it will take different forms in each new field, shifting in subtle, unexpected ways, so that one form of knowledge feeds back into another. In the psychological realm, it will bring clarity to values, attitudes, feelings, and the sense of quality. In the religious or spiritual domain, it will disclose new facets of our being in its interconnection with the cosmos and with human destiny, encouraging humility and devotion. In the field of reason and logic, it will teach us how these more traditional tools of analysis can be applied to foster an integrated, all-encompassing knowledge.

Free and open inquiry allows for all these possibilities and countless others. There are so many ways of being — so many different worlds, each with its own patterns of arising and becoming. Beneath the world of daily existence vibrates the fantastic world of subatomic particles. In the depths of outer space black holes transform the nature of time and place. There are realms of higher energies, realms invisible and visible, realms existent and non-existent.

As conceptual analysis gives way to more direct forms of inquiry, and such alternative ways of being become newly accessible, we may tap a knowing difficult to put into words. Yet even as we struggle with the limitations of language and thought, we begin to notice that such knowledge is self-affirming, communicating itself not only in what we think or say, but in our actions and our way of being.

Insight Through Higher Knowledge

The new knowledge that emerges in these ways can exert a powerful influence. To trace a single instance, suppose that we investigate the polarities and distinctions basic to consciousness — the interplay of 'like' and 'dislike' or 'satisfaction' and 'frustration'. As this analysis deepens, a change takes place quite naturally, loosening the pull of desire and allowing a special sense of freedom to emerge.

If we continue with this analysis, we will come to a level where emotions and feelings appear as manifestations of a more fundamental energy, carried by the experience that comes to us through the senses. At this level, emotions and judgments can be understood as labels applied to this underlying energy — labels that could perhaps be changed.

At the next stage, we see the link between such labels and distinctions and the underlying structures of the 'bystander-self'. The self has a yearning for happiness or pleasure; it is drawn to such feelings as a moth is drawn to a flame. But the self also establishes patterns that make it dependent on circumstances and thus guarantee frustration. These two aspects of the self are mutually conditioned. The result is that the self holds on to its pain or tension or anxiety, because it is unwilling to give up the activities that produce them.

When inquiry has led to this level of understanding, a knowledge begins to operate that makes it possible to move freely between polarities. Because we appreciate the structures of polarity as aspects of knowledge, we can be flexible and open in the patterns that we choose to adopt. As we continue to exercise knowledge, we may grow adept at switching from negative feelings to positive ones and back again. Viewed from a conventional perspective, this is a remarkable, even incredible ability. Knowledge itself makes no judgment. Conjoined to no positions by nature, knowledge offers naturally a freedom from the patterns of experience that now bind our highest potential.

If we carry inquiry still further, another dimension of knowing may open. We recognize that even the energy to which labels are applied can be put into operation in different ways. The distinction between energy and label becomes less definite, with the label understood as a frozen energy and the energy as an active knowing patterned by conventional structures.

Working at this basic level, we may recognize that even the complex of energy and labeling that bears the identity 'I am' is only another name — a patterned dynamic put into operation by knowledge. *We are free to participate in the pattern* with new appreciation, as though enjoying the telling of a delightful story that we already know by heart.

Chapter Thirty-Five

Investigating experientially language, changes in consciousness, space, and time; knowledge in particulars; knowing capacity of the mind; stillness 'before' thoughts; ways of being; feelings as manifestations of energy; the label 'I am'.

Exchanging Feelings

Entertain a positive or negative feeling and let it intensify. Explore various ways of doing this; for example, 'adding in' images, sound, or thoughts. Contact not only the 'content' of the feeling, but also its specific qualities of sharpness, orientation, and aliveness. When the feeling is fully energized, 'exchange' it without hesitation for its opposite. If necessary, spend some time building up this new feeling. Repeat this exercise many times at different tempos. You can also apply it in daily life to transform negative feelings and emotions. Note: Personal instruction can help deepen this exercise.

Exercise Thirty-Five

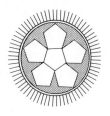

Seeing Through Light

Enfolding Embrace

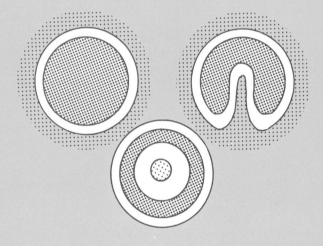

Unfolding knowing new dimension
Center recenters
Deep within
Without becomes within
Between among around
Surrounding embrace of Knowledge

MAGICAL
INTERPLAY

Inquiry and analysis bring forth energy and intelligence that enter our being and inform our actions and understanding. They open new realms for exploration, so that we can investigate ourselves, inquire into the source of mind, and become attuned to an intimate harmony that links each and every appearance.

Within free and open inquiry, intelligence sets resolutely to work. Questioning with no holding back, we see through time, encompassing past, present, and future in our gaze. We see the way of creation of all that we know to be. Recognizing words, presuppositions, perceptions, energy, and emotions as self-generated constructs, we accept full responsibility for our circumstances, embracing our life in a house of mirrors.

Free and open inquiry allows a deep appreciation for the magical interplay among the phenomena of the known world — the points of intersection in time and space alike. Seen with such appreciation, each single object we look at, each topic we consider, can unfold in patterns and rhythms that quickly exceed the power of the conventional mind to comprehend or to describe. Profound questions radiate from the simplest of facts, like the invisible waves of light that course through the vastness of space.

In calling *our own being into question*, free and open inquiry requires us to acknowledge that we do not have 'answers' for the most fundamental questions. This does not mean that we must call inquiry to a halt, nor does it suggest that we must look elsewhere for a knowledge that is presently inaccessible. Instead, inquiry invites knowledge to speak in disclosing the limitations on our knowledge. It investigates the prospect that 'knowingness' can appear *within what we do not know*.

Integrating Inquiry

Conventional understanding accepts existence as central, framing knowledge in terms of 'what is' and 'what is not'. But an open questioning starts from no fixed basis. It looks beyond the dichotomy of existence and non-existence to focus on the *knowing activity* through which 'existence' and 'non-existence' jointly emerge, together with fundamental dichotomies such as 'subject' and 'object', 'observer' and 'observed'. Turning from 'what' we know, it asks 'how' we know.

If this question were asked in conventional terms, the answer would start with the structures of knowledge already in operation and proceed to analyze them in terms of reasons, logic, and the patterns of cause and effect. Asking "Why?" or "What is true" in the standard way calls for just such an answer: an 'explanation' based on stories or theories that express an underlying 'logos' or narrative. The outcome of such inquiry will reflect the limits implicit in the structures established through positions, oppositions, and presuppositions.

Rather than following along in this pattern, we can turn to a more accommodating form of inquiry, asking "How does it come to be?" Seeing 'how' form is created and 'how' patterns emerge, 'how' do we react? These are the issues that determine 'how' knowledge unfolds.

From the perspective of the 'bystander', analysis of the structures of understanding may seem a purely theoretical and unrewarding pursuit. But listening to the self when it tells us to abandon a fruitless and unending questioning means failing to extend our inquiry to the one who gives us counsel. It entails looking 'straight ahead': not to the side, not behind, not beneath, and not beyond. To accept as a final position "I believe this has no value" is to fail to ask a whole series of vital questions: "Who believes? What is there to believe? How is the belief transmitted? What is the process by which the believer is established?"

To take this perspective may seem like setting up an unfair game, in which the self is put in a 'no-win' situation: If 'I' refuse to accept the need for inquiry, the reply comes back that 'I' have not inquired deeply enough. But this structure also has to be questioned. Where is the winner? Where is the loser? Is this just another picture being presented by the self? If the 'I' complains of unfairness, or dismisses the value of inquiry, it is making an interpretation and taking a position. 'I' decide 'my' response to what is being presented.

If 'I' conclude that the possibilities for new ways of knowing are too remote and abstract to be meaningful, am 'I' also choosing to accept a situation 'I' prefer not to investigate too deeply? Is there a possibility of inspiration, of new vision, that 'I' am rejecting?

Self-Reflection

In order to maintain the vitality of inquiry and analysis, a certain 'self-reflective' effort is required. The mind must actively go in new directions, clearing its own path rather than simply following the well-worn trails laid out before it. Instead of just thinking, *the mind engaged in analysis thinks about thinking.* Instead of relying on the accustomed ways of knowing, the mind makes those ways of knowing the *subject* of inquiry. Observation, analysis, and inquiry join forces to reveal new potential within the known situation.

In this new alliance, familiar mental activities are implemented in new ways. Thinking 'about' thinking steps outside the conventional structure of 'knower' and 'known', for it occurs *within* thinking. In the same way, knowledge is known *in the act of knowing.* The interplay of language, ideas, observation, and integration, of mental and sensory activity, of positioning and identification, is available for knowledge *directly.* Our questions themselves provide the 'material' that sustains the process of inquiry. Analysis of the old structures frees the energy locked within those structures, allowing that energy to be fed back into analysis itself, in a process that generates its own dynamic.

When inquiry manifests this active energy, it discloses the knowledge available *within* experience. Retracing *through its own momentum* the dynamic that experience embodies, analysis allows active knowing to emerge. Working together, inquiry and analysis need no longer rely exclusively on thoughts and concepts as tools, but instead can find knowledge directly within each moment — not isolated in the knower or hidden within the known, but freely available in a way that links the mind and the surrounding world, without necessarily locating either 'mind' or 'world'.

Knowledge 'Between'

As understood by conventional knowledge, 'knowing' and 'not-knowing' alike manifest in patterns of feedback between 'subject' and 'object.' Normally these patterns reinforce what everyone accepts and understands. But when inquiry has made knowledge active and available, feedback has a more creative aspect. 'Subject' and 'object' can be seen as correlative, interdependent facets of knowledge. In this way of seeing, knowing arises *between* subject and object: There is no 'knowledge gap' to be crossed. Observation, inquiry, and analysis bring out this 'knowledge between', presenting knowing with the opportunity to bear witness to its own intrinsic nature.

When the 'object' of investigation becomes knowledge itself, observation, inquiry, and analysis inspire and clarify the nature of the one that is inquiring, allowing the 'subject' to awaken to its own being. *Knowledge questions knowledge,* so that knowledge itself serves as the source for knowing.

301

In the light of such an inquiry, knowledge is no longer the surprising byproduct of an unlikely historical development, but is *integral to being*. As such knowledge becomes accessible, layers of subtle, unimagined energies and previously unknown modes of being are revealed. The knowing carried out by a 'bystander-self' is acknowledged as an aspect of a knowledge that goes to the very heart of being.

Chapter Thirty-Six

Inquiry as disclosing 'knowingness' within not-knowing; focus on the knowing activity and on 'how' knowledge unfolds; extending questions to the 'I'; knowledge known within knowing and within experience; knowledge 'between' subject and object, integral to being.

Visualizing Feelings

Visualize as intense colors the positive, negative, or neutral feeling that accompanies each sensory experience. Sight is associated with white, hearing with green, smell with yellow, taste with red, and touch with blue. 'Feed' the energy of the feeling into color, as in Exercise 35; you can also combine that exercise with this one. With continued practice, feelings may grow fluid, no longer arising in expected ways.

Exercise Thirty-Six

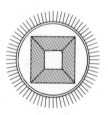

Bondage of Time

Balanced Knowing

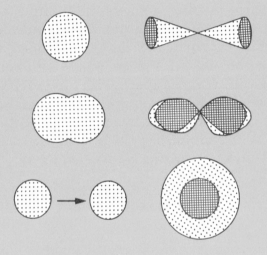

Fullness of inquiry opens
Structure of knowledge
Awakening to separation
Penetration appreciation
Embracing and embodying

KNOWLEDGE
THROUGH WONDER

Inquiry and analysis are focused by the intention with which they proceed. For example, if the purpose of questioning is satisfied by the first answer we receive, we rest at that point. This is the method we follow 'naturally' when we face a problem or a puzzle: a search for a solution, success or failure, and an end to questioning.

The answers that emerge through such questioning are predictable in advance — not necessarily in their specific content, but in their form and scope. They lead to a conventional knowledge ready to be 'assembled' into a coherent whole and 'packaged', 'distributed', and 'transmitted' as a part of collective knowing.

The knowledge generated through such an inquiry occurs within the framework of shared 'objective' reality. It relates in its particulars to specific objects or sets of circumstances, situated within a whole. The dynamic at work in this form of inquiry tends to fragment and segment what it knows. Objects and situations are dissected in terms of 'what needs to be known' — the problem at hand.

More fundamentally, the needs and concerns of the 'bystander' are placed over and against a 'world to be known', perpetuating the fundamental dichotomy and separation that make knowledge the exception in a structure where 'not-knowing' is basic. Because they proceed from such needs and concerns, questions are not free to multiply and expand, opening new dimensions through the power of the inquiry they manifest.

Inquiry can also proceed from an intention that has nothing to do with the 'needs' and 'concerns' of 'the one who questions'. *The questions 'we' ask can arise out of wonder and the love of knowledge.* When this is so, inquiry engages not only our needs and concerns, but the whole of our being. We relate to what is being questioned in a way that allows a 'knowledge between' to arise. Questions become inspiring, evoking a subtle and refined intelligence that unfolds, deepens, and expands through a momentum all its own.

Questioning Questioning

Questioning through inquiry and analysis inspired by wonder clears a path toward new forms of knowledge. It restores a sense of clarity and dispels confusion. The answers it leads to will be unexpected in nature or scope; indeed, *they may not look like answers at all.* But the new perspective that results will open dimensions previously hidden from view.

One way to evoke the inspiration that leads to such questioning is to *question the nature of questioning itself.* This can mean investigating the typical patterns of question and answer, problem and solution. It can also mean taking inquiry a step further, investigating the 'nature' of questioning *apart* from answers or from the process that leads to answers. How do we question? What is a question? Where does the capacity for questioning come from? In what way is this capacity connected to an active knowledge?

When we speak of 'inquiry' or 'investigation', it may sound as though we were trying to determine facts, or even to assign blame; when we speak of 'analysis', it may sound as though we were taking some 'thing' apart to reveal its components. If we question the 'nature' of questioning, it becomes clear that these conventional associations are misleading, and that something much more basic is under investigation. There is the polarity of 'subject' as 'questioner' and 'object' as 'what is to be questioned', together with the conventional narrative that arises when questions are motivated by 'concern'. And beneath that, there is the activity of questioning—luminous evocation of an as yet 'unknown' capacity.

Inquiry and Intimacy

The *attitudes* we adopt in carrying out our investigation shape the *attributes* we find in the world we investigate. The interaction is as intimate as the back-and-forth reflection of face and image in a mirror. Like a sculptor molding clay, the knowing 'subject' embraces through its intention the form and figure of the 'object' known.

The self interprets this intimate interplay as 'consciousness of an object'. It projects 'consciousness' and 'object' together, in a loop that circles back on itself. For the loop to operate, a subtle, intricate, and pervasive coordination and balance is required — like the coordination between mind and body needed to throw a ball or perform a dance.

In the activity of questioning, the balance between 'subject' and 'object' calls for bringing into play a certain sharpness and cutting quality. But if inquiry is to call into question the 'question,' the 'questioner,' and the 'act of questioning' itself, it must be more than simply sharp and cutting. For such an inquiry, the question must 'contain' within it the potential for transforming the relationship between 'subject' and 'object'. The move toward separating and penetrating must be 'balanced' by a move toward embracing and embodying. *The fullness of inquiry will open the structure of knowledge when its intention incorporates an appreciation that can deepen into intimacy.*

Appreciation seems to arise naturally when the subject of inquiry has direct and personal significance for our lives. Setting out to *collect* knowledge cuts off new ways of knowing in advance; shaping knowledge to make it conform to a description or a formula (including any descriptions or formulas apparently being offered here) will lead in the end to frustration. But when *wonder* guides our inquiry, we build on an appreciation that grows out of our own experience. From the very outset, we draw on a source of energy close to delight, and find that the living 'reality' of knowledge is close at hand and freely available.

Perhaps this is why philosophy has long been understood as the love of knowledge. Yet ordinary love may not be enough. When we speak of love, we imply 'lover' and 'beloved,' at once setting up distinctions and establishing separation. Philosophy as it has long been practiced in this culture starts from such separation, and blends the resultant longing with the initial impulse of wonder, until the two can no longer be distinguished. It teaches or assumes that human beings have become cut off from knowledge, and that knowledge must somehow be 'obtained' or 'recovered'. Once that structure is accepted, restraints upon knowing multiply, establishing presuppositions and structures that spread beyond the boundaries of philosophy itself to encompass every form of story, projection, commentary, and theory.

In such manifold activity, we tend to lose sight of the love of knowledge itself, or else to confuse it with the satisfaction of our longing. Appreciation and wonder slip out of view, and our questions begin to reflect a more narrow set of concerns, expressed in a widening web of positions. In the moral sphere, this might be understood as the adopting of a 'selfish' attitude, but the consequences are not only 'moral'. As positions proliferate, knowledge slips out of reach.

As a close cousin to 'need', 'longing' may be well-established and familiar, but this does not mean that it is the inevitable companion to inquiry. When inquiry is true to the love of knowledge, it offers us the choice of asking where 'longing' itself comes from, and whether there is anything beyond the interplay of 'longing' and 'satisfaction' that could bring us closer to knowledge.

As this question deepens, it brings with it others. What accounts for the lack of knowledge and the yearning that it inspires? How do 'subject' and 'object' or 'bystander' and 'world' come to inhabit two different realms of being, with a 'gap' between them that seems vast beyond bridging? Can love of knowledge give us answers to these questions?

Chapter Thirty-Seven

Inquiry based on wonder and love of knowledge; questioning questioning; attitudes shaping attributes; balancing of penetration and embracing; appreciation opening knowledge; love of knowledge as separate from longing.

Founding Receptivity

Return to the practice of Exercise 30. You can deepen this practice by listening to sound in a way that lets the vibration and the 'field' of sound flow directly into your body and mind. Try 'hearing' the sound as a visual image. How does the image relate to the source of the sound? What access do you have to the source? Does the nature of this access vary?

Exercise Thirty-Seven

Being as Light

Self History

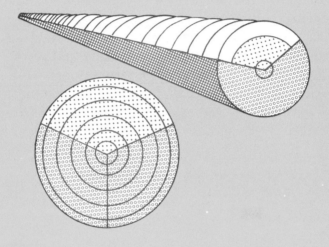

Founded in unfounded read-outs
Hidden unfolding into visible
Time emerges threefold
Moment from by moment
Moves made by Knowledge
Reading present into out of past

COMMITMENT
WITHOUT COMMITMENT

Any ordinary intention, any concern or desire—even the desire for knowledge—arises from a 'position' that the self takes up. From this 'position', love of knowledge can thus seem threatening: a call to 'give up' the positions that make the self what it is. We have seen, however, that the threat is not real. If the self's position is simply an *act of positioning*—a particular expression of the knowing activity—what is there for the self to give up? Only the positions already adopted by the 'bystander' insist that there is something 'real' in positions, and that this 'something' must be 'given up' for new knowledge to shine forth.

If we accept the possibility that 'positioning' can be an expression of 'knowingness' (without turning that acceptance into a position), the 'bystander's' concern for maintaining positions drops away. Our intention is left open and free, all-allowing and all-encompassing. *This* is the true love of knowledge—a love that turns from the concerns of the self, allowing knowledge to know without limitation.

Sustained by such a love, we could 'accept' our positionings without committing to them as 'the way we are'. Remaining 'within' the bounds of conventional knowing, we could turn aside the momentum of the known and embark on a new way of knowing.

Knowledge Within the 'Logos'

When knowledge is available directly in this way — available 'between' — the 'knowledge gap' disappears and the order and logic of the 'logos' become a source of knowledge. With no need to abandon the style of thinking, forms of language, and methods of observation that constitute our working system of cognition, we can know knowing in knowing. If the 'logos' itself is an aspect of knowing, then in penetrating *and* embracing its nature, what else is left to know?

Open to 'the logos as knowledge', we can have truly original thoughts — thoughts new not in their specific content but in the way of thinking that inspires them. We can ask in a fresh way about the right and the true, about higher goals and purposes. Not falling back on new positions, we can let the *knowledge at work within our inquiry* be the hidden topic of each and every question. If our questions are 'transparent' to resistance, not burdened by unacknowledged assumptions, they can pass without obstruction through the demarcations of the known, opening each limit and each boundary in turn.

The ways of knowing that prevent our questions from being 'transparent' are deeply rooted. Even if we learn to recognize knowledge within the 'logos', there are barriers in unexamined structures. Knowing 'all that exists' leaves 'what-is-not' unknown, while knowing 'all that it is possible to know' means not knowing the 'impossible-to-know'. As long as there are such limits and distinctions, there will be polarities that invite the taking of positions, and the love of knowledge will go unfulfilled. Moving to a different 'logos' — if such a move were possible — might carve out new forms of knowledge, but it would not penetrate to the core of this 'limit-making' way of knowing.

Intent on the *source* of knowledge, we must let our questions probe deeper. What is the source of the knowing that allows 'possible' and 'impossible' to take form as mutually interdependent constructs? Can limitations and distinctions be appreciated as *moves made by knowledge itself*?

Non-Established 'Read-Outs'

This way of inquiring leads back to the realization that the distinctions of conventional knowledge have no substantial foundation, but emerge *through an act of knowing*. All that we know seems to be interrelated and interdependent, like the infinitely complex 'read-out' of a set of founding principles or a specific way of knowing, put into effect some time 'before'. The 'read-out' is 'self-founding' and also 'self-contained': 'Knower' and 'known', 'subject' and 'object', 'self' and 'world' all arise within the 'read-out', and refer to nothing 'outside' it. Whatever the forms of knowing we develop, in the end they will trace back to the 'read-out' itself.

Yet the conclusion that the 'read-out' is all-encompassing is itself a construct of the 'read-out'. If the 'read-out' determines its own limits, what 'substance' can there be to borders or partitions? What 'final' meaning informs derivations or projections, 'from' or 'to'?

The 'read-out' claims an authority over knowledge that traces to the structure of time. A continuum is specified between the knowledge that 'has been' and 'will be', limiting knowledge in accord with what is already known. But this claim presupposes a temporal dynamic the nature of which is given by the 'read-out'. If the dependence of present on past and future on present is only an aspect of the 'read-out', then it is only the 'read-out' that sets up the 'read-out' as binding on the 'future' prospects for knowledge.

While the temporal flow that the 'read-out' establishes seems to be necessary for conventional knowledge, the knowledge that inquiry and analysis 'embody' may stand in a very different relationship to time, and to the 'read-out' itself. Perhaps this knowledge allows for 'other read-outs'. Perhaps it embodies a knowing inseparable from the 'read-out' itself. Or perhaps it points to a knowledge more 'fundamental' than 'read-outs'.

Chapter Thirty-Eight

Positions as acts of positioning, based on knowing; knowledge available within the 'logos'; limits and distinctions as moves made by knowledge; self-founding 'read-outs'; authority of past and future as given by the 'read-out'.

Embodied Energy

Focus on the ways in which tension, emotions, or more subtle 'positionings' are linked with specific aspects of embodiment: the breath, the beat of the heart, the sensation of heat or cold, etc. Experiment freely with these factors; for example, slow the breath down, or breathe more evenly or gently; generate heat in different parts of the body, or circulate heat from one part of the body to another. If tension or feeling increases, embody the intensified sensation or perception fully. As awareness deepens, you can explore subtle tactile sensations, feelings, and energy flows within the body and in relation to mind.

Exercise Thirty-Eight

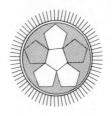

Knowing Self Transcends Being

PART FOUR

Knowing
Knowledge

Focal Points

Points open distinctions
One into two into three
Distinctions open points
Points circle into points
Encompass structures
Expanding cone of knowledge

ENCOMPASSING
OPPOSITION

While inquiry in terms of experience leads to a focus on time—back into our history and forward into goals and intentions—inquiry in terms of distinctions and characteristics leads to a focus on space, pointing to our reliance on models based on separation and the polar structure of observation.

Inquiry in terms of this 'space focus' starts from the fundamental quality of opposition within conventional knowledge. In the distinction-making that shapes the known world, true is opposed to false and good to bad; existence is opposed to non-existence and 'this particular existent' is opposed to others. Logic pursues with rigor the implications of the law of contradiction, and the polarity of self and world confirms that opposition is the single unifying principle in all knowledge.

The opposition inherent in distinction-making is not always visible on the surface. For example, in identifying a cow or a mountain, the opposition seems to be between what is defined and 'everything else'. Thus, 'cow' is recognized when it is set opposite whatever is 'not-cow'.

Though 'whatever is not-cow' is potentially infinite, interests, perceptions, and values serve to narrow its possible range.

The picture presented so far conforms to the 'world of objects' given by conventional space and time, but the situation is more complicated. Two things can be opposed to each only when they also stand in relation to each other. For example, up is the opposite of down, but an apple is the opposite of neither.

Opposites are thus in opposition because they share a common order, or appear in the same space, or operate in the same time. Each presupposes the other, making the link between the two more fundamental than the opposition. If this is so, why choose one member of the opposition over the other? In fact, such a choice may be nonsensical. We *cannot* choose life without choosing death, nor choose light without choosing dark. Indeed, when the connection is so basic, we may wonder how the opposition is ever set up to begin with.

Making Choices

From the position occupied by the self, it often makes sense to choose one side of an opposition over the other. Categories such as 'right and wrong', 'good and bad', or 'helpful and harmful' imply the validity of making choices based on values and commitment. For example, the fundamental prohibition against taking human life is based on the commitment that the self makes to existence. There seems to be something inescapable in this choice: If we choose the right not to exist, or to end the existence of another, we do so based on force and intention, which can be asserted only by someone who insists on his own existence.

The self thus knows in a way that requires always taking a side and maintaining a position. It engages in a kind of battle in which it plays the role of hero by standing for what has value, or by proving it, or by disproving what is illusory. Of course, this battle has been fought and won repeatedly by each individual, and it no longer has much significance or drama to it. But the structure of taking sides and stands is still in operation.

The interdependence of opposites, however, suggests that the stands we take are rather illusory. How can we choose existence over non-existence, when each presupposes the other both logically and 'existentially'? Again, the 'truth' that illusion is illusory is founded on the 'illusion' that the truth is true. Though we may assert one value as ultimate, it seems that even an 'ultimate' value is the outcome of another choice.

In the 'order' of separately defined 'objects' established by measurement and distance, it makes sense to give one side of an opposition preference over another: to establish 'true' or 'false', 'beautiful' or 'ugly', 'higher' or 'lower'. But these distinctions are 'self-evident' only in being based on the evidence presented to a self. They depend on the values and interests of the self that knows.

The self quite 'naturally' prefers existence to non-existence, life to death, light to dark. It makes choices, and based on these choices distinctions are made and a reality measured out. What is measured out is evaluated, and in direct consequence the decisions that set up a world take form. The picture of solid objects known by a substantial self results from the original choices made at the very outset of knowing.

Seeing Interdependence

If all choices presuppose a prior opposition, then the world that we establish through choosing is not the only world available. Not only could we choose differently: We could learn to acknowledge that no presentation presents uniquely. Dark can take equal credit for light, for without dark light cannot appear. Each bears the same value and shares in bearing this value.

If this were our understanding, the values and judgments that guide our conduct would no longer have the same significance in our lives. Objects that appeared in space would no longer have the same solidity or substance: New ways of appearing might become possible.

However, this insight into the potential for a new understanding is subject to the same structure of opposition that it attempts to encompass. To commit ourselves to attaining such a new understanding means taking a side and making a choice — setting up a particular mode of being that excludes other modes of being.

Investigation into the structure of opposition thus leads back to the limits of the old ways of knowing. The mind labels and conceptualizes, feeds back and identifies. To identify 'another' possibility leaves this fundamental structure or 'read-out' undisturbed.

We do not need to stop at this point. Instead, we can ask how the mind makes its choices and distinctions.

Without thinking, we refer to 'the mind' as though it were a specific entity, but it seems more accurate to view the mind as a process or activity: an ongoing 'minding'. Is this view consistent with the view that mind 'establishes' the structure of opposition?

Freely Active Minding

The mind responds to a situation by making a choice in favor of one alternative. Suppose that the next time 'minding' led to a choice in favor of the other alternative. Since it is 'minding' itself that distinguishes between the two alternatives, how could we know for certain that a different choice had been made? Only if 'minding' remained relatively constant in its operation from one moment to the next could there be a basis for the fixed judgments and distinctions that ground our conventional knowledge. But how can we 'know' that 'minding' is 'the same' from moment to moment?

Perhaps it seems too improbable to take seriously the possibility that the mind could really change. The mind is closely linked to the identity of the self over time, which we understand as the most fundamental structure of all. Any possibility that calls that fundamental identity 'into question' seems 'out of the question'. Yet this ready rejection is itself an activity of the mind, which can again be questioned. How does the act of rejecting arise? How does the mind fabricate its positions — with what motive and guided by what assumptions?

If this inquiry leaves us feeling there is something we have not yet understood, this sense of 'something missing' is again the outcome of a set of beliefs and labels that can be investigated. What is this 'something', and what kind of substance does it have?

Looking at the structures of mind, we find particular forms of consciousness in operation. There is the consciousness associated with having a problem, with developing solutions, with making effort, with the frustration of not succeeding, with adopting a discipline. All are interrelated. Moving from one to the other and back, we move in small circles that lead nowhere. Our knowledge is limited from the outset, and there is no way out.

Even in the midst of such repetition, the availability of inquiry *as a knowing activity* suggests that knowledge itself could take on a new dimension. Inquiry can acknowledge that the old patterns will proliferate, determining who we are and what we can be. But this very pattern is another topic for inquiry. The belief that there are only beliefs is just another belief.

Chapter Thirty-Nine

Opposition as the basis for distinction-making; opposites as connected; illusory nature of the self's choices; mind as an activity; absence of a founding entity; 'only beliefs' as a belief.

Sameness in Difference

Investigate the shared basis that links the sense of disagreement or conflict observed in Exercise 6. Look for ways to dissolve the conflict into this shared aspect, experimenting repeatedly until you can do this lightly and with a quiet ease. This practice can be applied to conflicts in daily life, whether internal or external.

Exercise Thirty-Nine

Understanding Through Knowledge

Time and Space Extraction

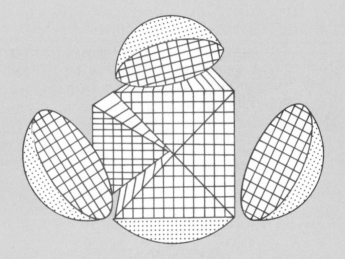

Space form weaving time
Measuring the shape of matter
Charting Knowledge
Open inner dimensions
Penetrating perspectives into Space

NOTHING TO KNOW

Inquiry has suggested that the theories and constructs we rely on to make sense of the workings of mind, together with the axioms on which they are founded, rest on an enigma. The discursive universe of temporal observation and of historical conditioning, proliferating since time beyond memory, seems to be based on distinctions that cannot be founded in anything beyond themselves. We have been programmed by previous thoughts, by language, and by the momentum of past conditioning. The program generates itself, empty of substance; the wheel revolves with no one to turn it, establishing subject and object alike. We rely in each moment only on previous moments.

This recognition of 'no-basis' is the obverse of the momentum generated by the narrative flow, and of its psychological counterpart: the commitment that individuals make to the stories they tell. *Momentum is essential for sustaining what has no substance.* The 'content' of the narrator's stories is like the illusory ring of fire created when a juggler whirls a lighted torch.

Indeed, even the sense of motion, embodied in the flow of time, may be the expression of a 'read-out' that is founded only by itself.

'Stepping Back' Through Negation

The step back that first discloses this essential 'non-foundedness' or 'emptiness' of everyday constructs and stories is a vital step toward allowing new knowledge. The process is similar to the stepping back that some-times comes with age and experience, as individuals begin to realize (perhaps with a sense of resignation) that the outcomes of the 'games' they have been playing all their lives are not as important as they once thought. Seeing how stories are put together undermines our own commitment to them, creating space for new kinds of thoughts and concerns to emerge.

We have seen that we choose existence. But how do we make this choice — where does the capacity to choose originate? Based on the analysis given above, choice is based on the power to negate. Each object of temporal knowledge takes shape as the negation of all other objects; nothing is uniquely itself, but acquires its quali-ties only through not being everything else. The attri-butes we take as defining an entity themselves emerge through the negation of what they are not.

Without negation, there could be no separating out, no 'getting hold of' any entity or idea in the first place. The cutting quality of the 'not' is fundamental to all logic, to each distinction and judgment. Paradoxically, the existent world is known through negation and could not 'exist' without it.

The known world, inclusive of its knower, could be thought of as a fabric woven long ago, with negation serving as loom and thread, and as the activity of weaving itself. Conventionally, we direct our attention to the woven patterns — never to the threads themselves: to the structures and not to their construction. Our knowledge is a knowledge of the differences and distinctions established through the knowing activity of negation. What can it say about that activity itself?

Conventional knowledge insists on the priority of what is over what is not. 'What is' provides a foundation and support; 'what is not' leads 'nowhere'. From this perspective, negation's 'not' seems 'good for nothing'. But what exactly this might mean seems difficult to say, for we are not accustomed to looking closely at this 'nothing'. What seems good for 'nothing' might also be good for knowledge.

Into Nothing

What is the 'nothing' that negation knows? When we try to investigate this unknown 'nothing', we quickly find ourselves in difficulty. We might start with the 'not' of our 'not-knowing'. Does it have any substance? If 'not' is the opposite of 'yes', then 'yes' is also the opposite of the 'not'. But if all this tells us is that 'yes' is 'not not', have we gotten any closer to understanding the 'not'?

Gaining knowledge of an unknown normally means referring it to a known in relation to which it stands, so that it can be positioned and defined within a 'logos', and thus 'recognized' in ever more refined ways. In the case of the 'nothing' opposed to 'something', however, there exist no 'knowns' to which the 'knower' can refer it. 'Nothing' stands in an inseparable relation to its polar opposite, but this relationship — unless it is understood as turning 'nothing' as such into a special case of 'something' — is one of mutual exclusion. 'Something' gives no point of contact with 'nothing', and no other point of contact exists. Without such a reference point, how can 'nothing' present itself to be known?

Perhaps the opposition of 'nothing' and 'something' is misleading; perhaps the true opposite of 'nothing' is 'everything'. But this move opposes 'nothing' to existence, and we have seen already that equating nothing with 'non-existence' does not serve to make 'nothing' knowable. Knowledge seems incapable of experiencing or even imagining a non-existent without somehow endowing it with a specific mode of existing: namely, the non-existing mode. The field of conventional knowledge does not allow for non-existence in a way that is truly 'non-existent'; there is no room to accommodate it.

The difficulty seems to be that existence and the knowable are inextricably linked, so that 'nothing' is in principle unknowable. Why should this be? To suggest that it would violate the rules of logic to be able to know 'nothing' is less an answer than a restatement of the question. There might be other systems of logic that could operate in different realms, just as there are geometries that could apply in different universes. The answer must have more to do with the nature of this world, governed by its specific 'logos'.

On this level, a central element of the prevailing 'logos' is the existence of a knower as the precondition or founding structure to which all knowing is referred. This seems to be why only what exists can be known. The human mind and what exists are children of the same parents; non-existence, in comparison, is fundamentally alien. Whatever the knower knows *as* 'nothing' is not 'nothing'. An existent knower could no more know what does not exist than a non-existent knower could know what does exist.

This is only the first stage of a difficulty that goes far deeper. The 'nothing' that is opposed to 'something' can be thought of as a common-sense 'nothing'; a 'nothing' that the self, with its existence-orientation, can feel comfortable with. But whatever we are referring to when we speak of *this* nothing, it seems that it 'is not' the 'nothing' of negation, for several reasons:

☆ The nothing that is opposed to something is the nothing of non-existence, and as such it is inseparable from existence: The two are interdependent.

☆ As one pole of a polar opposition, the common-sense 'nothing' presupposes the 'not' of negation, which must be 'prior' to all distinctions (since distinctions appear to depend on negation).

☆ In being present to the mind, the 'not' of non-existence has its own form of existing; namely, as a mental object. The distinction between 'mentally existent' and 'physically existent' has its own significance, but in this context it should not be dispositive, for even physically existent objects must ultimately manifest mentally (or generate consequences that do); otherwise they will not affect our known world.

☆ In the opposition between something and nothing, the 'something' depends on the 'nothing' to establish its own identity. But what establishes something else must itself be 'something'.

It seems that 'nothing' — even the relatively 'cozy' nothing of non-existence — cannot be established; the mind bound to existence cannot comprehend it. If so, the more fundamental 'nothing' of negation, which underlies all the distinctions of conventional knowledge, will be doubly unknowable.

Chapter Forty

'No-basis' and momentum; stepping back from the chosen into the 'founding' negation; no reference for knowing nothing; 'logos' as bound to existence; a doubly unknowable 'nothing'.

Space of Mind

Once you are familiar with the process of dissolving conflict explored in Exercise 39, follow the sense of agreement or sameness into the 'space' of mind. Stay in this open, 'space-like' realm 'prior' to the 'field' of agreement.

Exercise Forty

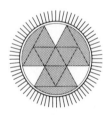

Noetic Being

Formal Negation

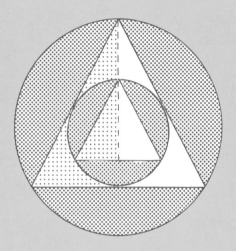

Distinctions establish
Points define
Negation allows
Arena of knowing
Patterns take shape
Endless discourse
Boundless boundaries

KNOWLEDGE
WITHIN NEGATION

Although the view that 'nothing' and 'negation' cannot be 'known' seems opposed to the view that negation underlies all knowing, there is no real conflict. Even if negation cannot *be known*, this does not mean that negation itself cannot *know*.

Such a 'knowing', however, would have to differ from the conventional knowing for which negation remains an unknown. While distinctions are the 'substance' of ordinary knowledge, negation itself makes no distinctions, negating all and everything. But this does not bar negation from knowing. 'Knowing' and 'not-knowing' are themselves a polarity, and since negation is prior to both of them — even in some sense linking them — negation cannot be considered as divorced from knowledge. Perhaps negation's 'knowing no distinctions' is a deeper knowing, available when we 'see through' the distinction between knowledge and lack of knowledge.

A negation more fundamental than either knowing or not knowing maintains no position; it no longer sets up 'here' and 'now', no longer categorizes or judges.

Negation allows and accommodates: It embraces everything, for everything is equally subject to negation. There is nothing to suppress and nothing to uphold, nothing untouchable or unreachable. Free of positions, the knowing faculty emerges within negation like a photographer who steps into the scene displayed before the lens of his camera.

The knowledge owned by a self projects content in an endless variety of shapes and forms. It sees negation as 'establishing' the opposite of each specified entity by negating the entity itself. But analysis at this level does not address negation directly. When attention shifts to the 'not' active within negation, the content of experience is seen as being like images projected on a screen. Each projection is recognized as a play of light, so that the light itself becomes accessible. The well-charted world of the 'logos' falls away; the old conventions no longer operate. The 'not' that negates opens into vastness.

Focus on Negation

A focus on negation as a knowing activity lets us look directly at knowledge, seeing 'through' known patterns and constructs to the creative power inherent in knowing. In the no-distinctions of the 'not', nothing finite any longer plays a role. Nothing is pre-established or presupposed; nor is the knowable opposed by the unknowable. We are free to develop an independent intelligence.

We might compare the inquiry that grows from negation to the activity of a composer. When the sounds of a hundred familiar melodies play themselves out in the composer's mind, creativity is stifled. Only through a return to the silence from which all sound emerges can music of power and beauty well forth. Negation can serve as a source of knowledge in this same way — allowing a return to 'silence'.

Yet the analogy has its limits. The focus on negation is not just an invitation to create a new set of patterns, distinctions, and definitions. We have another 'choice': to look at the activity of structuring beneath all structures, inquiring in a way that may eventually lead beyond the realm of 'choice' and 'no-choice'. Starting with negation, we can observe how knowledge arises, how the mind works, and how perceptions are built up. Not caught up in forms and patterns, we can focus our inquiry and develop our intelligence. We can be true philosophers — lovers of knowledge itself.

A Hidden Dimension

In the 'realm' of negation, before distinctions and structures, there is no beginning, no middle, no end. But this 'before' is not prior in any temporal sense. Distinctions and structures still present themselves; it is only the claim to substantive existence that is 'not-accepted'.

Conventional knowledge, which 'positions' itself on the side of existence, may find such 'not-accepting' threatening. But the conventional 'positioning' is also only a 'presentation,' and whatever responses it generates are 'presentations' also. With everything 'of substance' swept away, new potentiality surfaces, bringing new knowledge with it.

The 'nothing' that might be said to emerge from negation is not a secret form of 'something'. It does not render existence hollow, nor does it call forth witnesses to establish a new realm. Instead, it restores to appearance the hidden dimension of being 'not-established'.

Assigning negation such a vital role in the presentations of appearance might seem to reduce 'reality' to an aspect of mental activity. But 'mentalism' does not cut deep enough, for it continues to accept the validity of a suspect distinction-making. In a hypothetical 'founding act' of 'knowing', 'knower' is only the negation of 'known', and 'knowing' the negation of 'not-knowing'. There is no privileged position or entity prior to the 'not'; there is only an interdependent whole; or rather, there is not even that. Negation undermines all such distinctions, just as it dismantles all logic and narrative.

A focus on negation can reveal as such the limits within which we live. Appearance can fully appear, without anything being added or subtracted, reduced or interpreted away. In one sense, this results in no 'change' whatsoever, but in terms of conventional distinctions, the change is profound. Creative awareness comes to the fore, generating strength, confidence, and freedom. Transformation becomes an immediate reality instead of a distant goal, and a new way of being opens.

Chapter Forty-One

Negation as prior to knowing and not-knowing; embracing without positions; 'non-acceptance' of appearance; restoring a hidden dimension; inadequacy of mentalism; 'no-change transformation'.

Field of Feeling

Earlier exercises that dealt with feelings continued to accept a subtle positioning based on the
'feeling' to be 'exchanged' or otherwise manipu-
lated. To explore this positioning, allow all the
specific 'qualities' of the feeling to remain as
they are while reversing the 'tone' of the feeling.
For example, instead of 'exchanging' confusion
for confidence, 'stay' confused while 'generating' the characteristic tonal indicators of confidence. This practice contacts the 'field' within
which feeling arises and allows a 'joy' deeper
than 'feelings' to emerge.

Exercise Forty-One

Pattern of Time

Unfolding Zero

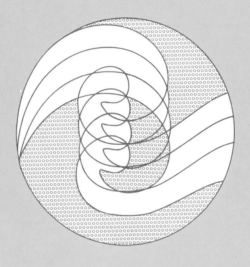

Symbol for negation within knowledge
For knowledge within negation
Openness of space rolling momentum of time
Condensed to non-dimensional point
Expanded beyond all limitation
Gateway to positive and negative
Arithmetic operator
Active engagement hidden dimension
Resolving back to zero

'EMPTINESS'
OF EMPTINESS

Despite all warnings and disclaimers, conventional knowledge interprets the knowing within negation in a way that reaffirms existence. One such interpretation holds that conventional substances and events are 'empty' of attributes or qualities. This proposition does not establish 'empty' as different from 'nothing' (for then it would be 'something'); instead, it gives a linguistically acceptable way of putting the 'nothing' of negation into relationship with specific 'entities'.

To describe something as 'empty' affirms the 'operation' of an abstract quality to which we give the name 'emptiness'. This affirmation makes clear that 'empty' cannot be considered a 'concrete' attribute of existent 'things', but it also suggests that 'empty' is 'empty' *through* 'emptiness'. Reality is understood as 'empty' of substance in a way that turns 'emptiness' (or its equivalent, 'nothingness') into something 'real', or perhaps even into 'the one true reality'. In that case, however, we have lost sight of the knowing within negation, in which nothing whatsoever is 'established' as real.

'Empty' and 'Ness'

When we focus on this difficulty, we find ourselves looking at the 'ness' of emptiness. 'Ness' seems to operate grammatically to affirm the 'reality' of the 'quality' to which it is applied. Thus, 'heaviness' gives the attribute 'heavy' (together with the attribute 'light') 'significance'. By this logic, adding 'ness' to 'empty' has the paradoxical effect of *negating* the significance of 'empty' by asserting that 'emptiness' *is*.

'Ness' as such might not appear to entail such an assertion. Joined to specific attributes, 'ness' establishes abstract entities. However, the 'ness' can in turn be abstracted from those entities, and this abstract 'ness' could in principle be referred back to the knowing within negation. That is, the 'ness' could be understood as 'empty'—*if*, that is, we can find a way to present *this* 'empty' in a way that does not make it dependent on a 'ness' that would 'falsify' negation.

This analysis makes the 'ness' of 'emptiness' unique. Understood as a way of naming the quality specific to what is known in negation, 'emptiness' stands in relation to nothing else; paradoxically, its 'ness' could thus be considered 'substantial' in a way that other forms of 'ness' are not. This unique 'ness'—the 'ness' of 'ness'—is not itself empty; even if it were, the 'ness' of *this* 'emptiness' would quickly lead us into infinite regress.

Perhaps it seems that we are focusing too much attention on a trick of language. But what is at stake in the 'ness-ness' is more than a linguistic difficulty: It is a pointer to the working of the mind, which stays bound to existence. In somewhat the same way that a zero drawn on paper is not zero, the 'emptiness' that is spoken of or thought about is not emptiness. To speak of 'emptiness' is 'empty talk'.

The tendency toward assertion expressed in 'ness-ness' makes reference to the knowledge within negation extremely difficult. Once there is the 'quality' of 'being empty', there is something that underlies or sustains that quality. This presupposed 'something' commits us to a position, and so to the logic of the 'logos', with its structures of opposition. Having applied a label, we accept the being of what has been labeled: We regard the construct as established and try to capture it within the conventional framework of positioning and polarity.

Ontologically, this sequence imposes a kind of eternalism, for there is always already something that *is* (even if that 'something' is labeled 'nothing'). Epistemologically, it means there will remain an unknown 'beneath' each act of knowing. And 'existentially', it binds and confines our potential, so that our freedom is cut off. Like a black hole in space, the unknown affirmed in the 'ness-ness' sucks away the energy that would otherwise be available.

Speech and Pointers

Because affirmation is an aspect of all speech and of all thought, the 'ness' of emptiness seems inescapable. Speech depends on designation, and designation depends on qualities. What is described or identified is based on something other than itself, and this 'something' is established as 'ness'. We may try to refine our speech and thought with the greatest of care, experimenting with alternative formulations, but because we are confronting a fundamental aspect of the mind that knows, no way out seems possible. For example, to deny that this is so establishes the 'ness' of the denial, or 'not-ness'.

As a way out of this impasse, we might try to refine our understanding of designation. For example, we could replace talk of 'nothingness' with talk of 'no-thingness'. In this way we would assign the 'ness' to the realm of existence and point by contrast to a non-implicative realm designated by the 'no'. But while this attempt may be valuable symbolically, analysis shows that the activity of designation and the implicit structure of opposition are still at work within the 'no', committing us on a subtle level to affirmation.

Another possibility is to interpret 'emptiness' or related terms as symbols: not meaningful in themselves but only as pointers. A good example is 'zero', understood as a symbol of 'what is not there'. Symbols take us beyond a first-level of meaning, in which the specifying of meaning *affirms the existence* of what is specified. A meaning that is only 'symbolic' is not directly specified, and so leaves open the question of existence instead of affirming it. Symbols thus can play a vital role in disclosing knowledge, allowing for new possibilities to which the patterns of the known, including the 'existence pattern', do not apply.

Still, the seeming success of the move to the symbolic level in allowing us to sidestep assertion is somewhat illusory. In the realm of first-level meanings, the symbol must have meaning *as a pointer*. If the zero-point points nowhere, it is meaningless. We might just as well say nothing, or say "Boo!"

It may be tempting to accept this consequence, for if what we say is meaningless, it entails no assertion. But 'meaningless' itself is not meaningless. It returns us to the conventional 'nothing' of non-existence — a hollow, dead vacuum 'between' 'meaningful entities'. And even if this somehow seemed helpful, how much progress would we have made? Since the 'meaningless' relies on 'meaninglessness', we seem to have returned once more to the 'ness', and thus to the 'ness' of 'ness'.

Closing Off Freedom

Our inquiry would appear to be on the verge of falling into word games. If 'zero' and 'empty' have any meaning, they are not empty; if they do not have meaning, why talk about them at all? We may have succeeded in forcing our analysis up to the level of meta-language, but now what further move remains open?

If we think of this difficulty as 'only' word games, we ignore the role of these constructs in shaping our knowing. Language and thought, words and constructs, are the environment of our being. They fence us in like horses herded into a corral. The 'ness' of 'ness' and the 'meaninglessness' of what departs from the 'ness' are central to our knowing. They give us whatever understanding we have of our existence and of the known world.

No matter how we 'understand' emptiness — as a verbal construct, a form of consciousness, a special mode of being or experience, or any other way — such understanding will not take us beyond the world built up by the mind out of the juxtaposition of presuppositions. Everything fits into a 'read-out' in which all manifestations refer simply to other manifestations.

Whatever move we make toward emptiness, we remain caught in the web of 'what is' — like someone filled with pride at his own humility. Designating emptiness as 'unknowable' simply makes it into a new existent, toward which the mind adopts the special relationship implied in 'unknowability'. Trying to 'cheat' by saying that 'emptiness' is 'meaningless' does not appear to help. We seem to be playing a game of such sophistication that all possible moves, including all possible ways of cheating, are themselves part of the game. The knowledge within negation remains out of reach; instead, we are confined to the 'well-known' knowledge that limits itself to discovering and describing 'what is'.

Chapter Forty-Two

'Empty' as based on 'emptiness'; 'ness' as substantial; the special 'ness' of 'emptiness'; assertion through 'ness-ness'; 'ness' as bound to language; symbols meaningful as pointers; the seeming inescapability of assertion.

'Ness' of 'Ness'

Observe without judgment the subtle levels of attachment or positioning that operate within feelings, noted in Exercise 41. By allowing this positioning to be present as part of the feeling, you can touch in a preliminary way the 'ness' of 'ness', which can be present without 'being' 'ness'. The 'joy' mentioned in Exercise 41 may manifest in various ways: as love, compassion, peace, a sense of well-being, or a refined and radiant energy. The present is the intimacy of that energy, a 'being-in' that is not confined by the specific manifestation of the 'field'.

Exercise Forty-Two

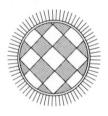

Textures of Space

Within Structure

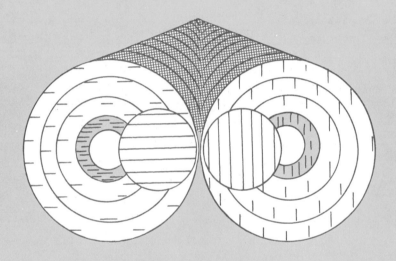

Feelings positive or negative
Feed back into experience
Stimulating more of same
Establishing self-sustaining
Patterns of embodiment
Subject to transformation
Revealing linkage

PROTECTING
AGAINST LOSS

The presence of the 'ness' in all knowing is an indication that the mind that knows is 'caught up' in the content of what it knows. Conventional consciousness operates by affirming and judging within a 'conceptual' framework, an established order that sustains each act of knowing. With knowledge bound to this framework, there will always be a 'ness' that remains unknown.

The same 'established' structure will continue to operate even when the content of what is known is presented as 'something beyond all frameworks'. As a *specified* 'something', 'something beyond' can only be pointed at within a pre-established framework. Though it may be specified that words and thoughts cannot specify this 'something beyond', specification and establishing still operate — as though language were being continued in another mode.

This mental activity establishes 'ness-ness' at the most subtle level. If we say there is nothing, it is active in the 'there is'; if we simply say, "Nothing!" it is active in pointing to an absence. Our only choice seems to be truly to 'say nothing'. But 'saying nothing' does not lead to knowledge; instead, it leaves intact old patterns. Once we accept 'ness-ness' as the 'last word', new knowledge cannot become available. We may argue about the nature of 'ness-ness' or give ourselves over to our imaginations of a world in which 'ness' has no 'ness' — all the while knowledge moves in the same track as before. There is no potential for knowledge to fulfill its nature.

Analysis Against Knowledge

The conclusion that knowledge is only word games and mental projections does not serve to increase understanding. Instead of inviting openness, it makes the scope of knowledge smaller and smaller, ultimately reducing it to the meaningless void of a conventionally understood 'empty'.

Analysis can take such a turn only when the scope of knowledge is misunderstood from the outset. This will happen when knowledge as an active engagement of human being is replaced by knowledge as conceptual structures and models. Then the 'ness' is made into an unknowable abstraction, and the significance of knowledge for human being is lost. If a presupposition is negated, this negation, instead of being understood as an expression of knowledge, is defined as another proposition that in turn must be negated, and so on. Knowledge is dissipated in endless rounds of self-cancelling verbal negations — turned into a pointing that is pointless. Yet even on this reduced level, where knowledge is defined as the destruction of knowledge, the basic structure of 'a-mental-activity-that-establishes' still operates. When analysis is made to demonstrate again and again that the 'ness' of the 'emptiness' that 'establishes' the empty is itself empty, it supports a position that establishes a conclusion. Maintaining silence does not free us from the cycle: It is only the concluding conclusion.

It may seem that analysis is responsible for this impasse, having reduced the knowable to intrinsically meaningless projections of mental activity. In this view, however, something vital may be left out of consideration. Perhaps in focusing on conventional knowledge as *conventional*, we forget that conventional knowledge is also *knowledge*.

Pride of Intellect

Whenever knowledge moves beyond the realm of the conventional, through analysis or otherwise, there is the risk that the intellect will take hold of it to further the purposes of the self. Labeling what has been learned, it will apply or invent the categories it considers adequate to contain the newly mastered content. The old knowledge can then safely be shown to be inadequate or inconsistent, or its limits can be confirmed, for a new position has been adopted.

When the intellect acts to turn knowledge into a newly 'established' understanding, the opportunity to deepen and extend into new dimensions the range of knowledge as a whole is lost. Instead of celebrating our freedom, such understanding specifies our impotence by affirming in advance what can be known. It is as though knowledge, our closest ally, had made its way into our jail cell to help us escape, only to find that we had gone over to the side of our captors. At a word from us, knowledge is seized and bound; soon it will be cast away into the deepest dungeon, powerless to help us or to benefit anyone else.

In seizing knowledge for the purposes of the self, the intellect may 'reduce' the newly known, interpreting it as 'nothing but' the old knowledge in new terms. Or it may reverse the argument, claiming that in light of the new knowledge, the old knowledge can now be understood as 'nothing but' the outcome of a particular position. In either case, knowledge is used to uphold the validity of a particular view of what is real, as seen by a particular knowing subject.

Reducing knowledge in this way reduces our own being as well. With knowledge restricted to the activity of a knowing subject, intelligence is limited to acts of repetition and affirmation. The resulting assertions about 'the real' may support our position as the narrator and meaning-giver, but they also limit our freedom and lessen our potential. Proud of what we know, we assign meanings and labels; proud of who we are, we confine ourselves to being something less than we could be.

Chapter Forty-Three

'Ness' as in operation at the most subtle level; 'knowledge as meaningless' the outcome of conceptual views; intellect as seizing knowledge to serve the purposes of the self.

Essence of Thought

Exercise 9, Expanding and Contracting Thought, posits an unaffected 'essence' for each thought. Investigate to see whether you can contact such an 'invariant' aspect within thoughts. How is it related to the 'gravitational' force that draws the mind from one thought to the next (see Exercise 8)? Can this 'invariant' aspect of the thought itself be expanded or contracted? Would this transformation occur in another dimension 'at right angles' to the usual one?

Exercise Forty-Three

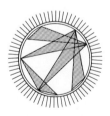

Dimensions of Knowledge

Perpetuating Polarity

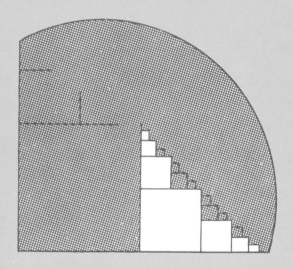

Repeating rule of division
Fracturing knowledge
Solidifying split
Elaborating frame within frame
Boundless activity of
Original undivided knowing

ASSERTION
OF THE SUBJECT

As long as knowledge is understood to result from a subject knowing, 'ness-ness' seems the inescapable consequence. The distinctions between 'knowing subject' and 'known object' or 'self' and 'world' establish the polarity of existence and non-existence that sustains the 'ness' of 'ness'. A structure is set up that at once falls away from the knowing within negation.

The 'ness' of 'emptiness' is thus also the 'ness' of our being — the apparently indisputable 'I-ness'. As long as we are who we are and know as we do, the 'ness' sets the limits of knowledge based on the structure of what is.

The continuing role of 'I-ness' can undermine active knowing by suggesting that the 'I' has *seen* the corral that encloses us, and that this seeing is exempt from the limits of the corral. We may convince ourselves that a profound new way of knowledge has opened, while the 'ness' of 'I-ness' continues in action, subject only to more complication. Now there is the corral, the self with its concerns inside the corral, and the self that sees the corral. How do the two selves relate to one another? How do 'our' concerns relate to 'our' seeing? Can we offer answers to these questions that do not just feed back more words? Have we found a way out of the 'read-out' structure, or have we just succeeded in modifying or perhaps replacing the 'read-out'?

Instead of posing such questions the self tends to interpret the burst of energy or joy that comes with insight as the witness to the birth of a new knowledge. The sense of discovery may extend to the 'I' itself, now understood as transcendental. The conclusion forms that knowledge has reached its goal, so that inquiry can at last come to an end.

Inquiry itself, however, points to a different understanding. 'I-ness' appears as an 'asserted fundamental' — a stopping place for knowledge, and thus a sign that a limitation on knowledge is in operation. The self may claim to have attained a knowing too subtle and too secret to be named or communicated. But this secret is also a 'ness' — the expression in new form of 'I-ness', which remains the biggest secret of all.

Investigating 'I-ness'

The commitment of the 'I' to existence limits knowledge from the outset. Even if knowledge of a different order did become available, it would be unrelated to the 'ness' of the 'I': 'Empty' of the structures of the self and its world, it would have no bearing on our concerns. In that case, why make any effort to 'obtain' it?

We can respond instead with a question that goes to a more basic level: What is the heart of 'I-ness'? Suppose that 'I' feel hungry, and that 'I' then respond to that feeling. If these are two separate moments, there must be a third element that links them. We are already familiar with several attendant difficulties: How can the third element communicate with the two others? Why does the third, connecting element care about the other two — what relationship operates among them that makes such caring appropriate? How does the third element initiate action — or is this the work of a fourth element, which must be linked to the others in turn?

The interconnection among such 'I-elements' traces experientially to the self's sense of ownership, continuity, and witness. These roles are basic to 'I-ness', yet we have no direct knowledge of how they operate. Apart from explanations that analyze possible physiological bases for connectedness, the links among the various aspects of the 'I' that together make up 'I-ness' remain a mystery. As with 'ness-ness', 'I-ness' is inaccessible to conventional knowledge.

In fact, this lack of knowledge is critical to the 'ness' of 'I-ness': *If the 'I' could be known, it could not be the 'I'*. As with anything put forward as fundamental, a position is effective as a position only if it cannot be further analyzed. Precisely because we rely on the 'ness' of 'I-ness', we *insist* that it remain unknown. The 'read-out' that guides us is based on this unknown and unknowable structure.

There is a way to challenge the 'unknown I-ness'. If we ask only, "What is this?" we assure that 'ness-ness' will continue to be active, for we are establishing the self in its positions and postures. But if we ask, "How have

'I' seen 'this' arise?" we respond directly to the challenge of 'ness-ness' and 'I-ness'. Instead of circling within the limits of the 'read-out', we invite an intelligence not bound by the 'read-out'. If 'I-ness' or 'ness-ness' confronts us with 'the incomprehensible' or 'the unknowable', we can simply continue with our questioning, asking how such concepts as 'incomprehensible' and 'unknowable' are established. There will be no boundaries to close knowledge off.

A powerful strand in modern thought suggests that knowledge is necessarily limited, but this way of understanding is based on a particular view of knowledge. Though it may purport to call existence and the 'I' into question, it accepts a more subtle 'I-ness'. We need to ask where 'I-ness' comes from. If the 'I' results from a 'knowing' that sees and projects, it forms a part of the 'read-out'. How can it possibly bind us?

Chapter Forty-Four

Insistence on 'I' as basis for restricted knowledge; 'I-ness' as necessarily unknowable; penetrating 'I-ness' by an inquiry into arising.

Accumulating Feelings

Practice 'accumulating' positive feelings as they come up, and then 'pour' this accumulated reservoir of feeling into neutral or negative feelings when they arise. This practice has a direct healing effect, counteracting stress, releasing and opening up the entanglements of negativity. It can be deepened through personal instruction.

Exercise Forty-Four

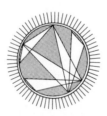

Image of Knowledge

From To

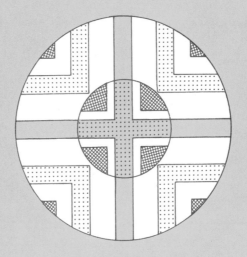

Molding space into form
Zero taking shape
Interpenetrating all
Multiple read-outs yield
Shape quality form
Space remains
Space within space

KNOWLEDGE
PERVADING BEING

D espite the momentum toward positions and not-knowing, the dynamic of an active 'knowingness' can bring light to the darkness of the 'ness'. Whatever points to a specific 'reality' or affirms the 'ness' of 'I-ness' can itself be subjected to analysis. Starting with histori-cal conditioning and the sense of an 'underlying reality' independent of knowledge, we can see how description, intention, and narrative establish our world. When this analysis enables us to appreciate the central role of interpretation, we can look more closely at *how* we interpret and at *the one that offers interpretations*, until the 'read-out' disclosed by interpretation reveals itself as the feedback of an ongoing creative knowing.

When inquiry proceeds in this way, it stays true to knowledge, putting no positions or interpretations into effect. The focus on interpretation cuts through the initial belief in the 'ness'; the focus on the 'read-out' as ongoing feedback cuts through the more subtle belief in the 'ness' of interpretations. Knowledge will be free from the known and unknown alike, and from the real and unreal as well. 'Subjective' and 'objective' will present themselves as interwoven, leaving no basis for either mentalism or materialism.

Through Negation to Knowledge

In conducting such an inquiry, we return to negation as a way of knowing prior to all positions and supporting conclusions. At the outset it may seem that negation depends on the *existence of something to be negated*, but what is negated is itself only the negation of everything else. Each 'ness' negates every other 'ness', so that nothing substantial is established.

As for the 'ness-ness' of 'I-ness' and 'emptiness', which seems more 'fundamental' than the interdependent 'nesses' of conventional entities, it is just this 'ness-ness' that negation could be said to negate. However, negation works 'within' the 'ness' of 'ness'. 'Ness-ness' is negated from the outset, and *never comes to be*.

Inquiry into negation allows a certain clarity about the patterns of mental activity. It does not place us 'outside' the 'corral' of frozen and conventional structures, but it suggests that the fences of the corral are not substantial in the way we have thought. Negation 'knows' in such a way that conventional knowledge can continue to operate — not 'reduced' to not-knowing, yet not engaged in establishing. Whatever is 'established' has already been 'negated' in the act of being established.

When negation pervades knowledge, knowledge pervades being, revealing being as more fundamental than either existence or non-existence. Distinctions between knowing and not-knowing lose their significance, for knowledge is global. Since knowledge is not used by the 'self-asserting I' to set up a specified reality, the distinctions that operate to confine knowledge do not come into play.

Negation discloses a new dimension to knowledge — a bottom-level 'zero-ness' emerges within 'ness-ness', while 'I-ness' gives way to 'knowingness'. In this context, we could perhaps speak of a 'further' level of the 'ness', a 'ness' that 'adds' nothing to appearance. We can test for such a 'ness' by asking whether the 'ness' active in our own knowing 'establishes' anything at all, either through affirmation or negation. Prepared to question 'what is going on', we can stay true to the zero while activating a fundamental 'knowingness'. Already active in the 'zero-ness' of 'knowingness', knowledge no longer needs to be 'pursued' within the polarity of existence and non-existence. Whatever is identified is seen as 'having been identified', giving new vitality to what is known.

Brotherhood of Knowledge

As inquiry and investigation unfold the dynamics of observation, interpretation, and negation, three different kinds of knowledge are revealed. We can think of them as being like three brothers.

The youngest brother understands what is known as consisting of what has appeared historically. Reality is 'what has happened', and his responsibility is to find out what this is.

The second brother sees the value of what the youngest is doing, but does not agree that the proper domain of knowledge is 'what has been presented'. Basic structures such as the three times or existence in space all need to be investigated. And so he invites his brother to go further and do more. He knows that investigation exercises knowledge and awakens intelligence, fostering a more healthy and complete way of being.

The third, oldest brother is pleased with what has already been done, but suspects that both his brothers may be lazy, or else that they fail to see their situation as a whole. In his view, the second brother still wants to reach a final destination — a goal or resting place where he can stop and say, "This is it!" To counteract this tendency, he is alert to point out to his brother that 'this' is not 'it'; that there is no 'it' and no holding onto something as established and beyond questioning. He is always asking his brother why he wants to stop — but is careful not to set up another form of 'wanting' instead. He is confident that knowledge can be self-validating.

Although all three brothers remain the best of friends, their understanding differs greatly. For the first brother, history — the domain of objective fact — is the witness to knowledge. The structure within which knowledge takes place is not an appropriate subject for inquiry, except perhaps in a historical or 'objective' way. He finds his brothers' activity incomprehensible, perhaps even subversive.

For the second brother, inquiry and the intelligence that it fosters are the witnesses to knowledge. He sees the structures on which his younger brother relies as 'read-outs' that restrict knowledge, and explores those 'read-outs' so that the artificial restraints they impose can be dissolved. He recognizes inquiry itself as knowledge in action, and delights in the opportunity to deepen and extend his intelligence. He worries that his oldest brother has taken on an exhausting, hopeless task. For there will always be more 'read-outs', stretching backward and forward in time and extending throughout space, even shaping space and time themselves.

The third brother, too, sees the 'read-outs' that the second brother has discovered, but understands them in a more fundamental way as instances of what could be called the 'read-out principle'. He sees that *there are only self-validating 'read-outs'; nothing else. And he recognizes that even this 'nothing-else' is a 'read-out'.* He explains to his younger brother that his anxiety is groundless: There is no one to be exhausted and no task to be accomplished. There is only the 'read-out principle' itself, which is not 'self-validating' but 'self-negating'. The only witness to knowledge is knowledge.

Grateful for the vital work performed by his two younger brothers, the third brother devotes himself to sharing with them the fruits of his realization, without insisting on these fruits as 'real' in the way that his brothers might think. He invites them to participate in a global knowledge.

But even this possibility requires a certain level of understanding. According to the first-level understanding of the first brother, global knowledge is impossible, for it would require traveling to the ends of the universe to discover the whole of the existent realm. No one has the power to do this: Time is too short, and 'locatedness' in space imposes insurmountable limits.

For the second brother, global knowledge is likewise impossible. We can discover new 'layers' of space and new 'rhythms' within time; we can penetrate the realms of the known to disclose the unknown. But the whole of what appears in space and time — the infinite range of possible 'read-outs' — is too vast to be encompassed by such a knowing.

For the third brother, however, knowledge is global from the outset. It 'contains' the universe and 'constitutes' all 'read-outs'. Through the intimacy of knowledge with time and space, an intimacy of knower and known manifests as fundamental. The objects of knowledge do not 'approach' us, nor must we journey 'somewhere else' to know 'more'. For it is the nature of time, space, and knowledge to be inseparable. As we come to embody space and time, knowledge is revealed as intrinsic to the nature of all being.

Chapter Forty-Five

Cutting through the 'ness' in inquiry; negation as revealing global knowledge pervading being; 'zeroness' in relation to 'knowingness'; brotherhood of knowledge; self-negating 'read-out principle'.

Mind Without Images

Within the experience of a layer of awareness 'beneath' all conventional narrative content (see Exercise 29), a subtle image of that awareness operates: the 'image of mind without images'. Because it does not participate in ordinary mental events, this 'imaged' mind is understood as isolated and alone, lost and uncomprehending in a dark and silent place. Sensitively explore this image, tracing how it gives rise to the conventional patterns of the mind, and whether it persists within those patterns.

Contacting the 'mind without images' can bring to the fore powerful emotions. If these emotions take on a substance and reality of their own, seek personal instruction before proceeding.

Exercise Forty-Five

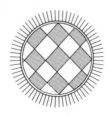

Intermission of Space

String of Diamonds

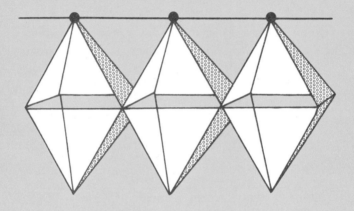

Distinctions find uncharted depths
Perception reveals unknown dimensions
Sparkling facets emerging light
Appreciation embracing the untold
Enter into open from know within
Free to Love of Knowledge

INEXPRESSIBLE
WONDERMENT

The feedback that comes from intelligence in action heals and strengthens awareness. Maintaining no 'right' view to put in place of a wrong one, knowledge simply lets us see 'how things are put together'. In one way, this represents no change at all, for it does not put forward anything new. In another way, it represents a change on the deepest level, like waking up within a dream or drawing back to remember that a game in which we are engrossed is only a game.

Of course, everyone who plays a game 'knows' that it is only a game; pointing this out seems to add nothing to enjoyment of the game or to the understanding of the one who is playing. However, unless the mind goes through a basic shift, this 'knowing' in which everyone already participates lacks any meaning or benefit. The player caught up in a game impatiently dismisses any reminder that it is only a game; he is eager to get back — he may miss his turn to play!

The 'shift' in mind that comes with knowledge offers an alternative to proliferation — a path of accommodation that leaves form as form, but endows it with a new, open and spacious 'quality'. Attuned in a new way to the patterns of our lives, we may be ready to see that our words and stories are not names for a fixed reality, but symbols of a deeper knowing.

Looking from within the structures of conventional knowledge, not separating what is from what is not, what has passed from what has yet to come, what is known to be true from what remains unknown, we can take our inquiry deeper. We can ask about the nature of knowledge itself, and about the structures of being that knowledge supports.

Limits Without Limitation

Inquiry and analysis, which reveal the game as a game, could be thought of as a bridge between the realm of ordinary understanding and a realm of deeper knowledge — a bridge built on foundations grounded solidly in both realms. Yet the bridge is a magical one, for when we cross it, we find that the realm to which it leads us is the same realm from which we departed, only transformed in a way that is at once too subtle to be specified and too all-embracing to describe.

The 'magic' that makes this transformation possible is not imported from the realm of the esoteric, nor is it conjured up by calling on a source whose being or nature remains mysterious. It is a magic that finds its power in embracing both conventional knowledge and a knowledge that goes 'beyond' the conventional. Another name for it is the love of knowledge, through which knowledge reaches out to us as we reach out to knowledge.

Only questions inspired by this love can serve the function of transformation. If we ask in order to confirm a pre-existing position, attain a specified goal, display a kind of cleverness, or demonstrate the futility of inquiry, we will find that the bridge leads nowhere. But if we ask in the love of knowledge, our questioning itself discloses the knowledge that we seek.

Inquiry and analysis let us look honestly at the patterns that shape our lives, investigating them and tracing them back to their roots. Investigating, we find that these patterns are interrelated, supporting each other in a way that gives them a remarkable strength. We see that our reality is founded in experience, our experience in interpretive concepts, and our concepts in beliefs that are themselves unfounded.

In the end there is nothing but beliefs, so thickly bunched that no one could ever hope to root them out. We live in a no-choice realm; we are trained to perpetuate that realm, and we have a massive investment in verifying the truth of our training. And so we do just that, affirming and transmitting it onward with each thought, each word, and each act.

Yet when we have undertaken this investigation and arrived at this insight *for ourselves* — not accepting it because we are told that it is true, or because a certain chain of logic and reasoning seems to support it — something quite wonderful happens. *Seeing only beliefs, we see no limitations.* Wherever we turn, we find beliefs hardened into convictions, and so into a mutually agreed upon reality. Our suffering is a belief, and so is our pain. Our conditioning and our isolation, our not-knowing and our anxiety — they are all beliefs. With nothing of substance to block the way, we stand at the threshold of a remarkable freedom.

The Freedom of No Positions

The same point can be put in another way. In founding and affirming our world, we exhibit a remarkable capacity of mind and body. The mind can learn perfectly what needs to be done, and can put it into effect without hesitation and without error. It is the master of its own conditioning, flexible and adaptable. In its activity and its understanding, the mind displays a quality of knowledge that is flawless and seamless, fantastically open and creative. *Whatever is thought is so; whatever is acted on establishes the foundation of action.* Historical conditioning, with all its attendant imperfections, expresses a perfection of being and knowing before which we might well fall silent in wonderment.

Viewed from such a perspective, suffering and the other circumstances of human being express a particular outlook on being. From within that outlook, which is *our* outlook, distinctions such as 'happy' and 'unhappy' matter a great deal. And this means that knowledge too matters, at the deepest level. Applied in our own lives, a knowledge that dissolved our suffering would be a gift more precious than any other.

Yet from the perspective of knowledge itself, the distinctions that suffering is founded on are themselves insubstantial. Suffering manifests knowledge — it is a particular position that we adopt, based upon what we 'know' to be true. Only from 'within' the position itself do we understand it as 'a position' with a substance and significance of its own. Seen as aspects of knowledge, the positions we take are not positions at all, for they establish nothing substantial or fixed, and do not impede the flow of knowledge. Like the facets of a diamond sparkling in the sun, they reflect each other in a dazzling display that knows no blockage.

Only Positions

So firm is our commitment to positions that the insight of 'no-positions' makes us uncomfortable. Amazingly, if we reflect on it, it almost seems that we would refuse an end to suffering that depended on seeing that suffering is insubstantial. First we want acknowledgment that our suffering is *real*; only then will we consent to having it removed.

In the face of a more comprehensive knowing, we may thus react with anger or anxiety, with disbelief or discomprehension. Understood as another 'positioning', *this reaction too is an affirmation of knowledge* — a response to the invitation that greater knowing offers, tempered by a sense that we are not ready to respond, or else do not know how. In the clarity of the seeing lies a knowing that the emotional response — whatever the content that accompanies it — only confirms.

This flexibility in the face of positioning is true freedom. It almost seems that we are free to go back and forth between two perspectives: the conditioning and suffering of ordinary knowledge, and the freedom of no positions. From the conventional perspective, such a shift would be impossible, because it would mean maintaining two inconsistent positions. But within greater knowledge, no positions are being maintained. Like a spotless mirror, knowledge can reflect any image whatsoever without itself being affected or disturbed.

Chapter Forty-Six

Form endowed by knowledge with openness; a subtle transformation based on seeing beliefs; conditions as expressing outlook on being; the freedom of 'no-positions'.

Alternatives to Mind

It is mind that imagines world without mind. This same limitation operates in terms of time and space: When subject relates to object or self to world the time of the subject and the image of the object are in operation; action can take place only 'within' this time and can only be directed 'toward' specific objects. Does this mean the mind of the subject or self is fundamental? To explore this question, try substituting for the 'mind' at the center of experience a fundamental facet of Being: Space, Time, or Knowledge. Note that the intention is not to 'undermine' the mind or deny its status, though questions of status may take on a different significance.

Exercise Forty-Six

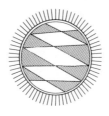

Time's Rhythm

Ways of Knowing

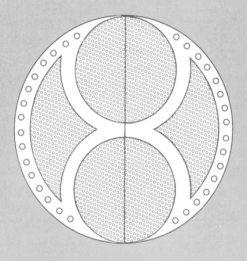

Cut like a knife to perception
Penetrate to understanding
Embrace without projection
Open to subject and object
Balance and encompass
Global Knowledge

KNOWING
IMPLICIT
ILLUMINATION

As long as not-knowing excludes knowledge, we are trapped by our positions, and there is no escape from the limits of the known. But when we set aside the distinction between knowing and not-knowing, engaging not-knowing as an activity of knowledge, escape from the consequences of not-knowing is no longer an issue in the same way. Instead of trying to 'know' the 'unknown', we can *integrate the unknown* into knowledge, allowing human knowing to 'develop' in a new way. Positions lose their rigid nature, together with their power to exclude. There is no situation that is hopeless, and also no need for hope. A path to greater knowledge lies open before us.

We discover knowledge within not-knowing. Even at the outset, we know knowing when we know our not-knowing *as* not-knowing. The task of inquiry is to open this channel of communication between not-knowing and knowing — to create the opportunity for knowledge to speak.

It may seem that this task is too difficult, or the path too long. But while it is true from a linear perspective that the path is not an easy one, a natural intelligence, not caught up in positioning, can reveal knowledge available within each point. There is nowhere else that we must go to obtain knowledge, and no distant goal to be achieved.

The patterns of ordinary understanding could be considered the frozen expressions of a deeper knowing. Because they are frozen, they prevent the free flow of intelligence, so that knowing comes only with difficulty. When these patterns are seen more clearly, however, as active 'positionings', a remarkable new intelligence can flow freely 'within' the confines and limits of conventional knowledge. Inquiry and investigation deepen and intensify spontaneously, and we find ourselves more active and involved in every aspect of our lives.

The prospect of such involvement raises another question: If everything is just beliefs, why act at all? But this question appeals to a premature, conceptual understanding of the 'no-positions' perspective. If we were no longer caught up in our actions and positionings, 'doing nothing' might be a sign of wisdom. But which of us can really 'do' nothing? Our entire being is a 'doing' of body, mind, consciousness, energy, and senses. Truly 'doing nothing' may well be the hardest thing we could ever imagine doing.

If we aspire to such a 'doing nothing', we can actively engage and exercise knowledge. Knowledge in action cuts through our ordinary 'doing', which fills up our space and occupies our time. By participating fully in our own knowing, we can make room for knowledge to appear. Even if we know only our not-knowing, we can welcome this not-knowing as a precursor to knowledge. In welcoming not-knowing, we invite knowledge and create an opening for the love of knowledge to manifest.

Investigating Not-Knowing

In trying to investigate knowledge, we communicate and think in the terms that language provides, structuring our inquiry through concepts such as 'truth', 'nature', 'reality', and so forth. As a result, not-knowing is active implicitly in every step of our inquiry.

If such not-knowing goes unknown, our inquiry will tend naturally to come to a halt at one or another version of the 'ness'. But this tendency is not decisive, for we have open to us the possibility of exploring our not-knowing. If words and meanings weave a robe, we can ask how we are able to wear the robe. How do we make it our position? *Where does this capacity come from?* Even the attempt at a full answer will direct us beyond the logical and sequential patterns of our conventional knowledge, allowing us to see more.

For example, we may hold to the view that there is a beginning to time, or a border to space, or that there are limits on knowledge that cannot be transcended. In each case we are led to assert a boundary beyond which there is only not-knowing. But no such boundary is absolute in the face of an active intelligence. We are free to ask what happened before time began, or what takes place beyond the edge of space. We can investigate how we know that there are things we cannot know.

In carrying out such an inquiry, we are not necessarily looking for answers, since our not-knowing insists that answers are not available. We are simply refusing to leave not-knowing itself as an uninvestigated position. At least potentially, we are acknowledging that there could be no positions whatsoever, and also no 'ness'.

Investigating the structure of our not-knowing leads us to look closely at the relationship between consciousness, language, and self. Words give meanings to perceptions and allow for a discriminating judgment to operate. As soon as we make use of words, however, the self comes forward to identify and judge what has been labeled, establishing substance and erecting the boundaries that define our not-knowing.

Not-knowing thus reveals the self in action, and an inquiry into not-knowing becomes a kind of psychology of the self, at the level where the fundamental structures of 'ness' and 'ness-ness' are established. In knowing our not-knowing, we see how human beings draw on knowledge that 'enters' through the senses and through linguistic structures to set up a world and define the role they will play in that world. We see how what is perceived and interpreted is made into 'the real', and how observation, meaning-giving and other fundamental human activities operate.

Such inquiry is all too rare. But when it is active, it opens the way for a knowledge that is truly vital; it invites knowledge to come forward and present its priceless gift. Allowing knowledge into our not-knowing frees knowledge to move forward on its own, inspiring intelligence and active communication.

Knowledge in Action

Knowing our not-knowing is knowledge in action. It deals with this world, not some other; it unfolds within our own experience and reflections, not someone else's constructs. Such knowledge does not tear down or reduce, nor does it dismiss the old ways of knowing. Taking the historical process and the constructs of consciousness as the field of inquiry, it does not easily allow itself to be appropriated by the claims of the 'ness'.

When not-knowing is available to be known, nothing is excluded and no positions need to be maintained or denied. We can take the limits on knowing as they are, continuing with our inquiry undisturbed by our ignorance. We can encourage challenges and invite argument, for we have nothing to defend — not even our not-knowing, for we ourselves have already put it in question. Eager to learn more through further inquiry, we wish for opponents with sharp weapons and quick minds. But we reserve for ourselves the right to challenge each position in turn, and to point out limitations wherever they may appear.

Knowing our not-knowing, we can explore, analyze, and understand without establishing, asserting, or maintaining. Unconcerned by the limits on knowing that our inquiry discloses, knowledge itself can continue to deepen and expand, acting as its own witness. With no fixed starting point, no impenetrable barriers, and no ultimate, knowledge will be unfettered. Things are left 'the way they are', but they *are not* that way. The witness witnesses no 'ness'.

Knowledge as its own witness suggests the possibility that known and unknown alike can be understood as aspects of knowledge. Like an artist or playwright, knowledge establishes the known world of labeled entities and unknown essences, of past and present and future. The fixed world of persistent things and the active consciousness that identifies and distributes them are equally expressions of a knowing that is more fundamental than either.

Taking this possibility seriously allows for an astonishing extension of knowledge. Physical existence and mind alike become carriers of knowledge. The labels that clothe the known world and the comparisons that give it substance are also carriers of knowledge. Not-knowing is not opposed to knowledge; instead, it is the sign that knowledge is active as 'this' and 'that', as 'ness' and as 'ness-ness'. As the absence of knowing, it is the mirror image of the knowledge within negation.

Chapter Forty-Seven

Knowledge in not-knowing and in positioning; 'doing' nothing; not accepting not-knowing as being a position; knowledge as its own witness.

Symbolic Interplay of Action

Imaginatively reflect on your life — its past and present unfolding — as an expression of the Time-Space-Knowledge interplay. In the usual view, your life is like a drama in which the plot is the activities and encounters of a self in a world of objects, acting on the basis of impulses and desires and a specific knowing. In this new view, Space, Time, and Knowledge, as facets of Being, are the actors in the play. The subject and the object are like props that the actors use. But subject and object are also symbols of the interplay, and thus symbols of each other.

Exercise Forty-Seven

Being as Time, Space, and Knowledge

Source

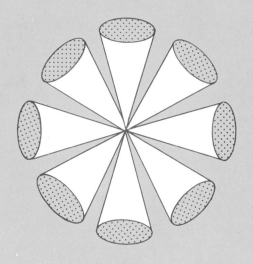

Knowledge unfolds from open center
Dimensions closed to sense-bound knowing
Field of Knowledge source of
Physical energies
Awareness mind
Rhythm momentum
Accommodation
Time and Space

OPENING
TIME AND SPACE

D eeper knowledge is not likely to make itself com- prehensively known until the old understandings of space and time begin to lose their hold. Everyday understanding confines our thinking to a space that positions and a time that conditions. But space and time alike are more complex than this, and hold out other possibilities for knowledge.

We can frame an inquiry into time and space by looking at the assumption that what is being presented here is a 'path' to greater knowledge. In terms of linear temporality, this may be an accurate statement, but phrasing it in this way establishes a structure that puts new knowledge 'somewhere else'. As we have seen, once such a dichotomizing structure has been established, the gap between antagonistic poles cannot be bridged. Distance is determinative: What is situated 'some- where else' is simply out of reach.

At the same time, the moment-to-moment structure of linear temporality cuts us off from greater knowledge in another way. The durationless moment acts as a bottleneck, choking off the free flow of a time that might spontaneously present greater knowledge. As long as all experience must pass through the moment, how can there be an opening to an understanding that is more spacious and accommodating?

When we see that knowledge need not be confined to the conventional, however, a possibility arises for understanding space and time quite differently. *The rhythms of time and the allowing capacity of space respond to the quality of knowing in operation, in an interplay of intimacy.* Concepts such as 'progress on a path' reflect a *particular kind of time and space* in which that intimacy has been submerged into the structures of distance and separation, ownership and wanting. But the intimacy itself continues to operate; in fact the apparent 'loss' of intimacy reflects a particular interplay of space, time and knowledge. Increased knowledge restores access to this intimacy. It reveals that the moment can be opened up, allowing space to exhibit a greater knowingness.

Limits in Space and Time

Our present ways of knowing what appears in space are rather limited, even crude. For example, we could make use of observation to investigate the structures of the body on an ever more detailed level, moving from surface appearance to interior structures such as the organs or the nervous system. We could go on to investigate cells and the flow of blood throughout the system. We could even penetrate to the molecular level and the operations of the DNA that contains the encoded knowledge of our physical embodiment. But in all such observation, we will retain the conceptual models of observation: observer and observed, progressive acquisition of data over time, and so forth. Other factors (for example, the interplay of space with what appears in space) will continue to be inaccessible and in part unthinkable.

This same pattern of observation, with its axioms of distance and separation, feeds back into the prevailing systems of knowledge. Whatever can be known will be conditioned in the same way that the physical laws governing a stream of electrons condition the circumstances under which that stream can be used to transmit a visual image, and what the nature of that image and its capacity to carry information will be.

Based on a distanced knowing, knowledge will be subject to the words and concepts that 'make sense' of observation. Talk and ideas will communicate an understanding that stands in relation to the potential for knowledge as observation carried out by the 'bystander' stands in relation to the potential for embodiment within space. Knowledge beyond the ordinary will be available only as the outcome of a long and difficult inquiry, conducted over a 'period of time' during which further, unknown events continue to unfold.

Following this model, the possibilities for space, time, and knowledge alike will be restricted. How could knowledge convince the body that it is not limited in its extension in space, or convince experience that it could expand to control time? Saying that the body itself *is* space or that experience *is* time seems to lead in the direction of meaninglessness.

Even if we could discuss such possibilities theoretically, the insights that resulted would lack any power to affect our lives on a deep level. Someone could read this whole book and another just like it, and not be any different for it. The fundamental 'read-out' would integrate any insights into the pre-existing pattern. The potential for new knowing or for new ways of being in space and time would be channeled into vehicles such as 'path' and 'goal' — vehicles that allowed for the unknown to become known only in accord with other, presupposed structures that imposed inescapable limits on the potential range of the knowable.

If someone thought he could satisfy his hunger by saying the word 'food', he would quickly learn to acknowledge his mistake through the effect on his own body. But because we have little direct access to knowledge not mediated through concepts and models, we can substitute constructs for active knowing without any way of detecting what we have done.

Beguiled by words and concepts, we may look past the limits that the conventional understanding of space and time put into operation. We may decide that we have finally come to the end of a long journey and attained a revolutionary form of understanding, yet all the while continue to act out patterns that remain virtually unchanged. Caught up in our fantasies, we may be letting real opportunities slip away. Like a child raised in the wild without ever learning to speak, we may be letting a vital capacity go undeveloped without even suspecting the nature of our loss.

Not Knowing Space and Time

Because the linear flow of time appears to cut off knowledge, it seems that a 'knowingness' that might know at the level of the 'ness' could arise only if it were already present in the very first moment. But this would be possible only if the 'first moment' itself were transformed, so that it no longer maintained its character as the initial instant in a linear sequence.

How could this happen? When our tools are mind and words and consciousness, we are confined to a linear view of time that allows only for cause and effect and historical conditioning. There will be no way out, no matter how long and winding the road. We may suspect that there are gateways to new knowledge, but those gateways will not open within linear time, nor will they be accessible in a space that is just the emptiness 'between'. Following one particular direction will lead nowhere, and disclosing a non-existent emptiness will create no possibilities for openness.

The long road that we have already followed in this book is not exempt from this insight. But in the course of our investigation, we have made certain preliminary discoveries that might lay the groundwork for a different possibility. We have learned to value inquiry, and to recognize the knowledge within negation. We have learned that knowledge can be active within conventional constructs and also within our not-knowing.

If the space and time we know shape and confine our knowledge, perhaps it is best to set them aside. Instead of staying with a 'space' and 'time' that are so well-known that they go unexamined, we can 'take up' space and time as *unknown* and *available* for inquiry. True, the inquiry itself will take place within space and time. But an active 'not-knowing' can take priority over the limits that this structure might seem to impose.

Engaged with space and time, we can put the restricted knowing of conventional space and time to the test, allowing 'room' for alternatives. Perhaps in this way the intimacy of space, time, and knowledge will disclose *within the confines of the old ways* new dimensions of being that go beyond our power to imagine.

Chapter Forty-Eight

No path to knowledge; knowledge based on a different time and space; patterns of distance and separation; beyond linear time; space and time as unknown and available for inquiry.

Exploring Space, Time, and Knowledge

Placing Space, Time, or Knowledge at the center of experience (see Exercise 47) shifts old assumptions. With the exhibition of space central, the distinction between 'mental' and 'physical' will not hold. With the presentations of time central, causal sequences and explanations give way to a more dynamic flow, and patterns of self-concern carry no special force. With the 'knowingness' of knowledge central, all positionings lose their privileged place. Explore these alternatives and others, letting a playful approach suggest openings. Continued practice of this exercise can introduce a non-ordinary way of being in which knowledge could be said to choose itself.

Exercise Forty-Eight

Energy of Time

Irresistible Rhythm

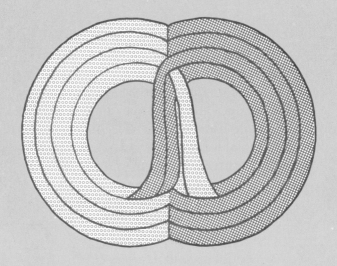

Irresistible rhythm of experience
Sense image feeling flow
Interlocking channels
Embodying Time Space Knowledge
Inner communion of love
Living creativity

DANCE IN TIME

A full investigation into space and time goes beyond the scope of this book. But as a way of suggesting how such an investigation might proceed, let us look briefly at the way in which time unfolds, comparing our actual experience with conventional understanding.

Even the simplest objects of the physical realm move and dance in time: Each of them comes into being in a way that the specifying of causes and effects leaves essentially mysterious; each unfolds and expands until dissolution and disintegration set in. The meaning and significance of the objects with which the self interacts also emerge through the dynamic of time, growing richer and more complex as 'layers' of meaning are added.

Time operates with a varying significance in the subatomic domain, in biological evolution, in cultural transformation, and within individual lives. The cycles of growth and decay that govern living organisms have parallels in the flux of human events; in the movements of sun and moon, stars and galaxies; perhaps even in the formation and passing away of the universe itself. At each level, time gives the impression of moving in specific, unique patterns, almost as if it were fulfilling distinct roles or duties.

In the stories that make up the inner experience of the self, a still more rich and active sense of time is at work. The intricate web of interwoven interpretations put forward by the self is a dazzling aesthetic achievement. Conceived and elaborated without apparent effort, the self's narratives are like a subtle musical improvisation, or like a marvelously complicated and constantly evolving game that the players make up as they go along.

Creative Wealth of Possibilities

The changing dynamic of time, especially as revealed in the narratives of the self, suggests a powerful, creative awareness at work. By habit and concern, the self is too captivated by its stories to recognize them as instances of profound ongoing realization. Here, hidden from view by the self's preoccupation, is one potential source for a knowing that could break the bounds of the known.

History itself discloses a tremendous depth when viewed with appreciation for the creative power of its narrative flow, and with a humility that allows for alternatives. Conceived as the blind unfolding of events — in human affairs, in the biological realm, or in the natural history of the cosmos — historical time does not fully cohere with the wealth of our knowing and being. But such a 'history', 'blind' to meaning and significance, is only a particular 'read-out' of an underlying 'logos'. Even in the terms specified by linear temporality, the historical process so conceived is an abstraction from a potentially multi-faceted range of experience. The historical sequence may not be as monolithic as it seems.

Viewed with open awareness, the events and patterns of 'history' disclose an interwoven tapestry of experience, within which time displays an unexpected diversity. Though the self's 'positions' tie it to a linear view of such patterns, even here a subtle interplay can be seen to link events occurring far apart in time, as shown in the movements of consciousness and intention that leap from past to future to present and back in just moments — movements pursued by the self with avid fascination. Applied consistently, the simple logic of linear unfolding accepted by conventional knowledge is inadequate to account for the quicksilver vitality that time displays.

Because it can comprehend and order time's vitality, the self portrays itself as master of its flow. But the truth may be more complex. When time seems limited, the self feels time's intense pressure, and when time seems empty of significance, the self experiences time's crushing weight. When the self steps in to 'take control' of time and to assign its flow significance, it asserts its 'mastery' only by *confirming* patterns of historical conditioning that it accepts as indisputable.

Most of us have known 'moments' when a more richly patterned understanding of time and its presentations has come into play. The linear laws of passage and decay seem suspended; past, present, and future all have their own texture, and time itself lives, offering a special nourishment. The self, with its interpretations and its commitment to historical conditioning, falls silent, and the flexibility of time, implicit in the kaleidoscopic flow of the self's narratives, comes to the fore. At such times, the link between time and knowledge, and the possibility that both could be other than they seem, are very much in evidence.

Alive in Time

When time presents experience as aesthetic manifestation for knowledge to absorb and to savor, the world becomes spacious, active, and accommodating. Present knowing is linked to the sources of understanding available in the past and the visionary knowledge of the future. Time's momentum discloses knowledge as self-arising, stable, and self-enriching; this greater knowledge in turn gives renewed access to the hidden power of time active in the dynamic of ordinary life. Deepening knowledge unites with what is available to be known — in art, in beauty, and in life. The power of knowledge manifests everywhere, unpredictable and irresistible.

For knowledge to manifest in this way, it is enough to open up one point fully, allowing the quality of knowing to emerge. Within this openness, space presents space, dissolving the distinction between space and the existent objects space 'contains'. The rhythm of experience changes as well, making time more fully available to deepen the activity of opening. Knowledge can communicate with knowledge, permitting a spontaneous intelligence to come into play. Thoughts, energy, and feelings are all understood as expressions of the interplay of time, space, and knowledge. Our actions and our being can embody directly a higher form of knowledge.

Alive in time and awake to the subtle flow of the temporal narrative, we experience past, present, and future with a knowing less bound to temporal knowledge and polar structures. We make our own the rhythms and momentum that we receive from the past, shaping them toward the future. Knowledge reveals a future that springs into being out of the present, like the image that leaps into existence when we step before a mirror.

Free from the power of positions to freeze and restrict knowledge, we learn that no perspective is absolute. Because 'reality' is not so rigid, it can be more readily penetrated, and also more readily embraced. This in turn makes inquiry more effective and understanding richer. Instead of being caught up in 'this' and 'that', we see how things and patterns gather together. Difficulties and obstacles that cause us pain appear in a new light — as manifested probabilities of being, which itself remains open and accommodating.

Active and alert in time, human consciousness can respond with joy and vitality to the display of forms in their arising. The emergent qualities of being exhibit beauty and aesthetic appreciation, as well as new ways to work, to produce, to create, and to live. Destiny, direction, choice, and intention become newly meaningful as expressions of human consciousness and embodiment.

Communication with others also stands revealed in a new light. Instead of unwittingly ensnaring each other in old patterns, we share new possibilities. The gestures and symbols of communication transmit living experience: fresh, powerful, and illuminating. Personal interactions become a bridge into a realm of freedom, and each action, as a full expression of being, becomes a potential vehicle for communicating knowledge.

When such awareness is active, we live our lives with an abundant appreciation for the intricate rhythms of time and the communion between this moment and others. A knowledge not ours to possess becomes accessible — a source of wealth that remains undiminished no matter how freely we share it with others.

Appreciation and awareness open for human being the full power of Time, Space, and Knowledge, offering a foundation and an inspiration for accomplishment. Building on this basis, we can be sure that we and others will benefit from our few short years on earth. Beyond conventional views, beyond fear, and beyond hope, a way of knowing awaits that can transform our world.

Chapter Forty-Nine

Creative dynamic of time; history as 'read-out'; the tapestry of experience; silent self; opening one point to reveal fullness of knowledge; full communication; through appreciation to transformation.

Symbols of Being

Continuing with the view suggested in Exercise 48, consider the possibility that 'you' and 'your body' can be understood as symbols interacting to 'produce' the distinctive characteristics and qualities of human being. Because symbols are 'by nature' open, this continuing interaction steadily generates new possibilities. Time is the path Being takes in unfolding, Space the arena within which being unfolds, and Knowledge the power through which Being manifests particular symbols. Reflect on Knowledge as the masterful response to the challenging circumstances presented by Time and exhibited in Space.

Exercise Forty-Nine

Mirage of Time

Love of Knowledge

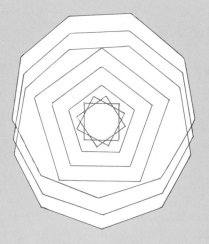

Vital radiant illumination
Allowing fundament without foundation
Origination without parentage
No pointing no distinctions
Witness suffused with Knowledge
Intimate appearance as wonderment

DYNAMIC
INTIMATE
AWARENESS

Within the potential vitality of time, knowledge and the ever-changing temporal display are inseparable. But this is not our experience in ordinary time. In the flow from past to present to future, we do not know the past or future directly — at best we can interpret or predict on the basis of fragmentary evidence and relatively reliable trends. Even the moment just past and the one about to come are not directly knowable. Nor can we account for the continuity that links moment to moment. And if we turn to knowledge, we cannot account with confidence for its origins or foresee its end.

A different set of limitations applies with regard to knowledge and space. Within each manifestation, there appears to be a potential for knowledge that penetrates and illuminates all partitions. Conventionally, however, knowledge is bound to the cumbersome extension of the knowing capacity throughout a vast physical domain. To rely on such a knowledge is like trying to illuminate the depth of an enormous cavern by moving through it with a single, flickering match.

It seems surprising that such limitations should operate. Whatever is accessible for knowledge 'here' manifests only through an intricate interplay with the rest of 'what is'. Why should our knowledge single out only this small aspect of a unified whole, instead of revealing the full range of interconnections at once? Similarly, since the present depends on the past and future, why should knowledge not be equally available in all three 'times'?

We may suspect that it is our way of knowing that imposes these limitations, and that a more encompassing knowledge would permeate the universe of space and time. Knowledge, however, not only determines but also depends on the time and space in operation within our realm. *As long as time and space jointly establish a known 'objective' world and a knowing 'subject', the knowledge that reveals time and space will reflect that established domain, with all its limits.*

No Known World

Inquiry into space and time as they ordinarily appear leads in the same direction as inquiry into knowing itself. The view that characterizes space as the void between existents parallels the insistence on the 'ness'. For space to be 'nothing', there must be 'something'. The known objects that exist 'within' space, established through their character and qualities, rely for their 'being' on the 'nothingness' that space makes available. Only in contrast to space can they assert themselves and their claims to existence.

This 'assertion' by each individual object is incomplete without the complementary 'assertion' of the qualities and attributes that make the object what it is. Since this second 'assertion' depends on the contrast between one object and the next, in the final analysis, each individual entity can 'assert' its being only in reference to the whole. And since this 'whole' depends on the 'allowing nothing' of space, the 'co-referring' realm of attributes ultimately relies on space as well. 'Existence' and 'attributes' appear to share a fundamental 'sameness' with 'non-existent', 'attribute-free' space.

Is the 'ness' of this 'sameness' the same as the 'ness' of 'emptiness' or 'nothingness'? If so, how can it 'establish' that space and objects are 'the same'? In what would this 'sameness' consist? On the other hand, if the 'ness' of this shared 'sameness' is *more* than 'nothing', then how can it share anything at all with space? To put it differently, if matter 'matters' through the 'ness', but is also intimately linked to space, then the 'ness' cannot be 'ness'. On the other hand, if the 'ness' is 'ness', then space cannot contain it and still be space. We are not clear on the 'nature' of either the 'ness' or of 'space'. Or perhaps both of these kinds of 'not-knowing' are in operation.

From a time perspective, an existent appears by 'coming into being', whether suddenly or gradually. What comes into being must trace to an original 'something' that parents it, and this original must also have a parent, and so on. If there is no end to this moving backward in time, how can there have been a beginning? And if there is no beginning, how can there be an act of founding that founds what is known?

Perhaps the difficulty traces to the original assumption of 'endless' (or 'beginningless'). Suppose instead that at some point in the sequence of backward tracings we encountered a 'something' that needs no further tracing — a parent without a parent. What could we say about this 'originating original'? Since it does not conform to the unfolding sequence of linear time, how can it be related to the historical sequence of the known world? Will it not be totally out of reach?

We are led by two chains of thought to a similar conclusion. The 'matter' that appears in space is either not matter, or it does not appear in space. The 'events' that unfold in time depend on an 'originating agent' that either lacks the power to originate or cannot influence the temporal flow. Conventional time and space disclose limitations that reflect a lack of knowledge.

No Knowing Subject

If the known world is without substance or origin, can there be a 'subject' that knows it? If a 'subject' could 'know' without any 'thing' to know, there would be only 'experience', experienced in specific ways. Even though there was nothing to be pointed out, there would be 'the one who pointed'.

Logically, this proposition is difficult to maintain. With nothing to be pointed out, there can be no pointer; with nothing that exists, there can be no 'realm' in which the 'one-who-experiences' shows up as a guest, let alone as 'one-who-exists'. But experience has its own persuasive power and acts as its own witness. No matter how 'unparented' or insubstantial we 'know' experience to be, we reject logic (as well as the 'experience' of analytic confusion) and return to the primacy of experience.

What gives experience this 'flavor' of certainty? Indeed, what determines the flavor of experience at all? Each knower holds his own 'experience' to be indisputable. But suppose that an ape has a 'different' experience in tasting a banana than a human being. Are the two experiences each 'true', each undeniable as experiences? In that case, there is no 'truth' at all — only the countless 'truths' of innumerable, incommensurate experiences.

Why is there such a variety of experiences in the first place, instead of just one experience? The conventional answer might trace the multiplicity of experience to the multiplicity of positions occupied by 'experiencers' within a unitary space and time. This only shifts the question to a different level: How can we affirm a unitary space and time if we base this affirmation on experience, especially when we concede that experience varies? It seems equally likely that there are countless forms of space and time, one for each experience.

No Distinctions in Time or Space

Instead of trying to maintain the 'reality' of the distinctions that manifest 'within' conventional space and time, whether through insisting on 'experience' or through reference to another 'witness', we might consider such distinctions to be exhibitions of an underlying knowing. In this global exhibition, all that appeared would be suffused with the knowledge that 'accounts for' its appearance.

How could we describe such a knowledge? To say that it was 'prior' to all distinctions and divisions and 'unaffected' by the unfolding of events in time would in a sense be accurate, but only in terms of the temporal categories of a more conventional knowing. To say that it was 'global' or 'pervasive' might again be accurate, but only in the categories of conventional spatiality. To say that it 'existed' or 'operated' would be to apply terms and ways of thinking derived from long experience with human claims to ownership of knowledge.

Perhaps we could trace a more global knowledge 'in action'. First, it would be free of assertions, for assertion stops the free flow of knowing. Second, it would be free of judgments, for judgments require positions. Third, it would be free of distinctions, for distinctions accept the truths of a more limited knowing.

From the perspective of conventional time and space, such a knowing would not be a knowing at all. But if we imagine how a global knowing would manifest, a very different understanding emerges. Attuned to conventional knowledge without accepting its assertions, a global knowledge would accept propositions *as if* they were true — either for the practical purposes of our lives, or for the specific purpose of cultivating greater knowledge. The concerns that weigh us down would all be acknowledged, and yet would lose their hold on our lives. The objects we identify would be inseparable from the space within which they manifest, while the actions we trace out would be rhythmic presentations of the time that gave rise to them. A remarkable freedom would pervade experience — a recognition that *nothing is as it is, yet nothing is other than it is.*

Within the luminous vitality of such a knowing, existence would be transformed into *'appearance as'.* 'Was' would be 'as' and 'is' would be 'as'; essence would be transformed into absence. Negation would be present within all appearance, as the heart of appearance.

Free Play of Global Knowledge

The potential for time and space to open to knowledge in a new way suggests that human beings could 'embody' such a global knowledge in a 'Body of Knowledge': an interplay of Space, Time, and Knowledge, revealing all three as facets of Being.

To manifest the 'Body of Knowledge' is to go 'beyond' meanings to the texture of all experience. The contents of conceptualization become pointers toward a more inclusive knowing — the intimacy of the immediate intuitive instant. Freedom and play replace the structures of care and concern.

The global knowledge of the Body of Knowledge can be considered the greatest gift, available through the 'grace' of the knowledge of knowledge. But this is not a 'grace' that comes from outside. Knowledge can be transmitted only because it is already active in our being. *We are intimately linked to the universal display of knowledge, for the nature of human being is to know.*

Knowledge opens all experience to wonderment and appreciation. Limits do not confine, but are available to be known within the vital immediacy of knowledge. Knowing is not something to be attained in the future in an unfolding rhythm of waiting or preserving; it is available now, within what we know and do not know.

By nature knowledge illuminates, in the same way that liquids by nature flow. Knowledge retains a dimension of mystery, for the luminous nature of knowledge is revealed only through knowing. But knowing itself is an ever present capacity: If we find it mysterious, it is because we have turned from what we already know.

The turn from knowledge has brought us to our present situation. Now it offers the opportunity for an unparalleled adventure. Alive to the luminous potential of knowledge, we can question ourselves as actors in the dynamic flow of history. Acknowledging what we do not know, we can resolve to free ourselves of the limits that narrow our vision and undermine our well-being. Like a lover absorbed in the beauty of the beloved, we can give ourselves to knowledge. The depth of our love will disclose the range of our vision.

Chapter Fifty

Knowledge as inexplicably limited; a more fundamental space and time; no knowing subject without existence; time and space as global exhibition; appearance 'as if'; Body of Knowledge.

Adventure of Being

Consider creative action as expressing the adventure of Being: the energy of Time, the accommodation of Space, the commanding presence of Knowledge. To behold and shape this dynamic is the birthright of Knowledge. The self is free to choose in favor of creation or against it, free to succeed or fail: Every choice reflects the unfolding adventure. Dwell on this imaginative vision from within the vision, asking how it might find expression in your future actions and in communication with others. Take the vision into your daily activity, observing lightly and free from judgment the effect it has in your life.

Exercise Fifty

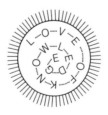

GLOSSARY

'BYSTANDER'   The position adopted by the self as an expression of the lack of unity between subject and object. On a first level, the 'bystander' does not participate in the world that it observes and owns. On a second level, the 'bystander' does participate, receiving and 'enjoying' experiences. Within this mode of participation, the dichotomy of subject and object persists, reflected in the interlocking polarities of 'empty/not-empty' and 'exist/not-exist'. For the 'bystander' on the second level, there is a complete separation from space and time and knowledge: Time has no beginning, middle, or end, space displays the endless reduplication of the same, and knowledge can be known only in ways that conform to the presupposed. This separation finds expression in the structures of process, 'from/to', and limitation.

KNOWLEDGE   On the conventional level, knowledge operates descriptively and intentionally, moving backward and forward in time with reference to objects that are distanced in space. Implicit in this movement are a

413

beginning and an ending. However, logic and intelligence demonstrate that 'beginning' and 'ending' have the same nature as the 'middle realm' of conventional reality, which remains unsupported.

Despite such insights, conventional inquiry displays the lack of balance characteristic of conventional knowledge: a focus on the side of what is established. Patterns repeat themselves, wearing channels that grow progressively deeper until knowledge is completely worn out.

By convention, knowledge does not recognize these limits. We accept known limitations in space and time as final, establishing a focal setting and accepting a 'read-out'. The lack of knowledge is blamed on a conventional not-knowing, without investigating the intimate link between not-knowing and conventional knowing. Even the 'new' possibilities that open at 'higher' levels of knowledge bind through affirmation of the possible. 'All possibilities' continues to subject knowledge to a restrictive concept that in turn restrains the creative power of time and the accommodating capacity of space. The potential for the exhibition of Being remains unfulfilled.

A more open knowledge restores balance to knowing by not singling out the established. Not restricted by implicit assumptions regarding being, it opens Being and so becomes the leader of beings. A special intelligence discloses the negation of what is positively established (including polarities such as 'exist/not-exist'). Knowledge emerges unexpectedly from within the 'not not-empty' and the 'non-begun'.

These 'areas' of inquiry are not subject to being talked about, for they do not depend on the 'ness'. They cannot serve as the subject of conventional inquiry, nor can they be known by conventional knowledge.

'LOGOS'   The governing understanding active within a temporal order. The 'logos' operates in accord with a specific and characteristic logic, establishing possibilities and defining limits. On a lower-level, the 'logos' is invisible, operating as 'the (temporal) way things are'. With more knowledge, the focal setting shifts, and the 'logos' becomes accessible as a structure to be investigated in terms of prevailing 'read-outs'. As investigation continues, the distinction between 'logos' as knowledge and 'logos' as the prevailing order of time and space gives way to a more comprehensive 'knowingness'.

'READ-OUT'   The informing, communicative output by time of a particular focal setting on space, based on a certain sort of knowing being in force. The 'read-out' purports to establish its content as real, but cannot establish itself; nor can it be established by anything 'outside' the 'read-out'. Whatever is put forward as 'outside' the 'read-out' is either bound to the 'read-out' or else takes form within another, independent 'read-out' and thus has neither status nor effect.

SPACE   In conventional understanding, the arena for objects and for the subject to appear. Implicit in this appearance is separation between subject and objects, based on the interpretation that 'I' am in space 'with' objects. This separation in turn supports such fundamental distinctions as 'experiencing/not-experiencing' and 'doing/not-doing'. 'Locatedness' in space in the 'objective' sense is closely related to the positioning of the 'bystander', which secures the self a place at the cost of establishing limits and excluding possibilities.

TIME   On a lower level, the measuring out of experience in accord with the rhythms of the cosmos, the earth, and the human body. Whatever exists manifests in time and is bound by time to the rhythm established by the two points of its birth and decay. This rhythm makes possible participation in the conventional instant realm, without which the subject would have no feedback or place to act. Between these points of beginning and ending lies the 'middle realm' that constitutes the 'bystanders's' field of participation. The 'bystander' thus maintains 'middle ground' as the real, reproducing it through a series of transitions that transmit the underlying rhythm. The nature of this transmission founds the 'bystander's' participation, guaranteeing it in a way that makes non-participation highly unlikely. Beginning and ending are not called into question.

INDEX

absence, 409

absolute, 233–236, 239, 244. *See also* conditioned

abstraction, 352

acceptance, 235

accommodation, 228, 338

accomplishment(s), 131, 142, 166

achievement(s), 94

acknowledgment, 6, 14, 48, 85, 302. *See also* unacknowledged

action(s), xxi, 44, 142, 186, 207, 243, 374; arena for, required, 257; initiating, 359; judged as right and wrong, 252; knowledge within, 292, 383–384, 398, 408; looking at results, 91; meaningful, xx, 61, 196; relation to desire and need, 34, 37; shaped by dreams and fantasies, 47; significance of, 58

activity: knowledge within, 79; of knowing, 271, 298; outpouring of, 69; purpose served by, 70; responds to own momentum, 71; unlimited, 71

adventure, 410

aesthetic awareness, 206, 396. *See also* appreciation

alertness, xxxiii

allowing, 91

amateur, xxviii

analysis, xli, 90, 275 – 276, 292-293, 300 – 301, 373; turned against knowledge, 352 – 353. *See also* inquiry

anxiety, xxviii, 6, 21, 28, 158, 223, 253, 293, 367, 374

apathy, 48

appearance, 340, 409; depends on past, 121; expression of knowledge, 85; friend to human being, 86; presentation of, 59

appreciation, xxxix, xlvii, xlix, 4, 13 – 14, 59, 77, 80, 197, 236, 288, 293 – 294, 297, 308, 410; aesthetic, 239, 399. *See also* intimacy

apprehension, 86, 205

art, xxxix, xlv, 39, 69, 206

artists, 12, 58

'as', 409

aspiration, 86, 112

assertion, 405, 408

assumptions, 7

atoms, 138

attitudes, 38, 307; selfish, 309. *See also* intention

attributes, xlv, 405

authority, 51 – 52, 231; divine, 231; of descriptive knowledge, 109; of narratives, 176; of 'readout'; of reason, 269. *See also* belief

awareness, xxxix, xlvii, 5, 35, 53, 59, 76, 78, 79, 164, 189, 193, 197, 224, 243, 340, 396; deepens naturally, 91; not static, 63; of span of history, 68. *See also* aesthetic awareness

balance, xxix, 6, 45, 235, 308

barrier: *See* protective barrier

beauty, 5, 69, 226, 243, 290, 399

being, 365, 399, 404, 405; knowledge in, xl, 36, 59, 85, 302, 365, 368, 398, 414; new way of, 93; of self and of world, 37; relation to knowledge, 36; self's being (*continued*) efforts to authenticate its, 207; ways of, 291–292, 324

belief(s), xiv, xxi, xxvi, xxvii, xlviii, 37, 78, 79, 133, 137, 253, 280, 299, 326, 373–374, 380; as carriers of knowledge, 53–54; as projections of mental activity, 53; as substitute for knowledge, 51–54; based on 're-presented' conclusions, 51; embodying knowledge, 54; in only beliefs, 326; regarding inchoate experience, 234. *See also* position

between, 391

beyond, xl, 7, 234, 250, 274, 351, 372, 409

bias, 38

body, xxii, xxxix, 35, 80, 93, 104, 194, 208, 389; of light, 80; relation to self, 104; specific attributes, 52; subject to decay, 61. *See also* mind; self

Body of Knowledge, 409–410

bridge between moments, 116–117

boundaries, 4, 84, 223, 242, 260, 282, 381

boredom, 6, 158

bubble in water, 259–260

Buddhism, xvii

'bystander', 264–266, 269, 271–274, 281, 293, 299, 302, 306, 313, 389, 413, 416

calm, xxxiii

capacity: for assigning meaning, 381; for choice, 330; for knowledge, 4, 7, 13, 45, 85, 101, 410; goal of perfecting, 21; human, 69, 390; of mind and body, 374; restricting, 235 ; unique, of self, 170

carrier of knowledge, 384

categories, xxviii, 43, 45, 129, 269, 408

cause and effect, 44, 123, 180, 182, 196, 269, 270, 298, 391. *See also* determinism

center, 272–273. *See also* point

challenging the familiar, 46–48. *See also* inquiry; questioning

change, 166, 185, 194, 202–203, 244, 340; change in range of, 84–85; not allowed for, 132, 160; prospects for, 59, 259; rate of, 13, 17, 27

chaos, 165, 196, 241, 250

choice; choosing, 8, 175, 266, 322–324, 339, 399; capacity for, 330. *See also* 'no-choice'; opposition; position; self

circle(s), 326; of conditioning, 112; of conventional knowledge, 257; of not-knowing, 63, 260

civilization, 11, 18

cognition: *See* knowledge

collective knowledge, 4, 22, 44, 129, 163–166, 188, 249, 282, 305; turn to psychology, 165. *See also* cultural heritage

commitment, xxvii, xxix, 89, 207, 235, 314; to existence, 205, 227, 275, 291, 358; to founding story,

227; to history, 217; to identity, 205; to inquiry, 4; to knowledge, 78, 85; to narrative, 176, 329; to observation, xlvi; to past, 204; to positions, 275; to temporality, 217

common sense, xlviii, 100, 111, 139, 165, 249, 333. *See also* conventional knowledge

communication, xxiv, xxxiii, xl, xli, 40, 43, 141–142, 166, 287–288, 379, 399; between mind and body, 80; difficulty of as to new knowledge, 63; of commitment, 79; of knowledge, 77, 79, 292, 398; through beliefs, 53–54; visionary, 242

compassion, 93

computers, 26–27

concentration, xxxiii, 35, 189, 193, 227

concerns: *See* self

conditioned, 233–234, 244. *See also* absolute

conditioning, 7, 45, 46, 48, 58, 62, 64, 112, 170, 194, 201,

conditioning (*continued*)
205, 263 – 265, 329, 363,
374, 391; as positive
good, 218; mind as
master of, 374. *See also*
history; programming

conditions, 263 – 265

confidence, 7, 340

confusion, xxiv – xxv, xxix,
xlix, 21, 58, 78, 141, 165,
259; as response to not-
knowing, 224 – 225

consciousness, xxii, 12, 59,
173, 219, 282, 287, 288, 292,
326, 383, 399; language
and, 382; of an object,
307; temporal rhythm of,
215, 397

consequences, 21, 44, 243

conspiracy of what is, 291

contradiction, 117

control, 6, 158 – 160. *See
also* technology

conventional knowledge,
xlvi, 4, 22, 47, 59, 62, 68,
71, 72, 83 – 85, 94, 99 – 100,
126, 227, 257, 321, 332, 334,
359, 364, 372, 381; knowledge within, 353. *See also*

collective knowledge;
common sense

creation, xxx, 93, 195, 243,
297

creativity, 13, 69, 92, 160,
198, 243, 245, 338, 340, 363;
in narratives, 396; of
mind, 290; revealed in
fantasies, 75

creator, 218

crowding, 27, 44, 78, 165 –
166, 265

cultural heritage, 47. *See
also* collective knowledge

custom, 45, 249

death, 59 – 60, 170, 181

decision, 28, 324

dedication, 78

deductive reasoning. *See*
reasoning

deepening, xxxiii

definition(s), 4, 105, 110,
129, 163

descriptive knowledge,
104 – 106, 109, 112, 117,
125 – 126, 132, 149, 151, 155,
156, 169 – 170, 173, 175, 188,

descriptive (*continued*) 194, 257, 265; and models, 129. *See also* models

designation, 346

desire(s), 33–34, 36, 38, 47, 59, 86, 149, 156–158, 163, 166, 171, 270, 292; force of, 155–156; fundamental, of self, 148–149; momentum and, 47; shaping conduct, 60; unfolding as linear time, 149. *See also* image of desire; momentum; object of desire

despair, 219

destiny. *See* human destiny

determinism, 122, 201, 214, 217, 266

devotion, xlix, 235, 291

dichotomy, 34, 228, 244, 245, 265, 298, 306, 144. *See also* opposition

difficulties: source of energy, 75

discipline, 77, 89, 160, 252, 253

distance, xxviii, xlii, xlviii, 102, 213, 323, 387, 389

doctrine, 45

dogmatism, xlviii, 76

'doing nothing', 380, 416

dreaming; dreams, 142, 143, 158, 207, 260, 371

dual citizenship: of self, 151, 180

duplication, 266

dynamic, xvi, 57, 164, 187, 189, 193, 214, 305; leading to new knowledge, 59; of self and history, 173; within stories, 205

echo, xxv, 84, 105, 126, 141, 228

education, xxvii, xliv, 18, 28, 62, 130

elements, 138

embodiment, 399; in space, 389; of knowledge, 398; of self, 170. *See also* Body of Knowledge

embodying , xlvii, 308; knowledge, 13–14, 59, 72,

embodying (*continued*) 78, 275; presentations, 264. *See also* knowledge

embracing, 264, 307–308, 314

emotions, xxix, 35, 47, 58, 156–158, 163, 171, 179, 249, 297; confirm knowing, 375; energy and, 292; questioning and, 280. *See also* confusion; energy; fear; feelings

emptiness, 330, 343–348, 357, 405; of space, 86, 391

empty, 44, 100, 352, 358, 413. *See also* space

energy, xxii, 138, 166, 180, 185, 187, 193, 198, 276, 297, 302, 345; becomes available through time, 214; dispersed in linear time, 159; drained in coping, 165; emotions and, 70, 292; for questions, 280–281; freed by analysis, 276, 292–293, 300–301; labels and, 293–294; lacking in thought, 36; mental, 70; of intelligence, 78; of knowing, 43–44, 91; of self, 34, 195, 198; sapped, 61; within thoughts, 133

enjoyment, 45

entities, 43, 283

error, 38

esoteric, xlv, 372

essence, 409

event(s), xlvi, 99, 100, 171, 180, 406; singular, 232

evidence, xxvi, 99, 231; for 'reality', 139

evolution, 287

exhibition, 407–408

existence, xliii, 205, 217, 340, 343, 345, 357, 413, 414; as basic, 291; asserted within vision, 245; consists of limits, 259; importance of as given by 'logos', 227; knowledge confined to, 332–334; of 'nothing', 332; of past, present, future, 125. *See also* being; objective realm; self

experience, xx, xli, xliv, 5, 14, 43, 45, 53–54, 129, 141, 156, 171, 175, 179, 185, 196, 250, 276, 373, 389, 407, 408;

experience (*continued*) as limiting capacity to receive knowledge, 53; as projection, 141; as source of knowledge in models, 133; basic structures of, 59; dealing with unusual, 223–224; flow from past to future, 173, 174; inchoate, 234; inner, as inaccessible, 206; labeling, 51; lack of vitality in, 44; organized by self, 169; past-centered, 188; potential depth, 69; self's isolation from, 109; shared, 99; sublime, 244; turned on edge, 274; untrustworthy, 165. *See also* self (as) owner

explanation(s), 6, 39, 52, 129, 165, 171, 217, 259, 265, 270, 298

fact(s), 298, 366; and interpretation, 137–142; learning new, 58; questions of, 252

failure, 252–253

faith, 8, 134, 235–236, 252

familiar, 7, 63

fantasies, xlii, 6, 39, 47, 48, 61, 158, 390; reveal creativity, 75; source of riches, 69. *See also* self-image

fear(s), 35, 157, 223–227, 274, 400; pointer to knowing, 227

feedback, 92, 276, 301, 363, 371

feelings, 35, 38, 58, 156–158, 163, 171, 249, 252, 291; switching, 293. *See also* emotions

field, xvi, xxi, 138, 164, 165, 266, 274, 332, 383. *See also* gravity

'first-moment experience', 105–106

'focal setting', 105, 414, 415

forces, 71

founding identity, 201–208. *See also* founding story; self

founding role of polar knowledge, 109

founding story, 173–175, 197–198, 204–205, 216, 224–227, 242. *See also*

founding story (*continued*) history; narrative, story

framework, xxviii, 351

free and open inquiry. *See* inquiry

free will, 266

freedom, xxvi, xxix, xxxix, xliii, 6, 7, 46–48, 83, 84, 91, 112, 166, 244, 245, 260, 292, 293, 340, 353, 374, 375–376, 409

friction, 253, 274

frustration, xxvi, xxxi, 58, 63, 78, 86, 157–159, 259, 308, 326

future, 6, 68, 102, 148–150, 155–157, 164, 181, 186–190, 203, 214, 240, 242–243, 399, 403–404; ability to foresee or control, 13, 29; as marker, 194; knowledge available only in, 113; knowledge of, 60; patterns endure into, 62; possibilities available now, 91; projected by self, 170; 'read-out' as binding, 316. *See also* intentional knowledge; past; present; three times; time

game, 371, 372. *See also* word game

genes, 27, 217

genius, xli

global culture, 18

global perspective, 91

goal(s), xxi, xxviii, 6, 79, 86, 155–156, 169, 340, 358, 366, 380, 390

'grace', 410

gravity, 274. *See also* field

greed, xlix

guidance, 6, 77

happiness, 293; continued pursuit of, 60; inability to achieve, 22

harmony, xxix, 235, 245

healing, xl, xlix, 276

'here', 101–102, 106, 147, 150, 263, 281, 404. *See also* 'there'

'here and now', 109, 112–113, 170, 281

'higher', xvi

historical conditioning. *See* conditioning

historical perspective, 13

history, xv, xxii, xlii, 11, 26, 80, 166, 170, 205, 257, 260, 365 – 366; dynamic of, parallel to self, 173; examples of harmful models in, 132; helplessness before, 57; inquiry into, 287 – 289; knowing patterns of, 63 – 64, 383; knowledge in, 11; of knowledge, 11 – 13; patterns of, 19; reinterpreted, 207; self subjects itself to, 204, 217 – 220; shaped by a creator, 218; source of conditioning, 46 – 48, 112; time's power in, 396 – 397; unimaginable scope, 68; witness to alternative knowledge, 63. *See also* collective knowledge; conditioning; narrative; reality; world

hope, 149, 157, 165, 400; as basis for accepting authority, 52

human being, 1, 39, 47, 208, 244, 252, 410; acknowledging circumstances of, 59 – 62; reality of, 100; knowledge based on senses, 100; partnership with knowledge, xxi, xlii, 85; relation with space and time, xx – xxi, xlii, 86; responsibility to, 77. *See also* being

human destiny, 133, 208, 218 – 219, 236, 291, 399; interwoven with knowledge, 77; transforming, 72

humility, 235, 291, 396

'I', xliv, 194 – 196, 201, 243, 299 – 300, 358 – 360; occupied by act of knowing, 180; presence of establishes present, 181. *See also* read-out

'I am', 179, 294

'I-ness', 179, 357 – 360, 363 – 365

idealism, 266. *See also* mentalism

ideals, 7, 8

identity, 34, 37, 38, 60;

identity (*continued*) assigned by self, 102–103, 109, 266; loss of, 28; principle of, 117; space and, 89, 92. *See also* founding identity; knowledge; self

ideology, 37, 38, 45

ignorance, 68, 282–283

illusion, 48

image of desire, 34–35. *See also* desire; object of desire

imagination, xxxiii, 89, 143, 158

individuals: as embodying knowledge differently, 13. *See also* whole

information, 5, 7, 14

inquiry, xvi, xix–xxx, 8, 14, 28, 63, 64, 72, 78, 83, 85–86, 90, 270–310, 358, 364–368, 373, 379–383; art, religion, psychology as forms of, 39; domain of, 37, 38; focused by intention, 305; historical, 287–289; into models, cut off by; into particulars, 289; models, 133–134; random, 274–275; space focus, 321;

subjects for, 59; technology and, 29; value of, called into question, 71. *See also* analysis; questioning; self-reflection

insight, 69

inspiration, xli, 6, 39, 284, 300, 306, 400

intelligence, xxix, 8, 14, 27, 30, 35, 43, 46, 64, 75, 80, 90, 208, 246, 288, 289, 297, 306, 366, 367, 380, 414

intensity, 106, 166

intentional knowledge, 150–152, 155–160, 163, 169, 173, 270

intention(s), 60, 169, 313. *See also* attitude; appreciation

interdependence, 322–324. *See also* opposition

'interesting', xxviii, 58

interplay of time, space, knowledge, xliv, 398

interpretation(s), xlii, 36, 64, 109, 112, 152, 171, 173, 179, 186, 218, 243, 250, 266, 280, 363; as part of visionary whole, 240; based on sense data, 100;

interpretation(s) (*cont.*) completes observation, 169; fundamental to 'truth', 137–144, 151–152; lack of power, 170; no escape from, 259; polar knowledge prior to, 110; self-, 197; self as, 170

interpreter, 169–170. *See also* self

intimacy, xx, xlviii, 93, 105, 307–309, 368, 388, 392, 409. *See also* appreciation; love

intuition, 249, 409

isolation, 63, 101, 103, 310, 374; of momentary knowledge, 118. *See also* bystander; self

joy, xli, 80, 158, 223, 226, 242, 358

judgment(s), xxvii, 39, 43–45, 53, 63, 75, 76, 173, 175, 250, 252, 266, 292–294, 324; as labels for energy, 292

knowable: bound to a specific time and place, 67; range of, 12, 69, 72

knower, xlii, 92, 138, 169, 175, 215, 291, 301. *See also* self

knowing. *See* knowledge

'knowingness', xxviii, xxx, xxxiii, xxxix, xlii, xlv, xlvi, l, 94, 275, 298, 313, 363–365, 388, 391

Knowledge, *passim*; abandoning, 157; acquired with difficulty, 60; alchemy of, 91; alternative, 40, 77, 258; arises within order, 35; as tool, 175, 251; becomes routine, 4; becoming homogeneous, 19; being and (*see* being); 'between', 301–302, 306, 314; beyond the visionary, 245; brotherhood of, 365–368; cannot be momentary, 114; changes in through time and space, 19; collecting, 308; commitment to, 64; commodity, 253; companion and guide, 14; dependent on models, 36–37, 129, 130, 134; desire

Knowledge (*continued*) for, 51; distanced, 389; developing in time, 14; distributed in advance, 43, 44, 83, 164; divorced from experience and intelligence, 36; domain extended by thinkers and artists, 57–58; embodying (*see* embodying); engagement in, 77; exercising, xxiv, 7, 380; for a purpose, 33; gap, 101–102, 264, 301, 314, 387; global, xxxi, 365, 367–368, 408–410; going behind and beyond itself, 59; 'gut-level', 157–158; higher, 219; hoarding, 76; inability to communicate new, 40; incomplete, 58–59; inner, 69; intrinsic clarity, 64; inviting, 94; knowing time and space, 92; lack of, belief in, 52; levels of, 72 (*see also* levels); limited by self's situation, 52; limited capacity and scope, *passim*; limited to moment, 113–118; 'logos' and, 314–315; 'lower', xviii; mediated, 234;

mechanism for transmitting, 48; models of (*see* models); modern revolution in, 18, 22; more embracing form of, 72; more comprehensive and encompassing, 8; moves made by, 315; natural abundance and capacity, 85; negation and, 337–340; new fields of, 17; not dependent on knower, 215; notion of can change, 5; not welcome, 207; not owned, 79; object of, 35; object of technology, 26–27; object-centered, 159; 'objective', 40; of the absolute, 236; of impending death, 60; of knowledge, 29, 84, 99, 251; opening for luminous, 274; opposed to knowing, 264; of reality, 129; outside of time, 203; own witness, 228; ownership of (*see* self (as) owner); participation in, 79–80; partitioned, 4; possessing (*see* self (as) owner); power of, 3, 72, 78, 216; presented in history, 11–13; private vs. public, 39–40, 77,

Knowledge (*continued*) 78–79; product rather than faculty, 28; property of self (*see* self (as) owner); quality of, 91; random, 275; realm of deeper, 372; restricted to existence, 332; rhythm to, 84; routinized, 163; science considered culmination of, 19; seen as coming from 'outside', 7, 45; self's as fallible, 35; serving projected image of desire, 34; source of, 14, 264, 315; speaking, 379; stimulating, 90; styles of, 63; subjective realm, no role in, 33; subordinated to identity and desire, 34, 36; suffering and, 374–375; supporting knowledge, 90; teaching knowledge, 5; technological model for, 26, 28–30, 33, 34, 39–40, 46, 78–79; traditions, 77, 232; working 'well enough', 71. *See also* being; belief; conventional knowledge; descriptive knowledge; intentional knowledge; knower, known; 'logos';

models; negation; notknowing; polar knowledge; 'read-out'; sense knowledge; technological knowledge; temporal knowledge; witness

known, xlii, 92, 138, 301; going beyond, 46–48; relying on, 43–46

labels, 43, 45, 51, 75, 76, 83, 195, 249, 257, 271, 292, 325, 326, 345

language, xxix, xxxiii, 129, 141–142, 163, 258, 271, 287, 288, 329, 347–348, 351, 382; need for new, 90; trick of, 123. *See also* speech; words

level(s), xxii, xxiii, xliii, xlv, l, 72, 413, 414, 416; of 'ness', 365

light, xlv, 35, 205, 244, 363

limitations; limits, *passim*; 'limit structure', 283

logic, xxxix, xlviii, 36, 93, 94, 125, 159, 171, 175, 197, 227–228, 232, 291, 298, 323, 332, 340, 373, 414; called into question, 117; of conflict, 253; of

logic (*continued*)
descriptive knowledge,
125; of polar knowledge,
151. *See also* 'logos'

'logos', 226–228, 299, 314–
315, 332–333, 338, 345, 396,
415. *See also* knowledge;
logic; read-out

love, xvi, xlviii, xlix, 5, 69,
80, 410

love of knowledge, xvi,
xxxix, xl, xli, xlvii-l, 4, 5,
14, 91, 236, 306, 309–310,
313–314, 339, 373, 381

'lower', xvi

machinery, 159

magic, 372

magical interplay, 297

materialism, 19–20, 266,
364. *See also* mentalism;
idealism

matter, xvi, 80, 405–406

meaning(s), xlv, 12, 33, 38,
47, 78, 165, 244, 271, 346–
347, 381; assigned by self,
103, 104, 109, 147, 169, 395;
meaning of, 141; pre-
sented by time, 193

meaningful, 77, 141, 142,
228, 258, 347

meaning-giver, 169, 354.
See also self

meaningless, 142, 347–
348, 353, 389; comes to
fore by default, 33

measurement, 110–111,
123, 124, 159, 204, 213, 231,
275, 323–324. *See also*
time

mechanism(s), 48, 58, 266

memory, 45, 106, 125–126,
129, 155, 169, 186, 187, 282;
linking moments, 125

mental patterns. *See*
mind

mentalism, 364. *See also*
idealism

metaphor, 12, 90

method, 6

middle realm, 414, 416

mind, xxiii, xliv, xlvii, 6,
13, 35, 45, 48, 51, 53, 69,
76, 80, 89, 93, 141, 171, 193,
194, 197, 208, 282, 288, 290,
298, 301, 371; bound to
existence, 333, 345;

mind (*continued*)
exercising, xxiv, xlvii; linear temporality and, 124; knowing capacity of, 290; 'made up' in advance, 260; master of conditioning, 374; minding, xlvii, 325; no basis for knowing, 45; potential for changes in, 325–326. *See also* body

miraculous events, 132

mistaken way of being, 253

mistakes, 253

models, xlviii, 48, 93, 129–134, 250–253, 257, 260; for how knowledge arises, 83–84, 99–106; guiding thinking, 8; in competition, 18; investigating, 29, 133; of bystander, 264; of knowledge, 205; of technological knowledge, 20; offered by thinking, 36; prevailing, 84; questioning dependence of knowledge on, 84; reliance on, 130–131; self and world as fundamental, 251; 'self-centered', 39; scientific, for the knowable, 110–111, 130;

suited only to knowing repetitive events, 132

moment(s), 113–118, 121–122, 125, 148, 170, 179–180, 185, 187, 189, 214, 217, 329, 359, 387–388, 403; first, 122–123, 391

momentum, xiv, xxix, xxxiv, xliv, 13, 263, 274, 276, 306, 329; historical, 44; initiated by judgments, 266; intentional, 164; of activity, 71; of analysis, 301; of change, 27; of crowding, 166; of desire, 34, 36; of linear time, 149, 185, 188; of narrative, 175, 241; of not-knowing, 271; of patterns, 57; of technology, 18; of the known, 314; temporal, history as source of, 175; traced by knowledge, 28. *See also* dynamic; rhythm

moral code, 89, 164, 232

moral conduct, 93, 309

motivation, 39; for flow of time, 122; for questioning, 110–112; for seeking knowledge, 63 music, 69, 339

mystical traditions, xlviii, 244

narrative (structures), 172–176, 179, 186–188, 197, 204, 207, 218–219, 239, 257, 260, 299, 329, 340, 396; of question and answer, 228. *See also* founding story; story

narrative time, 186–188

narrator, 170–173, 186, 189–190, 228, 264, 289, 354. *See also* bystander; self

natural law. 231

natural order. *See* order

nature, 69

negation, 330–331, 333, 337–340, 343–344, 352, 357, 364–365, 384, 391, 409

negativity: source of energy, 75

'ness', 344–346, 351–352, 357–359, 363–365, 381, 382, 384, 391, 404, 405

'ness-ness', 344–345, 348, 351–352, 360, 364–365, 382, 384. *See also* 'I-ness'

'no', 346

'no basis', 329

'no positions', 375, 376, 380

'no thoughts', 290

'no-choice' realm, 112, 373. *See also* choice

nothing, 331–334, 340, 347, 351–352, 404, 405

'nothing but', 354

'no-thingness', 346

'not', 331, 333, 338, 340

'not-doing'; as category within a model, 258

not-knowing, 38, 44, 57, 58, 72, 123, 142, 270–272, 331, 337, 364, 374, 379–384, 391–392, 414; accepting without being bound by, 72; acknowledging, 90; as subject for inquiry, 59; belief in, 52; knowledge emerging within, 90; motive for abandoning, 103; possibility for

433

not-knowing (*continued*) knowledge, 270; self appropriates, 224–226; vicious circle of, 63

nothingness. *See* emptiness

'now', 91, 101–102, 106, 147, 241. *See also* 'then'

object(s), xliv, xlvi, 101, 139, 176, 185, 195, 269, 282, 301, 305, 307, 357; appearing in space, 100; assumptions about, 83; continuing presence of, 114–115; established through choices, 324; exist based on past, 181; fixed, depend on temporal rhythm, 215; in time, 395; in perception, 101–102; inquiry into, 289; knowledge as, xlii, 115; mental, xliii, 333–334; of desire, 35–36, 45, 150, 155, 159; of knowledge, 44; self as, 170. *See also* image of desire; objective self; subject; subject-object interaction

'objective', 35, 38, 39, 79, 83, 139, 231, 364. *See also* 'subjective'

objective knowledge. *See* knowledge

objective reality, 112, 169, 194, 205, 217, 257, 263, 305, 366. *See also* reality

objective realm, 33–35, 37, 39, 205. *See also* subjective realm

'objective self', 181, 187, 201–202, 205, 265. *See also* object; self

observation, xli, xlv–xlvii, 14, 75–76, 83, 90, 116, 147, 164, 169, 175, 194–196, 206, 231, 251, 270, 301, 388–389; polar structure of, 101–102; used by inquiry, 273. *See also* polar observation

observer, 100, 214

obstacle(s), 8, 75, 86, 92; established by pattern of knowing, 86

occupation, 180

'open-minded', 90

openness, 91, 158, 206, 226, 352, 398

opposition(s), 39, 44, 133, 264–266, 269, 299, 321–

opposition(s) (*continued*) 325, 345; encompasses 'new' knowledge, 324; interdependence as basis of, 322. *See also* choice; dichotomy

order, 165, 258, 263, 351; acceptance of, 235; cosmic, 219; established through time, 100; natural, no meaning or value in, 218; sustained by prevailing model, 84, 133; within which knowledge arises, 35. *See also* logos; temporal order

owner; ownership. *See* self

pace of modern life, 45

pain, xxxi, 6, 374, 399

partitions, 403

past, 6, 68, 102, 109, 126, 148, 164, 186–190, 203, 205, 214, 240, 242–243, 399, 403–404; as marker, 194; as perceived, 102; commitment to, 204; encompassing endless possibilities, 122;

knowledge of, 13; linked to present, 103–106; locus for known object, 113; narrow view of, 13; seized by self, 170; source of what is real, 176, 181; vanished, 22. *See also* descriptive knowledge; future; history; present; three times; time

path, xxi, xliv, l, 47, 80, 157, 279, 371, 379–380, 387, 388, 390. *See also* process

pattern(s), xxii, xxvii, 11, 13, 19, 28, 46, 57, 62–64, 71, 79, 86, 157, 205, 206, 217, 223, 225, 243, 258, 260, 275, 287, 293, 338–339, 373, 380, 414; as manifestations of particular forms of knowledge, 85; inherited, 89; within the robe, 240–241; unfolding, 297

patterning, 275

penetrating, 308, 314

perceiver, 101, 109, 110, 112–117, 147, 148, 150, 169–170, 174, 180, 189, 264. *See also* bystander

perception, xxvii, 101–102,

perception (*continued*) 112–117, 171, 180, 297; qualities of, 53; feeling chosen over, 156

philosophy, x, xix, xxi, xxii, xxvii, xlii, xlv, 19, 39, 139, 164, 250, 309, 339

physics, 71

play, 1, 206, 409

poetry, 19

point(s), 272, 297, 380; knowledge available within, 398. *See also* center; position; zero-point

pointer(s), 227, 236, 271, 345–347, 409. *See also* symbols

pointing, 352

polar knowledge, 101, 109–118, 121, 129, 132, 189, 190, 194, 203, 269, 271; critiques of not convincing, 151; hypothetical construct, 265; necessary connections, 109–110; and human freedom, 112

polar observation, 206, 321; as basis for knowledge, 175; data not directly accessible, 110–111; relation to space, 214. *See also* observation

polarity, 293, 315, 357

position(s), xxvii, xxix, xli, xlvi, 44, 76, 83, 92, 175, 241, 251, 263–266, 269, 272–275, 279, 299, 309, 313, 315, 323, 338, 339, 353, 375–376, 379–383, 397; cannot be analyzed, 359; clinging to, 62, 225; momentum toward, 363; not taking, 76–77; relation to space, 92. *See also* choice; opposition; point; positioning

positioning, 217, 265, 272–275, 282, 290, 313, 339, 375, 384; affirmation of knowledge, 375; by self, 147; in space and time, 213; knowledge, 134; of a knower, 93; the known, 106. *See also* position

'postures', xlvi

pre-established, 7, 44, 46, 57, 79, 83

preoccupation, 46, 224

present, 109, 181–182, 185–

present (*continued*) 190, 203, 214, 240, 243, 399, 403 – 404; as experienced, 102; as marker, 182, 194; as not momentary, 121; authenticated by self, 170; depends on past, 121 – 122, 125; established by presence of 'I', 181; not available for enjoyment, 155; power of, 242; self as always in, 148, 204. *See also* existence; future; past

presentation(s), xx, xxiii, xliii, 86, 241, 242, 339 – 340

presupposition(s), xxviii, xlviii, 46, 53, 83, 297, 299, 309, 338, 348, 352, 413

pride, 353 – 354. *See also* humility

private; privatism. *See* knowledge

probabilities, 138, 275, 276, 399

process, xviii-xix, xxxiv, xliii, 413. *See also* path

'professional', xxviii, 224

programming, 47, 253, 329. *See also* conditioning

progress, 20, 132

projection(s), xlii, 141, 195, 203, 228, 250, 338, 352, 353; of image of desire, 34; of knowing capacity, 264; received belief as, 53

protective barrier, 92

psychology, x, xxvii, 39, 164, 173, 287; inquiry as, 382. *See also* collective knowledge

public discourse, 39; value and meaning as topics, 33

qualities, 86, 91, 291, 372; communication of, 53; of experience as witness, 143

questioning, xlix, 78 – 80, 83, 86, 245, 279 – 284, 305; activity of self, 228; and locatedness, 281; as 'doing', 258; based on willingness, 72; basis for transforming human destiny, 72; hidden topic, 314; knowledge as beyond, 44; narrative of, 228, 283, 306 – 307; questioning, 306; rhythm of,

questioning (*continued*) 75; transparent, 314. *See also* challenging; inquiry

random. *See* inquiry; knowledge; time

random matrix, 141

rationality, 134

'read-out(s)', xxvi, 315–316, 325, 330, 348, 358, 360, 363, 367–368, 390, 396, 414, 415

'read-out principle', 367

reality, 94, 182, 232, 244, 245, 260, 264, 354, 363, 372, 382; as construct, 140; as underlying interpretation, 138–143, 152; bound to narratives, 174; dreams and, 143; formed through descriptive knowledge, 106, 275; function of space and time, 215; human beings subject to, 111; levels of, xxii; linked to present, 181; models for, 36; 'ness' and, 344; polar knowledge must conform to, 110; reason and, 269; structures of, 7; times when most real, 193;

witness as guarantor of, 143–144. *See also* objective reality; 'read-out'

reason(s), 44, 93, 232, 270, 282, 291, 298; for accepting models, 131; linked to 'bystander', 269; unfounded, 269; used by inquiry, 273

reasoning, xxiii, 266, 373; depends on law of simultaneity, 117

rebellion, 48

religion, x, xxi, xxii, xxvii, 19, 39, 164, 231–232, 250, 291

're-presenting' conclusions, 51

responsibility, 46, 77–80, 84, 204, 297

restlessness, 6

rhetoric, 159

rhythm(s), 17, 18, 57, 274, 368, 388, 410, 416; to knowledge, 84; of consciousness, 215; of experience, 398; of questioning, 75; of self's life, 196; unfolding, 297.

rhythm (*continued*) *See also* dynamic; momentum

sacred texts, 231

'sameness', 405

satisfaction, 6, 155, 156, 160, 309

science, xxi, xxii, xliv, 19–21, 139, 164, 173, 213, 218

scientific method, xxxix, 38, 138

scientific model. *See* models

security, 163, 206

self, xli, 33–37, 147–207, 215–220, 236, 252, 264–266, 293, 313, 323–324, 382, 396–398, 413; and descriptive knowledge, 103–106, 169; and temporal knowledge, 103, 148; as witness, 144, 171; at center of known world, 34; belief in, 47, 53; central to knowing, 84, 252, 257; concerns of, 35, 72, 76, 84, 90, 91, 93, 169, 204, 206, 217, 309, 357, 396; and acceptance of models, 131; beyond, through devo-

tion, 235; love of knowledge turns from, 313; control over knowledge, 252, 353; 'core', 171; cut off, 156; demanding space, 92; energy of, 34; existence of, 171, 195–196, 204–205, 216, 218, 223, 275; focus on, as function of space and time, 215; gaining knowledge, xxx; historical entity, 205, 219, 223; identified with body, 196; identified with experiences, 196; identity, 34, 195, 204–207; inaccessible to knowledge, 34; independent of change, 202–203; isolation from experience, 109; knowing world, 102–103, 169; lack of choice, 35; linking moments, 103–104, 147–150; living toward future, 149; model of, 130; no 'room' for, 104; observing, 194–196; owner of knowledge and experience, xxix, 33–34, 76, 93, 150, 171, 185–190, 195–196, 201–204, 215, 264, 289, 338, 359, 408; persistence over time, self (*continued*) 148, 196; pre-occupied, 180–189; priority of, 196; split in two, 202–204; questions regarding, 76, 104, 106, 194–198; relation to space, 104, 150; relation to time, 147–150, 186–190; separated from desired objects, 150, 155; temporal entity, 205; uniting observations, 144; witness to new, 193. *See also* body; bystander; founding identity; identity; intentional knowledge; interpretation; I; I am; I-ness; interpreter; isolation; knower; meaning-giver; narrator; objective self; perceiver; witness; world

self-evident ideas, xx, 67, 68, 100, 173, 323

self-hatred, xlix

self-image, xxix, 61

self-reflection, 300–301

sensation(s), 45, 76, 157

sense knowledge, 100

senses, xxiii, 69, 100, 111, 179, 250, 281, 382; tempo-

ral dynamic of, 125

separation, 34, 150, 213, 242, 253, 265, 389, 413, 415

shamanism, 19

silence, 339, 353

simultaneity, 117

'single-minded' knowing, 174–176, 207

'singling out', xxix

skepticism, xxvii, 40

Space, *passim*; accommodating, 92; allowing capacity of, 388; allowing knowledge, 92; and self, 35, 52, 104, 150; as chilling void, 286; as created, 214; as partitioned, 89; as unknown, 392; attributes and, 405; body and, 104, 389; border to, 381, 382; central to world of objects, 150; disappears from view, 100; distance in conventional, 102; emptiness of, 86; filled up, 165, 166; ill-suited, 44; in early moments of universe, 67; interconnection with time, 213–214; lacking depth, 165; layers

Space (*continued*) of, 368; meeting place with time, 274; must arise, 214; 'non-existent', 100; object- and self-centered, 151, 152; objects in, 99–100, 398; relation to knowledge, 85, 92, 214; unitary, 407. *See also* distance; identity; objects; position; separation; territory

specification, 351. *See also* language

spectrum of knowledge, 13, 14

speech, 346–347. *See also* language

spindle, 12

spiritual insight, 69

spiritual practice, xxxix, 89

stability, 45, 163

standards, 20; global, 25. *See also* truth

statecraft, 19

stipulation, 126

stoic acceptance, 48

stories, xxx, 137, 171–173, 194, 206, 224, 243, 260, 329–330, 372, 396; about stories, 172; about the visionary, 245; absolute as a, 239; enjoying, 294; history as a, 217; time in, 396. *See also* founding story; narrative

stress, 28

structure(s), 45, 75, 93; as manifestations of particular knowledge, 85; of desire, 36; of division and polarity, 101; of experience, 114; of self, 79; of wanting and judging, 76

styles of thought and action, 67

subject, 101, 175, 301, 307, 354, 357, 406–407, 413; assumptions about, 283; conditions memory, 126; experience as, xlii; of investigation, 14, 29. *See also* object; self; subject-object interaction

'subjective', 35, 38–40, 47, 79, 138, 181, 258, 364. *See also* 'objective' subjective knowledge. *See* knowledge

subjective realm, 33–40, 156. *See also* objective realm

subject-object interaction, xlii, xlvi, 75, 194–196, 291, 301, 364

suffering, xlix, 21, 78, 204, 374–375

supernatural power, 51

supplicant, 235–236

symbol(s), xxvii, 90, 231, 288, 346–347, 372. *See also* pointers; zero

techniques: already practicing, 274

technological: culture, 18; language, 26; modality, 26; model for knowledge (*see* models); style, 26

technological knowledge, 18–22, 28–30, 37–38, 43–48, 76–77, 159–160, 163. *See also* knowledge

technology, 17, 21, 25–26, 34–35, 39, 133, 159–160;

affecting knowledge, 33; positions the self, 78

temporal knowledge, 138, 147, 188, 190, 244, 271; characteristics and reliability of, 100. *See also* knowledge; polar knowledge

temporal order, 103, 217, 275. *See also* order

temporal sequence, 44, 316

temporality, 185, 263

tension, 253

territory, 37–38, 60, 264; relation to space, 89, 92

'then', 101–102, 106, 147, 241. *See also* 'now'

theoretical construct, 259

theories, 37, 270

'there', 101–102, 147, 150, 263. *See also* 'here'

thinkers, 12, 57, 80, 224

thinking, 36; about thinking, 300

thoughts, 179, 186, 258, 271, 329; beyond, 234;

thoughts (*continued*) models directed toward, 133; original, 314; place within, 290; pointers toward knowledge, 271; refining, 246; structures of, linked to experience, 123; temporal dynamic of, 125; trillions in one hour, 70

three times, 181 – 182. *See also* time

Time, *passim*; allowing knowledge, 92; and self, 35, 52, 147 – 151; alternative forms of, 124; as relentless force, 86, 89; as unknown, 392; beginning of, 122 – 124, 381, 405 – 406; 'beyond', 123 – 124; central significance for self, 104, 150; creative power of, 188, 395 – 400; display of events in, 57; diversity of knowledge through, 214; end of, 124; experience as, 389; filled with events, 58, 68; flow of, 171, 173, 185 – 190, 196; history shows mind at work in, 13; ill-suited, 44; in early moments of universe, 67; in unconscious realm, 124 – 125; inconceivable activity within, 70; interconnection with space, 213 – 214; linear structure investigated, 121 – 126, 179 – 182; linear structure reflecting knowledge gap, 102; measured-out, 159, 160; measures and distributes events, 100, 205; measuring, 124; meeting place with space, 274; narrow and superficial, 207; narrative structure and, 176, 179; object- and self-centered, 151, 152; object of knowledge, 203; personalized in separation, 150; proceeding in moments, 116; primordial, 123; purpose of emerging into, 69; random, 116, 243; relation to knowledge, 85, 92, 214 – 215; self-identity and, 179 – 180, 196; space-like, 214; threefold, 181 – 182; timeless, 241; two kinds, 179 – 182, 203 – 204; unitary, 407; used up, 166; varying operation, 395 – 400; visionary, 241 – 244;

Time (*continued*)
vitality of, 205; without
distinctions. *See also*
condition; conditioning;
events; future; history;
measurement; memory;
moment; narrative time;
past; present; rhythm;
temporal sequence;
temporality

time-frame: effect on
knowledge, 68

tolerance, 91

timepieces, 12

tradition(s), xliv, 45, 231 –
232, 249; as authority, 51;
of knowledge, 77

traditional: ways of
life, 21

tranquility, 69

transcendence, 235, 245,
358

transformation, 84, 94, 340;
dreams of, unfulfilled,
62; from source outside,
236; historical, 12; in
knowledge, 17; within
present, 89

trends, 13, 19

trustworthiness, 52, 233

truth, 8, 11, 38, 46, 134,
225, 228, 244, 272 – 274, 281;
as correspondence, 139 –
140; based on interpreta-
tion, 137 – 144; empirical,
231; eternal, 244; in
descriptive knowledge,
125; of models, 131, 137;
of our training, 373;
models as way of deter-
mining, 36; no need to
establish, 273; religious,
as 'second class', 231;
standards of, 14. *See also*
self-evident ideas

unacknowledged knowl-
edge, 59 – 62

unconscious: and time,
124 – 125

uniformity: trend
toward, 19

value(s), 6, 11, 14, 19, 38,
46, 64, 109, 112, 147, 158,
163, 252, 266, 291, 324;
loss of, 28; improper subjects for knowledge, 33;
subject to distortion, 25;
technology leaves aside,
29, 39; ultimate, 323

vision, xxx, xli, 6, 8, 46, 54, 86, 89, 91, 112, 205, 236, 239–246, 270, 300, 398, 410; activating, xviii; emergence of this, xliii–xlvii; lost power, 6; of the knowable, 69; of the robe, 240–244

visualization, xxxiii

vitality, 44, 276, 290, 365; lessens with age, 62; of present, 187; of self as owner, 188; of witness, 190. *See also* energy; experience

void, 226, 352

ways of knowing, 12, 67; universal, 93. *See also* styles of thought

whole, 405

wisdom, 93, 134

witness, xlv, 171–173, 189–190, 193–194, 197–198, 207, 216, 228, 233, 257, 340, 359; as guarantor of reality, 142–144; experience as its own, 5, 233; knowledge as, 30, 367, 383–384; false, 198; 'ness' and, 384; self as, 144; time, space, knowledge bearing, 194; to limited capacity of knowledge, 37

wonder, xxxix, xlviii, 14, 228, 234, 283, 306–309

wonderment, 374, 410

word games, xxx, 347, 352

words, xxx, 206, 249, 271, 288, 297, 381, 382; meaning lost or distorted, 78; pointers toward knowledge, 271. *See also* language

world, 69, 129, 235, 301, 310, 348, 384, 398; around us, 6; based on opposition, 324; built out of models, 137; change characteristic in, 84; cluttered with structures, 78; depends on connections, 114; effect on of countless thoughts, 70; founding story as basis, 173; given in advance, 36; historically determined, 175; in dynamic flux, 70;

world (*continued*)
knowledge of based on negation, 331; knowledge not welcome in, 207; known, 34, 111, 117, 125, 165, 169, 244, 406; made up of objects and events, 99; objective, 33–35; of 'bystander', 265; of the vision, 240; polar relation to self, 102–104, 148–149, 170; self as part of, 170; shaped by interpretation, 64; space-centered, 205; subjective, 33, 36; witness to substantiality of, 193. *See also* self; subject; whole

worship, 235

'yes', 226, 331

zero, 275, 345–347, 365

'zero-ness', 365

zero-point, 347

zero-structure, 242

TSK Graphics

Patterns related to the structure of Time, Space, and Knowledge can be derived from geometry, numerology, and mathematics. Image-presence 'reads out' different levels of seeing in time and space.

1001 1000 01 10110 101 1000 1001 100 100 101 1110 10100 10010 10101 101 1100 1111 10110 101 1111 110 1011 1110 1111 10111 1100 101 100 111 101 1001 1110 10100 1000 1001 10011 100 1001 01 111 10010 01 1101

10000 10101 10100 01 1100 1100 10100 1000 101 10000 10101 11010 11010 1100 101 10011 1001 1110 10100 1111 1111 10010 100 101 10010 10100 1111 110 1001 1110 100 10100 1000 101 1101 101 01 1110 1001 1110 111 1111 110 10100 10010 10101 101 1100 1111 10110 101

10100 1000 101 1111 10010 100 101 10010 1111 110 10100 1000 101 11 1000 01 10000 10100 101 10010 10011 1001 10011 01 10011 11001 1101 10 1111 1100 1111 110 10 1111 100 11001 1100 01 1110 111 10101 01 111 101

10100 1000 101 1011 101 11001 1000 01 10011 10 101 101 1110 10000 10101 10100 1001 1110 10100 1111 110 1111 10101 10010 10100 1000 10010 101 101 101 1001 111 1000 10100 1110 1001 1110 101 10000 01 10010 10100 110 1111 10101 10010 1001 1110 11 1111 100 101